BECKETT AND CONTEMPORARY IRISH WRITING

Samuel Beckett is one of the most important figures in the history of Irish literature and he continues to influence successive generations of writers. In *Beckett and Contemporary Irish Writing*, Stephen Watt searches for the "Beckettian" impulse in Irish literature by tracing the Nobel Prize winner's legacy through a rich selection of contemporary novelists, poets, and dramatists. Watt examines leading figures such as Paul Muldoon, Brian Friel, Marina Carr, and Bernard MacLaverty, and shows how Beckett's presence, whether openly acknowledged or unstated, is always thoroughly pervasive. Moving on to an exploration of Beckett's role in the twenty-first century, the study discusses ways in which this legacy can be reshaped to deal with current concerns that extend beyond literature. Encouraging us to think about Beckett's work and status in new ways, this landmark study will be required reading for scholars and students of Beckett and Irish studies.

STEPHEN WATT is Professor of English, Theatre, and Drama at Indiana University, Bloomington.

BECKETT AND CONTEMPORARY IRISH WRITING

STEPHEN WATT

CAMBRIDGE UNIVERSITY PRESS
Cambridge, New York, Melbourne, Madrid, Cape Town,
Singapore, São Paulo, Delhi, Tokyo, Mexico City

Cambridge University Press
The Edinburgh Building, Cambridge CB2 8RU, UK

Published in the United States of America by Cambridge University Press, New York

www.cambridge.org
Information on this title: www.cambridge.org/9781107404502

First published 2009
First paperback edition 2011

A catalogue record for this publication is available from the British Library

ISBN 978-0-521-51958-8 Hardback
ISBN 978-1-107-40450-2 Paperback

Contents

Illustrations

Acknowledgments

Beckett and Contemporary Irish Writing is hardly the sole product of the author whose name appears on the title page. No book is. Books require the support, intelligence, and affection of friends and family, colleagues, and, in the case of writers who also happen to be teachers, administrators who provide them, in the best cases, not only with hospitable places to work, but also with something every bit as valuable: time. That is precisely what the College of Arts and Sciences at Indiana University and its former dean, Kumble Subbaswamy, provided me with. Thanks, Swamy. And thanks, too, to my wife Nonie and to my children, Caitlin and Brendan Watt – Caitlin provided me with fine proofreading, and Brendan with needed respites from work for rounds of golf. My putting is still horrible, but I'm working at it – thanks for the tip about my posture and stance.

My colleagues at Indiana – Susan Gubar, Ed Comentale, Shane Vogel, Alex Teschmacher, and Ellen MacKay – performed the thankless task of reading chapters in manuscript form and gave me wonderful responses. I am privileged to have such dear friends. The suggestions of my former students Aaron Jaffe and Craig Owens helped me shape the book's coda on Beckett as a twenty-first century tourist attraction, a version of which appears in *Modernist Celebrity*, edited by Aaron Jaffe and Jonathan Goldman. Andrew Kincaid's work on tourism and urban development in Ireland has proved a revelation to me. Thanks for sharing your unpublished research with me, Andrew. My thanks, too, to the staffs of the Emory University library and the Irish Museum of Modern Art, and to Jane Powers, Paul Muldoon, and Thorsten Sandberg of Sweden Post Stamps for helping me secure illustrations for the book. Of course, Ray Ryan, Maartje Scheltens, Paul Stevens, and the staff of Cambridge University Press have made this experience a painless and entirely pleasant one, and I shall be forever grateful to them.

My largest debts are to Tony Roche and Des Kenny. Tony's book on contemporary Irish drama and Des's constant supply of books he thought I should read – and he is unfailingly right about such things – exerted an enormous impact on my thinking. Tony generously invited me to speak at the Synge Summer School in 2006 and to contribute an essay to his *Cambridge Companion to Brian Friel*, which served as the urtext of chapter two of the present book. My sincerest thanks to you both.

An early, much shorter version of chapter three on Bernard MacLaverty appeared as "Beckett, Late Modernism, and Bernard MacLaverty's *Grace Notes*," *New Hibernia Review* 6 (Summer 2002), pp. 53–64.

Introduction: Beckett, our contemporary

> I had agreed to review this production … on RTÉ Radio One's arts programme, *Rattlebag*, on a date which suited us both: 11 September 2001 … The following week, an Irish publication protested that as 9/11 unfolded RTÉ radio was broadcasting a review of Beckett's *Krapp's Last Tape* … What struck me forcibly was the greatness of Beckett's play in being adequate to the awfulness of the historic moment, its ongoing prophetic ability to address world events long after its composition.
>
> –Anthony Roche, "Samuel Beckett: The Great Plays after *Godot*" (2006)

> NELL: Actually, I think they have little to offer us anymore–
> JUDITH: Who are you talking about?
> NELL: Giacometti. Beckett. All the rest of them! They're dead. We're alive. What we know now comes to us from the future.
>
> –Thomas Kilroy, *The Shape of Metal* (2003)

Tony Roche told me the story, recounted above, about appearing on the radio to discuss a production of Samuel Beckett's *Krapp's Last Tape* just hours after al-Qaeda's attacks on America.[1] As he recalled in a recent essay, his decision to go through with the radio interview was not universally admired: Was it appropriate to "go on" given the enormity of the events on September 11? Didn't his appearance suggest a kind of insensitivity to the gravity of the moment? More significant, I think, was the implication that topics such as the theatre – and Samuel Beckett – just didn't matter at such a critical historical moment. Media outlets and their listeners ought to concern themselves with more serious things – dare I say, to use an expression susceptible to any number of unfortunate connotations, more *relevant* things?

Just a few hours before Tony began his trek to the RTÉ studio in Dublin, I was brewing coffee at my home in the American midwest, preparing breakfast, getting my children ready for school, and packing my notes for a seminar on Samuel Beckett and Harold Pinter. As is typical on such mornings in our house, the news show *Today* was droning away on a television in the background, offering its mildly diverting, but largely ignored soundtrack to the minor chaos of eggs being scrambled, misplaced notebooks being found, and backpacks being overloaded with the myriad necessities teenagers require. This morning evolved differently, though, as pictures of the first burning skyscraper in midtown Manhattan stopped me in my tracks. One of the program's hosts admitted his uncertainty about the fire's origin, and the earliest reports from the scene speculated that a small commuter plane had accidentally struck a building, one which, as we all know, was later identified as the North Tower of the World Trade Center. In the time between my leaving home and arriving on campus some fifteen minutes later, reports came over the radio that more planes – large passenger jets, not single-engine "puddle-jumpers," as my father used to call them – had crashed into the WTC's South Tower, into the Pentagon in Washington, and into a remote field in Pennsylvania. More people had died; more confusion, more grief. The seminar convened as scheduled and, not surprisingly, it began with expressions both of shock over these attacks and anxiety over what they might portend. We decided nonetheless to move on to Beckett and plodded through the day's reading with considerable awkwardness, far more than that typical of a group of new post-graduate students meeting for the second time in the term. Given the events of the morning, one of the students found *Waiting for Godot* – the principal focus of the session – far too depressing. She eventually left the seminar, then dropped all of her courses for the remainder of the semester.

The seminar pressed on.

Much as it had with Tony Roche, this odd conflation of horror and Beckett struck me as meaningful almost immediately, and I found myself – as I now recognize more clearly some years later – responding to the moment in ways inflected by my experience of reading Beckett or watching his plays in the theatre. After my sorrow had abated – and after I experienced the relief of learning that my brother-in-law, whose company was housed in the WTC, had been out of town on a business trip that morning – Beckett seemed to speak to a new reality born in the rubble and tragedy of September 11. Something, as Clov informs Hamm in *Endgame*, was indeed "taking its course." Perhaps oddly, I began to regard the events of this terrible day as paralleling the scene of Beckett's late prose piece *Ill Seen Ill Said* and echoed by Paul Muldoon, a poet greatly affected by Beckett, in the opening lines of his elegy "Yarrow" from *The Annals of Chile* (1994). Namely, events were set in motion that produced ineffable senses of encroachment and of an irreversible process under way that would forever alter our feeling about living and the everyday. Muldoon's "Yarrow" begins with just such a sense:

> Little by little it dawned on us that the row
> of kale would shortly be overwhelmed by these pink
> and cream blooms, that all of us
> would be overwhelmed ...[2]

Some force or thing akin to the pink and cream blooms of yarrow slowly enveloping the kale – and the world – in Muldoon's poem was asserting itself upon life in America and the West more generally. This malignant force, however, was hardly fragrant or floral, but more craggy and obdurate like the stones that "increasingly abound" in *Ill Seen Ill Said*. Violence was "gaining" on us and, in the ruthless play on words in Beckett's late text, there was "none to gainsay" or "have gainsaid" this fact. "Ever scanter even the rankest weed," Beckett's narrator observes in an echo of *Hamlet*, describing the shrinking green space of his – and our – world.[3] Beckett seemed, in short, wholly adequate to the task of discerning a changed structure of feeling in the contemporary world in which such senses of encroachment and an all-too-familiar absurdity seem almost overwhelming.

Of course, not everyone would agree with this assertion. Moments from the final curtain of *The Shape of Metal*, Thomas Kilroy's vivacious octogenarian-sculptress announces a view of Beckett that contrasts sharply with Roche's – and with mine. As Nell Jeffrey declaims in the second epigraph above, Beckett and his friend Alberto Giacometti, who once designed a tree for a revival of *Waiting for Godot*,[4] have nothing to say to a new generation hurling toward a future of dizzying technological advancements, ever-intensifying political tensions, and – perhaps – the conditions of man's "extinction." Considering the prominence in Nell's memory of meeting both artists in Paris in the late 1930s – she refers to it throughout the play, adding more details with each retelling, including their inebriated debate over the importance of a good pair of boots – this pronouncement comes as something of a surprise. Over sixty years later, her recollection of this encounter is still vivid, and within the play's narrative her repudiation of its importance might be explained by her daughter's feminist taunt that "You are a great artist. You don't need a male example, never have ..."[5] But protest its importance as she does, Nell recalls this meeting often: it is indelibly traced in her mind, and she returns to it on an almost daily basis.

The difference between the opposing positions staked out by my epigraphs – Beckett possesses enduring relevance for the twenty-first century; Beckett has "little to offer" it – only partially illuminates the project of this book. Indeed, Beckett may grow even more meaningful in a century that is still in its infancy because unlike Didi and Gogo in *Waiting for Godot*, as the events of

September 11 so strikingly demonstrate, we cannot comfortably bide our time as the stones of barbarism advance, or wait patiently for the next Hurricane Katrina to arrive. The latter point informed numerous responses to the November 2007 productions of *Waiting for Godot* in the "weed-choked fields" that were once a neighborhood in New Orleans' Lower Ninth Ward. As Jed Horne reported, in this ravaged place Beckett's play was "weirdly, eerily expressive of the continuing fiasco in which New Orleans finds itself" – an "emblem of Bush-era incompetence" – as it awaits the next storm.[6] Reporting on these performances of *Godot* for *The New York Times* – it was produced at two different venues in New Orleans – Holland Cotter felt that in such a locale "The soul of *Godot* isn't in Vladimir's cry at being marooned in nothingness, but in something he says later in the play: 'Let us not waste our time in idle discourse! Let's do something, while we have the chance!'"[7] Only time will tell if proactive doing or further worrying is justified, and in its later chapters this book confronts ways in which in the present century Beckett, for reflective good or commercial ill, is being refashioned into our contemporary: at some times as a low-comic analogue to present-day political misadventures and buffoonery; at others as a tourist attraction, a one-man theme park who draws euros and dollars, however deflated, to Ireland.

In much of what follows, however, I also hope to illuminate the ways in which Beckett has *already* demonstrated his importance to contemporary Irish and Northern Irish culture, in particular to representations of "the Troubles" in the latter half of the previous century. And, much like Nell's rich memories of Paris in the 1930s, the title of this prolegomenon "Beckett, Our Contemporary" originates in my first encounter nearly a half century ago with Jan Kott's classic study *Shakespeare Our Contemporary* (1964). My allusion to Kott's book is intended neither as a frivolity nor a homage, although his articulation of Shakespeare's *King Lear* with Beckett's *Endgame* remains as compelling today as it was when he wrote it. Like many of Beckett's narrators, or John Banville's, I may be accused of suffering an unfortunate compulsion to explain myself and exhaust all the possibilities of my chapters' titles (titles, like names and words, as the following pages will corroborate, are something of an obsession with me). If so, my unease, at least in part, speaks to the susceptibility of such an idea to responses of bemusement or indifference. That is to say, of course Samuel Beckett is our contemporary. As he lived from 1906 until 1989, readers who have attained the age of, say, thirty or more, hardly require a reminder that he lived in their time, that he *was* their contemporary. I seek these readers' forbearance, asking that they withhold their verdict about a critical enterprise that, by comparison to Kott's assertion of Shakespeare's contemporaneity, might seem tepid or even superfluous.

This book concerns itself not only with twentieth-century writers born before World War II who share affinities with Beckett or, in some cases, employ him or his characters as one or another device – playwrights, poets, and novelists contemporaneous with his later years and works – but also with a newer generation of writers who have discovered in Beckett values quite different from those privileged by the postwar generation. Because the term "values" in this instance is quite purposefully vague, it might prove useful to identify something more specific like dramatic *form*, a radical "value" that emergent playwrights of the later 1950s and 60s like Harold Pinter, Tom Stoppard, and Sam Shepard have acknowledged as crucial to their development. Among other things, Beckett's dramatic form exhibited a kind of subtractive calculus that, as Stoppard once underscored in revisiting his first viewing of *Waiting for Godot* in 1956, "immobilized" audiences "for weeks": "Historically, people had assumed that in order to have a valid theatrical event you had to have x. Beckett did it with x minus 5 ... He's now doing it with x minus 25."[8] Shepard experienced a similar epiphany, once remarking that shortly before he began to contribute to New York's burgeoning "Off-Off-Broadway" movement in the early 1960s, he was barely more than a theatrical neophyte guided only by his experiences of high school productions and the model of *Waiting for Godot*, which a "beatnik" had causally given him to read: "We were listening to some jazz or something and he sort of shuffled over to me and threw this book on my lap and said, 'Why don't you dig this, you know?' ... It was *Waiting for Godot*. And I thought, what's this guy talking about, what is this? And I read it with a very keen interest."[9]

However significant, as *Waiting for Godot* certainly was for a postwar generation of young playwrights, more than dramatic structure or the conventions of theatrical minimalism were and are at stake. Beckett, for example, has exerted an obvious and profound impact on postwar philosophy. In this regard, given my invocation of Kott, it might seem incongruous to agree with commentators like Alain Badiou who recently – and rather feistily – disparaged nihilistic readings of Beckett's *oeuvre* as reflective of a "two-bit, dinner-party vision of despair" which should be "repudiated."[10] "Negation," Banville similarly observes in his contribution to *Beckett 100 Years: Centenary Essays* (2006), an anthology celebrating the centenary of Beckett's birth, "is not nihilism,"[11] even if commentators like Theodor Adorno writing about the Holocaust and *Endgame* understood this relationship differently. Given Kott's reflection on the operations of a "grand mechanism" of cruelty in his chapter on *King Lear* and *Endgame* in *Shakespeare Our Contemporary*, he rather amazingly advances a view of

Shakespeare that at times complements Badiou's understanding of Beckett. Glossing a line from Prospero's monologue in *The Tempest* – "And my ending is despair" – Kott insists that despair "does not mean resignation," supporting his inference with a line from *Antony and Cleopatra*: "My desolation does begin to make/A better life."[12] Thus, as we shall see, although evocations of the Holocaust and a more nihilistic Beckett occasionally surface in Northern Irish writing, a testament to Beckett's enduring importance to both an old century and new millennium, recent writers find a multitude of other meanings – and beauties – in his work.

Another provenience of "Beckett, Our Contemporary" is far less complicated than disagreement over Beckett's putative nihilism. And, again, it is hardly "news" that Beckett's work has inflected the thought of, among others, Adorno, Badiou, Gilles Deleuze and Félix Guattari – and that Jacques Derrida once famously rationalized that because he felt so close to Beckett he was unable to write about him. Many of these matters demand our attention and will receive it, particularly in the chapter that follows. Equally important, though, and in some ways an analogue to Beckett's prominence in European philosophy, are the influential writers who have turned to Beckett to explain the history of Irish literature or, more broadly, to define irreducible qualities of Irishness and the Irish experience. The former topic might be regarded as an addendum to, or gentle correction of Vivian Mercier's influential book *The Irish Comic Tradition* (1962) which, at almost the same time Kott was adducing similarities between *King Lear* and *Endgame*, attempted the unlikely project of demonstrating how Beckett's writing reveals a "continuity with a [Gaelic] tradition of whose very existence he is hardly aware."[13] In *Irish Classics* (2001), Declan Kiberd seems at times to hazard the even more daunting enterprise of tracing the presence of Beckett in Irish writing centuries *before* Beckett was born. In the early pages of *Irish Classics*, destitute seventeenth-century bards resemble "Beckettian tramps who once had learning but now face a deteriorating situation"; lines in seventeenth-century Gaelic poetry proclaiming the banning of poetry are "deeply, richly poetic" in a manner that will "become familiar" in Beckett's work; and "moments of animation in [Irish] culture" from the seventeenth century to the mid-twentieth parallel "Samuel Beckett's bleak aphorism that it is the search for the means to put an end to things which enables discourse to continue."[14] Beckett is not only *our* contemporary, Kiberd seems to suggest, he has been nearly every major Irish writer's contemporary for something like four centuries. In these and other ways, Kiberd's Beckett, who during my days as a post-graduate student in the 1970s was indexed in bibliographies as a French author and then later, in a more colonial register, as a British one, has now been repatriated by a new generation of Irish scholars. And, as my coda about Beckett and tourism explains, in the twenty-first century he is being made more Irish every day.

Paul Muldoon's view of Beckett complements Kiberd's. In a series of Oxford lectures published as *To Ireland, I* (2000), Muldoon argued that Irish writers have developed a "range of strategies" for "dealing with the ideas of liminality and narthecality that are central … to the Irish experience."[15] In extrapolating his concept of "narthecality" from the architecture of early Christian churches, in which the narthex was a porch or vestibule leading to the nave, Muldoon offers the tantalizing addition that a narthex in the early Church was reserved "for penitents and others not admitted to the Church."[16] If "liminality" in rites of passage defines the condition experienced by initiands "betwixt and between" social categories or formations – a condition shared by Vladimir and Estragon, the narrator of "The Expelled," and many other characters in Beckett's work – then narthecality identifies the site of such a condition. Why those sequestered there cannot be admitted or pass through the threshold – the berm between the assembled congregation and the margin, between town and lonely road, between life and death – and who or what denies them such progress are both more varied and less important than the condition itself and its location. And moments later in *To Ireland, I* – a title that like "Beckett, Our Contemporary" is also an echo, in this case of Donalbain's line in *Macbeth* – Muldoon proclaims Beckett the "Lord of Liminality." What does such a Lord do? How does he exert his power? Recalling one definition of the privileged term *gnomon* in the opening of "The Sisters" from Joyce's *Dubliners* and its reappearance in *Krapp's Last Tape*, Muldoon implies, much as Kiberd does, that Beckett casts his considerable shadow over Irish writing, perhaps as a kind of ghost. After all, the *bec* in Beckett's name may be "construed as a version of the Old English *boc*, a 'beech' that lies behind 'book.'"[17] Taken together, in these tropes Beckett is the "Lord" or shadow or ghost that presides over Irish liminality and the writing that expresses it; in a more arboreal figure, he is the wood or beech from which paper is manufactured and on which Irish writing exists. In a more Freudian register, Beckett resides in a mystic writing pad, a deep etching in a waxy substrate lying below recent Irish writing and Irishness itself.

All these metaphors aside, on the most literal level Kiberd and Muldoon are surely right. While perhaps not omnipresent, Beckett has appeared prominently in Muldoon's poems and others by Derek Mahon and Anthony Cronin; in novels and short fiction by Banville and Bernard MacLaverty; and of course has influenced a rich canon of contemporary

Irish plays by Brian Friel, Martin McDonagh, and Marina Carr, to name just a few. While Mahon produces such evocative poems as "An Image from Beckett" and "Beyond Howth Head," poems which offer extended rejoinders of what, in the latter, Mahon's speaker terms Beckett's "bleak reductio,"[18] a contemplative diner in Cronin's "Lunchtime Table, Davy Byrne's" reflects upon the occupations of his companions and imagines that Joyce and Beckett "give a cachet/To jobs concerned with handouts, trade and art."[19] A weary passenger in MacLaverty's story "At the Beach," from the collection *Walking the Dog and Other Stories* (1994), quips to his wife that in addition to the usual "Wake for Meals" card in the travel kit provided by the airlines they have another, "We give birth astride the grave," and later in the same volume a man who likes to imagine himself as Beckett contributes a recipe for boiling an egg to a cookbook. While McDonagh famously takes the title for *A Skull in Connemara* (1997) in his "Leenane Trilogy" from Lucky's speech in *Godot*, Beckett makes an unlikely appearance near the end of Peter Sheridan's memoir *44 Dublin Made Me: A Memoir* (1999) in the company of African-American blues artists Leadbelly, Howlin' Wolf, and Sonny Boy Williamson because, for the teenaged Sheridan in the 1960s, *Waiting for Godot* was a "two-hour blues song of unbearable pain."[20]

Even if Beckett does not make a cameo appearance within this or that text, literary critics and reviewers seem to find him there anyway, which allows publishers to employ his celebrity for their own purposes on dust jackets and covers. So, for one critic Banville's *Eclipse* (2000) is marked by its paradoxical "Nabokovian lushness" and "Beckettian asperity," and for another, more academic reader of *Eclipse*, Beckett amounts to Banville's "other ghost" in a novel haunted by all manner of ghosts and specters (as much of Banville's work is).[21]

Reviewers of both Marina Carr and McDonagh's plays detect traces of Beckett at every turn, even if Carr herself seems at times chary about the comparison. While, on the one hand, conceding her admiration of Beckett's "black humor" and going so far as to deem her earlier work the product of her "Beckett phase," Carr has claimed more recently, on the other, not to be "hugely influenced" by the "great Irish playwrights of the past," a group which includes Beckett.[22] Nevertheless, commentators consistently characterize her early work *Low in the Dark* (1989) as derivative of Beckett's theatre, particularly in the physical restriction of the character Curtains, which in turn allowed the actress to discover a "new freedom for her voice." Sounding a bit like Muldoon, reviewers found Patrick Mason's 1998 Abbey Theatre production of *By the Bog of Cats* ... set in a familiar "Beckettian no-man's-land" to register its protagonist's occupation of a "liminal space" between society's big house and the tinker's shabby caravan.[23] More recently, writing in the *Guardian* Lyn Gardner describes Carr's *Woman and Scarecrow* (2006) as a "Beckett-like deathbed drama," a sentiment shared by numerous reviewers.[24] Many of the same characterizations have been used to describe McDonagh's canon – his Beckettian humor, for instance, and the haunted self-consciousness of his characters – and Christopher Murray has asserted that the "weakest parts" of *The Cripple of Inishmaan* (1997) occur precisely where "bits of Beckett obtrude."[25]

At this exceedingly early point, however, much like the narrator of *Ill Seen Ill Said*, I am tempted to interpose the cautionary term, "Careful." Be cautious when making claims that promise exactitude or even the "meremost minimum" intellectual certainty about who or what Beckett and the Beckettian are, to borrow a phrase from *Worstward Ho*. It is because of this caution that I inserted that ever so slight comma in the title of this brief commentary – "Beckett, Our Contemporary" – a comma Jan Kott's study of Shakespeare lacks. A comma, of course, scarcely provides the pause this topic requires. When reflecting upon the challenge of playing Mouth in *Not I*, the difficulty of delivering lines so rapidly that they seem "spewed out," Jessica Tandy observed that if Beckett "puts a comma [in the script], he means a comma there. And Beckett puts his four dots in when you need to take a breath."[26] My puny comma is intended to provide such space for a needed breath, a surrogate of the "four dots" any actress playing Mouth so desperately needs. In what precise ways (*pause*) *is* Beckett our contemporary? Can emphases of asperity or spectrality, of grotesque comedy and/or "philosophical cruelty," convey Beckett's influence – or adequately describe Beckett's work itself? Even this hedging, uncertain formulation implies that there is an essential, unchanging Beckett to uncover who spans the time between, say, *Whoroscope* and *Stirrings Still*. Among others, Alain Badiou has insisted that this is not the case, that with the publication of *Comment C'Est* (*How It Is*) in 1961 Beckett began a new moment in his writing and thinking. Not surprisingly, then, the signifier "Beckett" and its adjectival form "Beckettian" require our attention: What does it mean to call any writer or literary work "Beckettian"? How do we understand this adjective and manage its connotations?

So, the lone comma – perhaps there should be five or six – represents the need to slow down, to work through ideas more carefully, one of which I have labored to avoid and inserted hesitantly in the preceding paragraph: "influence." An enterprise like this one must confront the idea of literary and cultural influence, however anxiety-producing such a confrontation promises to be in the wake of Harold Bloom's well-known meditations on the issue. In his 1997 "Preface" to *The Anxiety of Influence* (1973), a preface that anticipates his later devotional tract *Shakespeare: The Invention of the Human* (1998), Bloom advances several formulations of influence that bear upon this conversation. He argues, for example, that the "largest truth of influence is that it is an irresistible anxiety: Shakespeare will not allow you to bury him, or escape him, or replace him," and that "Joyce, Burgess, and Fraser in their different ways acknowledge the contingency that Shakespeare imposes upon us, which is that we are so influenced by him that we cannot get outside of him."[27] Such influence for writers like Henrik Ibsen, according to Bloom, engendered a "horror of contamination." For Bloom, "influence," as it appears in Shakespeare's own writing, might mean "inspiration," or, more determinatively, it might signal "the flowing from the stars upon our fates and personalities." Muldoon's *gnomonic* shadow of influence, then, might in other metaphorical registers characterize the actions of Lear's wanton gods who torture us for their sport, or reveal a contaminant that parasitically insinuates itself into our anguish, or identify the "sheeted dead" whose "gibber" is as foreboding as that of the Romans Horatio describes in *Hamlet* and the Northern Irish prisoners at Long Kesh Muldoon similarly refers to as "sheeted dead" in his verse play *Six Honest Serving Men*.[28]

In the pages that follow I try to account for these possibilities insofar as Beckett and contemporary Irish and Northern Irish writing are concerned, leaving it to others to conduct analogous investigations of contemporary French, British, and world literatures. On occasion, to employ the spectral trope common to such projects – Tony Roche's privileging of Beckett as the "ghostly founding father" of contemporary Irish drama, for instance – two other "ghosts" will make recurrent appearances, indeed, they already have: Shakespeare and Joyce.[29] As Bloom insists, we cannot escape Shakespeare – and neither could Beckett nor the contemporary Irish writers who have followed him. *Hamlet* and *King Lear* in particular are so much a part of a transnational cultural imaginary that they make Shakespeare unavoidable, and so, too, in Irish writing are *Dubliners*, *A Portrait of the Artist as a Young Man*, and *Ulysses*. In the pages that follow, I hope to make an analogous case for the large shadow, or contaminative viral potential – or just plain importance – of Samuel Beckett to contemporary Irish writing.

In this way I hope to extend the projects of Vivian Mercier, Declan Kiberd, Paul Muldoon, and others by considering cultural texts produced after the mid-twentieth century. In a later chapter these include works by Marina Carr and Sam Shepard, whom I regard as a kind of honorary Irishman by virtue of the premiere of his 2007 play *Kicking a Dead Horse* at the Abbey Theatre, and the Abbey's abiding interest in his plays. In three earlier chapters, however, I want to pay particular attention to the often more subtle cases of Brian Friel, Bernard MacLaverty, Paul Muldoon, and Derek Mahon, excavating Beckett and connotations of the Beckettian in post-1968 Northern Irish work, much of which represents the historical impasse known as "The Troubles." For as capacious as Mercier, Kiberd, and Muldoon are, none of them sustains an engagement with Irish writing beyond the mid-century and such figures as Flann O'Brien, Louis MacNeice, Patrick Kavanagh, and a few others. "Coverage" or encyclopedic reach is not the aim of this project and, consequently, the roster of writers discussed in the chapters that follow is not a long one, although many more will be included than the titles of my chapters might seem to suggest. More important will be refinements of matters that have only been sketched roughly above – Beckett's dark humor, liminality, expressive underdevelopment, ghostly influence, and so on – all of which are undertaken in the next chapter.

This chapter begins, however, with another motif that runs throughout this book: the adequacies and copious inadequacies of literary criticism – the latter made more conspicuous by any project that attempts to assess the contemporaneity of a writer, or any figure for that matter, from the past. Obviously, "influence" can scarcely be conceptualized as "anxiety," but equally misleading is the very notion of an intellectual trajectory that proceeds in only one direction: from past to present. If Beckett – or Shakespeare or Joyce – is our contemporary, it is not only because he has pressed himself upon us, but also because we have made him our contemporary or *needed* to make him so. In the process, we may also have "retrofit" such writers in the same way an older building is "brought up to code" with new overhead sprinkler systems, widened entrances and exits, and other improvements. In the process, though, we may have modified the original in outrageous ways – sprinkler systems are one thing, fuchsia-colored carpeting with puddles of lime-green paisley is quite another.

Nothing is "pure and simple" in Beckett, to echo a refrain from *How It Is*, and neither are the myriad ways in which Beckett ... is our contemporary.

NOTES

1. Anthony Roche, "Samuel Beckett: The Great Plays after *Godot*," in *Samuel Beckett 100 Years: Centenary Essays*, ed. Christopher Murray (Dublin: New Island, 2006), pp. 65–66.
2. Paul Muldoon, *The Annals of Chile* (New York: The Noonday Press, 1994), p. 39.

3. All quotations from *Company, Ill Seen Ill Said*, and *Worstward Ho* come from the volume Samuel Beckett, *Nohow On* (New York: Grove Press, 1996). Page citations will follow quotations in the text.
4. James Knowlson discusses this in *Damned to Fame: The Life of Samuel Beckett* (New York: Grove Press, 1996), p. 433. Nell's emphasis of the pair's midnight walks and their "spificated" condition perhaps owes more to Anthony Cronin's extended discussion of the "midnight promenades" of Beckett and Giacometti in *Samuel Beckett: The Last Modernist* (London: HarperCollins, 1996), pp. 279–81.
5. Thomas Kilroy, *The Shape of Metal* (Oldcastle: Gallery Books, 2003), p. 56.
6. Jed Horne, "Is New Orleans *Waiting for Godot*?" *The Huffington Post*, November 14, 2007: www.huffingtonpost.com.
7. Holland Cotter, "A Broken City. A Tree. Evening," *The New York Times*, December 2, 2007, p. 21.
8. Mel Gussow, *Conversations with Stoppard*, rpt. in *Beckett Remembering Remembering Beckett: A Centenary Celebration*, eds. James and Elizabeth Knowlson (New York: Arcade Publishing, 2006), p. 283.
9. Kenneth Chubb and the Editors of *Theatre Quarterly*, "Metaphors, Mad Dogs and Old Time Cowboys: Interview with Sam Shepard" (1974), rpt. in *American Dreams: The Imagination of Sam Shepard*, ed. Bonnie Marranca (New York: PAJ Publications, 1981), p. 191.
10. Alain Badiou, "The Writing of the Generic," rpt. in *On Beckett*, trans. Nina Power and Alberto Toscano (Manchester: Clinamen Press, 2003), pp. 3–4. All quotations from this essay, from "Tireless Desire," and from "Being, Existence, Thought: Prose and Concept" come from this volume and will be followed by page numbers in the text.
11. Murray (ed.), *Samuel Beckett 100 Years*, p. 127.
12. Jan Kott, *Shakespeare Our Contemporary*, trans. Boleslaw Taborski (New York: Norton, 1964), p. 341.
13. Vivian Mercier, *The Irish Comic Tradition* (New York and London: Oxford University Press, 1962), p. 76.
14. Declan Kiberd, *Irish Classics* (Cambridge, MA: Harvard University Press, 2001), pp. 14, 17, 21. All quotations from this volume will be followed by page numbers in the text.
15. Paul Muldoon, *To Ireland, I* (Oxford: Oxford University Press, 2000), p. 5.
16. Muldoon, *To Ireland, I*, p. 18.
17. Muldoon, *To Ireland, I*, p. 15.
18. Derek Mahon, *Collected Poems* (Oldcastle: Gallery Books, 1999), p. 53. I will offer a more sustained reading of these two poems in a later chapter on Mahon and Muldoon.
19. Anthony Cronin, *Collected Poems* (Dublin: New Island, 2004), p. 82.
20. Peter Sheridan, *44 Dublin Made Me: A Memoir* (New York: Viking, 1999), p. 263.
21. Brian Duffy, "Banville's Other Ghost: Samuel Beckett's Presence in John Banville's *Eclipse*," *Études Irlandaises* 28.1 (2003), pp. 85–106.

22. See James F. Clarity, "A Playwright's Post-Beckett Period," *The New York Times*, November 3, 1994. In her interview in *Reading the Future: Irish Writers in Conversation with Mike Murphy*, ed. Cliodhna Ni Anluain (Dublin: The Lilliput Press, 2000), Carr suggests the influence of Eugene O'Neill and Tennessee Williams, something evident in her turn to models of Greek tragedy and to the memory play form of *The Mai* (p. 44).
23. See Sarahjane Scaife, "Mutual Beginnings: Marina Carr's *Low in the Dark*," and Bernadette Bourke's "Carr's 'cut-throats and gargiyles': Grotesque and Carnivalesque Elements in *By the Bog of Cats ....*" in *The Theatre of Marina Carr: "before rules was made,"* eds. Cathy Leeney and Anna McMullan (Dublin: Carysfort Press, 2003), pp. 14–15, 139.
24. Lyn Gardner, "Woman and Scarecrow," *Guardian*, June 23, 2006.
25. Ashley Taggert, "An Economy of Pity: McDonagh's Monstrous Regiment," and Christopher Murray, "The Cripple of Inishmaan Meets Lady Gregory," in *The Theatre of Martin McDonagh: A World of Savage Stories*, eds. Lilian Chambers and Eamonn Jordan (Dublin: Carysfort Press, 2006), pp. 166–67, 91.
26. Knowlson and Knowlson, *Beckett Remembering*, p. 237.
27. Harold Bloom, *The Anxiety of Influence*, 2nd edn. (New York: Oxford University Press, 1997), pp. xviii, xxvii.
28. Paul Muldoon, *Six Honest Serving Men* (Oldcastle: Gallery Press, 1995). Scene VI begins: "And all the while the sheeted dead did squeak/and gibber in the cages of Long Kesh/the walls of which they'd smeared with their own keek" (p. 16).
29. Anthony Roche, *Contemporary Irish Drama: From Beckett to McGuinness* (Dublin: Gill & Macmillan, 1994), p. 5.

CHAPTER I

Beckett and the "Beckettian"

> We should not let Beckett's death impose upon his work the kind of finality, or separative integrity, which I believe it so thoroughly resists. We should not assume that we can now understand or possess that work, as readers, teachers, actors or directors, or legislate his legacy too narrowly on the basis of such an assumption.[1]
>
> –Steven Connor, "Over Samuel Beckett's Dead Body" (1992)

> After a remarkably vital period in the 1970s and 1980s, literary criticism in the English-speaking world became sluggish in the 1990s ... Today, literary criticism is very much a tired-dog if not entirely dead-dog discipline. Maybe this is a little too glum.[2]
>
> –Joe Cleary, "The World Literary System: Atlas and Epitaph" (2006)

In his introduction to the Norton edition of *Shakespeare Our Contemporary*, Martin Esslin reaffirms a disciplinary imperative that, after undergoing a process of refinement, will inform this essay and those that follow. The problem is that the discipline Esslin practices is literary criticism which, in Joe Cleary's diagnosis, seems almost dead, languishing from exhaustion and losing ground to younger rivals, the most formidable of which is an exciting "world literature" study with the potential to "liberate comparative literary studies ... from its customary Western European and 'romance languages' straitjacket."[3] Among its virtues, as Cleary summarizes in reviewing two books on the topic, world literature study aspires to "reinvigorate traditional literary history by marrying it to literary geography," particularly the uneven urban terrain of world capitals and the inverse relationship between their economic power and the cultural capital they have accrued. Early twentieth-century Dublin, for example, a scene of armed resistance to colonial hegemony and finally civil war, produced artists of world-class caliber; by contrast, Belfast during the same period opted to "tie its fortunes to London and to remain a provincial city," thereby enjoying relative economic prosperity and greater stability, yet forfeiting any "significant place in the annals of modern literature."[4] Cleary tempers his generally sanguine report on this intervention with reservations, yet there is no denying his admiration for the interpretive potential of world literature study, something brought into sharper relief when juxtaposed to the enervated discipline it might just replace: "At a time when literary criticism has so often reduced itself to ritual semiotic joustings or mock battles of no consequence, this [intellectual] work has the courage to think big and take risks."[5]

This *does* sound a little glum.

To be sure, humanistic disciplines have suffered of late from a kind of malaise or, to change metaphors, intellectual atrophy. But is it necessarily true, as Pascale Casanova charges in *The World Republic of Letters* (1999), a book motivating many of Cleary's indictments, that literary critics invariably practice a "radical monadology," or that only the "global configuration or composition" of the total literary carpet – and "that alone" – is capable of "giving meaning and coherence to the very form of individual texts"? To address the former issue, traditional literary history of a formalist bent may indeed regard each work as a "perfect unity that can be measured in relation only to itself," but if this were the only conception of textuality that obtained over the past fifty years, such enterprises as semiotics or new historicism would never have been launched.[6] No doubt a "new method of interpretation," as Casanova claims, *can* be derived from the understanding that "the writer stands in a particular relation to world literary space by virtue of the place occupied in it by the national space into which he has been born." In particular, she emphasizes that Beckett, "despite the fact that few writers seem further removed from the reach of history, for the course of his career – which led him from Dublin to Paris – can be understood only in terms of the history of Irish literary space." Hence, the "dual historicization" she proposes might revive literary history as it also "allows us to describe the hierarchical structure of the literary world and the constraints that operate within it."[7] Taken together with *The World Republic of Letters*, Casanova's later study *Samuel Beckett: Anatomy of a Literary Revolution* (2006) and its trenchant reading of *Worstward Ho* recalls for me, perhaps perversely, the punch line of Nagg's monologue in *Endgame*, which compares an imperfect "WORLD" to an expertly stitched pair of trousers. Which is finally greater or more impressive: the "world republic" of letters with its forays into the larger literary marketplace and its "dual historicization" of writers; or, to borrow from the subtitle of Casanova's later book, Beckett's "literary revolution"?

In my view, however, it is possible to attain results similar to the kind Cleary applauds – the refocusing of attention to the accumulating cultural capital of cities like Belfast, for instance – by revising the literary criticism he derides. A less risky ambition than the world literature project, perhaps, or an instance of starting small before thinking in larger terms, such an intervention might never completely exonerate the discipline from the charges Cleary levies, but let's be fair: the best literary criticism always aspires to more than a blinkered monadicism or a rehashing of the "preciosities and trivial arcana" to which academic philosophy has been reduced for Banville's jaded protagonist in *Shroud* (2002).[8] At the same time it would seem foolish to deny the discipline's past and the shortcomings Cleary outlines. To fly past these nets, literary criticism must recalibrate its terminology, resist imprecise generalizations and claims – and, one hopes, take less interest in inciting "mock" battles of negligible intellectual consequence (let's just save these for the meetings of academic departments). Such redactions, of course, assume that the object of literary critical attention is still culturally significant; that is to say, from the perspective of a hipper cultural studies, it may not be the discipline of criticism that's "dead-dog," but rather literature itself. Sketching the contours of an intellectual moment after the "golden age of cultural theory" has passed, Terry Eagleton wryly observes that "In the old days, the test of what was worth studying was quite often how futile, monotonous and esoteric it was." By contrast, in some circles the only criterion of an object of study is "whether it is something you and your friends do in the evenings," a standard that excludes almost nothing from critical exegesis: French kissing instead of French theory (Eagleton's enviable witticism), body piercings, "gangsta" rap, television, and almost anything that can be located in everyday experience.[9] I have no wish to disparage this broader cultural study, although the pages that follow have little to do with it until we arrive at the golf courses and *faux* Big Houses in my "Coda." Moreover, a demonstration of the ways in which Samuel Beckett's writing informs contemporary Irish writing need not fetishize the esoteric and should be capable of commenting on everyday lives in Dublin, Derry, Belfast, and elsewhere. The question is, "How?"

To rise from its sickbed, literary criticism, to return to the introduction of *Shakespeare Our Contemporary*, must first engage Esslin's analogy between the work of its practitioners and that of historians: "The writing of history and, above all, literary criticism can, and must, always be understood as an attempt to find in the past aspects of human experience that can shed light on the meaning of our own times."[10] In the most compelling chapter of *Shakespeare Our Contemporary*, as I have mentioned, Kott acts on this imperative, explaining how both the dramatic form and "philosophical cruelty" of Shakespeare's *King Lear* exceed the conventions of early modern tragedy even as they approach the grotesque comedy of Beckett's *Endgame*.

Nearly a half century later we may no longer be persuaded by readings of Beckett couched in the trappings of absurdism, even if, like Charles Lyons, we recognize that there was no "clearer way of addressing Beckett's texts in the 1960s than seeing them related to the existential search for self-definition in which the human figure … attempt[s] to forge an operative image of the self."[11] A contemporary generation of Irish and Northern Irish writers tends to read or perhaps, as Bloom would have it, *misread* Beckett – and Shakespeare – differently, in an unavoidable act of "poetic misprision,"[12] and it is the purpose of this project to delimit these readings while tracing the ways in which Beckett's work "belongs to and continues to compel the thought of our time …"

Steven Connor completes this thought by citing the "repeated and insistent discovery of the impossibility of disembodied thought" as the primary reason for the contemporaneity of Beckett's canon.[13] Yet such a keen insight about the relationship between embodiment and thought in Beckett – as we shall see, embodied thought leads inevitably to a corporalized language, with all the deficiencies this implies – amounts to only one thesis about the matter. At the same time, it also reveals a critical tendency inherent to such an assessment: namely, the need to totalize an *oeuvre* that, in a different essay written shortly after Beckett's death in 1989, Connor conceded "thoroughly resists" the assignment of a "separative integrity" or essentiality. Equally problematic, the imposition of historical delimitations of the ways in which Beckett remains vital to contemporary Irish literature can prove a daunting and, at times, almost counterintuitive task. In his meditation on *Endgame* and *King Lear*, for example, Kott seems not so much to adduce Beckett's similarities to Shakespeare but, paradoxically, to underscore Shakespeare's affinities with Beckett, thus inverting the trajectory of Esslin's prescription by showing how the present explains the past as much as the past illuminates "our own times." And within this temporal reversal even more interpretive danger looms, a peril as inherent to interpretation as it is to memory for Banville's self-conscious narrator in *Athena* (1995): "How can I say for certain what I felt or did not feel? The present modifies the past; it is a continuous, insidious process."[14] Beckett begins *Proust* (1957), his most profound meditation on memory, with a similar observation about its transformative capacity: "There is no escape from yesterday because yesterday has deformed us, or been deformed by us."[15] Esslin's literary criticism, that privileges the past's ability to inform the present, thus needs to be reconceived as a process that, like memory, also runs in the opposite direction as the present modifies, even deforms, the past, as revisionism in some instances has done and an unbridled presentism could do.

In the preface I alluded to a similar temporal inversion in such recent studies of Irishness and Irish literature as Declan Kiberd's *Irish Classics* and Paul Muldoon's *To Ireland, I*. A little more should be said about this. While for Casanova "classics" embody "the very notion of literary legitimacy" and possess the greatest cultural capital, for Kiberd, less given to metaphors of the marketplace, a classic is "news that stays news" long after it has exerted a profound impact in its own time.[16] (The concept of an "Irish classic" would seem, from Casanova's perspective, almost oxymoronic, for "classics" in her world republic of letters possess transnational cultural capital.) In an almost Herculean labor, Kiberd surveys Irish writing from bardic poetry of the seventeenth century and the works of Jonathan Swift and Oliver Goldsmith in the eighteenth through such later "classics" as Lady Gregory's *Cuchulain of Muirthemne*, J. M. Synge's *The Aran Islands*, James Joyce's *Ulysses*, Flann O'Brien's *At Swim-Two-Birds*, Kate O'Brien's *The Ante-Room*, and Patrick Kavanaugh's *The Great Hunger*. Given this ambition, it seems at first blush surprising that none of the book's thirty-five chapters devotes itself exclusively to Beckett; later, though, it becomes clear that this is neither an omission nor a defect in Kiberd's argument, but rather a sign of Beckett's presence throughout.[17] Indeed, Beckett looms *everywhere* in *Irish Classics*, most intriguingly, perhaps, in poetry written centuries before his own because, for Kiberd, both early Irish literature and the work of more recent writers like Kavanagh and Beckett reveal their hatred of "the language of masters." This hatred catalyzed an "estrangement from their own language"; led to the eventual refinement of an "expressive underdevelopment"; and, in a phrase rich with interpretive possibility, motivated their cultivation of an irreducibly Irish aesthetic space made – recalling Emily Dickinson's evocative phrase – "sumptuous by destitution" (590).[18] Thus, Irish space *is*, to a great extent, Beckettian space.

Kiberd's appropriation of Dickinson's "sumptuous destitution," a leitmotif in *Irish Classics*, provides a stabilizing rubric in this chapter for what otherwise might result in excursuses rivaling Molloy's random jaunts on his bicycle. That is, the discussion that follows will be organized by phrases and keywords advanced by some of Beckett's most incisive students to which several of my own will be added. As Robert Scholes reminds us, a properly *critical* reading – of Beckett or any writer's work, or of almost any cultural form – must finally "get somewhere, must open some new perspective on the text read, and not simply double or repeat the text respectfully." A critical reading should aspire to greater "exorbitance," venturing out of the ambit of an individual text, however impossible it is to stand outside of textuality per se.[19] My later readings of Brian Friel, Bernard MacLaverty,

Paul Muldoon, Derek Mahon, Marina Carr, and others are intended to "get somewhere," to move beyond influential understandings of Beckett's contemporaneity like "sumptuous destitution" and "embodied thought."

But prerequisite to any speculation about Beckett's contemporaneity is the reaching of some consensus about the first term in the title of this book – Beckett. For how could Beckett help us "get somewhere" with any writer's work without even a provisional agreement about what we mean when invoking his name (or aegis)?[20] Beyond its obvious reference to that historical personage who was born in Foxrock in 1906, lived much of his life in France (dying there in 1989), and produced a now familiar canon of texts attributed to him, the referent "Beckett" remains startlingly open to interrogation even though, as A. Alvarez predicted years ago, by the time the twentieth century had run its course as much was written – or *seems* to have been written – about Beckett as about Christ, Napoleon, or Wagner.[21] What do we understand "Beckett" to mean? When "Beckett" is modified as an adjective to characterize a writer's work – "So and so's play or novel is Beckettian" – how do we manage its range of connotations? Such questions are fraught by the necessity of hypostatizing a separative integrity or essentiality for the very works Connor describes as resistant to such formulations. Moreover, any attempt to decode the Beckettian in this post-Barthesean, post-Foucauldian intellectual moment – more authorial adjectives to unpack! – must consider concepts like the "author function," binarisms like closed literary "work" versus more semiotically open cultural "text," and constructions of an intertextual production of meaning incompatible with the image of a solitary Romantic laboring on a chapbook. That academics and theatre reviewers wield terms like "Beckettian" with the celerity with which they employ the most mundane of adjectives, as I have just done, isn't of much help. They presume we know what they mean, and we seldom press them for more specificity.

In what amounts to the equivalent of doctors urging the display of warning labels on cigarette packets or vials of prescription drugs, scholars have further complicated the matter by issuing thoughtful admonitions about the deployment of authorial adjectives. In *Modernism and the Culture of Celebrity* (2005), Aaron Jaffe historicizes authorial adjectives in the modernist moment – Joycean, Woolfean, Firbankean, Eliotic – as functioning like "imprimaturs" that in toto "comprise a makeshift register, an inventory ... charged with the utmost degree of connotative aura." This situation, he argues, is "homologous with a conception of literary value articulated in much of modernist literary criticism."[22] Outside of this economy, one in which the names of the gods of High Modernism can be exploited to valorize some writers' works and not others, an author's name becomes both "a means of universalizing a continuous, ontological restatement of the author function" and a promise to condense a writer's production by "digest[ing] the entire work of reading."[23] And authorial adjectives promise even more when this digestion evolves into a broader interpretive claim.

In this regard, it matters little whether one is discussing creative or critical work, as authorial adjectives function similarly in both domains. Speaking of the Russian theorist Mikhail Bakhtin, whose *oeuvre* is complicated by the works he may have produced with two close friends, Simon Dentith dismisses the idea of "constructing a 'system' out of his work" as a thoroughly "misplaced ambition." Part of the difficulty, Dentith maintains, is that while Bakhtin is a "wide-ranging, imaginative and suggestive writer," he is not a "systematic one" – whatever this means. His value to us now, therefore, is "certainly not that of a ready-made interpretive system which can be 'applied' to a range of writing ..."[24] Neither can something called "the Beckettian" operate as a "ready-made interpretive system." Acutely aware of the stakes in the debate about authorship between affording "primacy to large, relatively impersonal and intersubjective phenomena such as 'codes' or 'discourses,' or to the agents who use them," Dentith finally settles on a theoretical middle ground in which writers possess sufficient agency "to inflect, negotiate and redirect the discourses at their disposal ... in at least partially intended ways."[25]

Fair enough. If one can conceive of Bakhtinian thought as the result of a partial intentionality, so too can "Beckett" and "Beckettian" be regarded as deriving from a more considered notion of invention. If literary criticism is not "book-keeping," as Beckett observed in his essay on *Finnegans Wake*, neither is it a gesture of obeisance to God-like creators.[26] Instead, one *could* imagine "Beckett" as signifying a nexus of inflections of and negotiations with, say, philosophical discourse on subjectivity or modernist discourses on textuality.[27] Yet such assertions of a limited agency scarcely seem "Beckettian" – or is it Beckettian enough? – when juxtaposed to passages like this one from *Molloy* in which Beckett's protagonist contemplates invention and arrives at a dispiriting conclusion:

> And truly it little matters what I say, this, this or that or any other thing. Saying is inventing. Wrong, very rightly wrong. You invent nothing, you think you are inventing, you think you are escaping, and all you do is stammer out your lesson, the remnants of a pensum one day got by heart and long forgotten ...[28]

In this formulation, expression cannot be the product of invention, in part because as readers of Beckett know, saying is always already ill saying or "missaying." But even if this weren't the case, even if words were not so – "What is the word? What the wrong word?" (*Nohow On*, p. 56) – inadequate, their enunciation may originate in a half-remembered pensum "got by heart" that can be summoned when required. Just as stammering may be the product of muscle spasms, or the effect of "disruptions in [that] part of the auditory cortex in which we hear *ourselves* speak,"[29] the process of invention is rendered as mechanical and dubious as it is "very rightly wrong." Molloy's rumination, then, articulates the "meremost minimum" conception of invention and, by extension, of authorship, leading us toward a dunciad of "tatter'd ensigns" and a Rag-Fair textuality of "impersonal" codes and discourses, none of them original.

This view of a diminished author endowed with only a smidgen of agency, however, or of one who traffics in second-hand intellectual goods, is still not quite reducible to a mutterer of pensums. As Paul Ricoeur reminds us, the classical model of education, of *paideia*, "consists in the *recitation* of the lesson learned *by heart*" in which "authority ... more precisely enunciative authority" is on conspicuous display.[30] Within such a pedagogy the student can be doubly manipulated by both the mastery of the teacher and the cultural authority of the lesson: the rules of grammar so central to formal language training, the canonicity of culturally valorized poems and plays, and so on. The desired outcome of such a pedagogy is an indelible imprinting or *tupos* so that culturally valorized bytes become fixed in a student's memory where they reside "available for activation."[31] Unfortunately, getting something "by heart" can also be the result of an even more extreme coercion, for "pensum" also connotes a lesson wielded as punishment, as in a teacher's dictum to an unruly pupil, "Write this sentence on the chalkboard 200 times." This sense of pensum surfaces early in *The Unnamable*:

> I was given a pensum, at birth perhaps, as a punishment for having been born perhaps, or for no particular reason, because they dislike me, and I've forgotten what it is. (*Three Novels*, p. 310)

All joking aside, when blurted out loud, pensums, like other "extracts of anxiety," have in actuality *not* been long forgotten, because, as Beckett asserts in *Proust*, "Strictly speaking, we can only remember what has been registered by our extreme inattention" (p. 18). In any case, a pensum amounts to a mechanical reproduction, a dusty spool on an old tape recorder. And the tape must be played before freedom can be secured: "Yes, I have a pensum to discharge, before I can be free, free to dribble, free to speak no more, listen no more ..." (*Three Novels*, p. 310). But can this moment be reached? And if not, what does this imply about authorship?

How about a sliver more of agency or something beyond the freedom to be deaf and mute? For Beckett in *Proust*, the pensum, like other "laws of memory," is "subject to the more general laws of habit" (p. 7). Habit is the "Goddess of Dulness" and, "if Habit is the Goddess of Dulness, voluntary memory is Shadwell, and of Irish extraction" (p. 20). From this point of view, voluntary memory emerges from a genealogy of comically skewered figures in both John Dryden's *Mac Flecknoe* (1682) and Alexander Pope's *The Dunciad* (1729). In the former, Mac Flecknoe, a stand-in for hack dramatist Thomas Shadwell, is "mature in dullness" from his "tender years" and, like his Irish priest-father, Richard Flecknoe, has been "confirmed in full stupidity"; in the latter, "e'er mortals writ or read," Dulness once ruled unchallenged. Diminished in an age in which comic ingenuity has usurped much of her power, she remains determined to restore her primacy: "Still her old empire to confirm, she tries,/ For born a Goddess, Dulness never dies." (Instead, she haunts "Rag-fairs" of intellect in search of second-hand goods). In *Proust*, involuntary memory has the wherewithal to oppose Dulness's dynastic ambition, as it boasts a revolutionary power capable of summoning the "real," Dulness's most formidable nemesis. The point of this brief stop at Dryden and Pope, however, is this: Is "the Beckettian" reducible to only a morsel of invention, a rusty tin of intellectual beans?

Such a question poses a significant impediment to definitions of the "Beckettian" by intimating that it might be decidedly un-Beckettian even to contemplate such a project, or that the inevitable end of such an endeavor is preciosity. For although Banville may be correct that "all" of Beckett's work, from Belacqua's fumbling in *More Pricks than Kicks* to the groping for speech in the poem "what is the word," is "first and foremost a critique of language,"[32] this same canon can also be seen to enact a critique of authorship from *Proust* to *Ill Seen Ill Said*. In the latter, Beckett depicts his central character by reference to the legend of Memnon – like a statue, the old woman is "erect" and "rigid" (*Nohow On*, p. 49) and later adopts a "Memnon pose" (p. 69)[33] – invoking the mythology of an object that sings at receiving the morning light:

> From where she lies she sees Venus rise. On. From where she lies when the skies are clear she sees Venus rise followed by the sun. Then she rails at the source of all life. On. At evening when the skies are clear she savours its star's revenge. (p. 49)

The sun, metaphor for poetic inspiration and life itself, is here something to be railed against and, while Beckett's text never ramifies all the dimensions of the legend, one might note that the twin Colossi of Memnon were not associated with song or poetry until *after* an earthquake in 27 BC partially collapsed the north statue. Singing in this case might more accurately be rendered as "singing" – as in the headline in Orson Welles' *Citizen Kane* when Kane marries the hopeless "singer" Susan – for, as one reference book explains it, this whistling tribute to poetic inspiration results from the evaporation of moisture in the pores and cracks of the statue's rock, making this "art" as subject to natural forces as pensums are to mechanical recitation.

Even so, even if invention can be reduced to a nonintentional natural phenomenon – and the resultant art amounts to a stammer or "song" – it must exhibit some identifying mark to be discernible as Beckettian stammer, as opposed to Stoppardian repartee or Pinteresque silence. Even so, we're not quite out of the woods yet. For what about Jaffe's contention that authorial names promise to distill an author's body of work? Is Beckett, unlike Bakhtin, more systematic, thus making such a condensation possible? Or, as Steven Connor avers, does Beckett's "preoccupation with repetition" constitute a kind of distinct identity:

> There are, to be sure, significant breaks in the chain of repetitions, moments when Beckett seems to achieve some real novelty amid the nothing new, but even these are liable to reversions – as when, for instance, the inhabitant of closed space who begins *Company* ends up crawling, like the inhabitant of the mud in *How It Is*.[34]

While no one has studied repetition in Beckett more intently than Connor, at times there exists in his meditation a circularity about the question of identity. On the one hand, some identity or essence, some essential Beckett, must exist; if it did not, any repetition would be totally illegible:

> For there can never be any such thing as pure or exact repetition. In order to be recognizable as such, a repetition must, in however small a degree, be different from its original.[35]

On the other hand, the terms "original" and "repetition" are forever in a kind of dialectical flux:

> Origin and repetition are to be understood as moments in an unending process of mutual definition and redefinition. It is for this reason that Derrida refuses to see origin and repetition in a relationship of simple presence and simple absence, the original being defined as a presence by the absent, potential repetition.[36]

Repetition, then, at times *may* approach Beckett's involuntary memory, whose brightness illuminates "what the mock reality of experience never can and never will reveal – the real" (*Proust*, p. 20); equally important, repetition delimits the signifiers "Beckett" and "Beckettian."

Repetition so construed relies upon suppositions of both an original and of a temporal process, the latter of which further complicates definitions of the Beckettian. Ideas about time almost always inhere in conceptions of

Beckett or any other artist, as they do in both Banville's thesis about Beckett's career enacting a critique of language and my conviction about his similar preoccupation with invention and, by extension, authorship. Such assertions presume continuity through time by implying that "Beckett" in 2007 is largely the same as Beckett in 1957 or 1937. The result, at the risk of veering toward the tautological, is decidedly *un*Beckettian: "We are not merely more weary because of yesterday," he says in *Proust*, "we are other, no longer what we were before the calamity of yesterday" (p. 3).

But because most readers are *not* like Beckett's Watt, not predisposed to exhaust all logical possibilities in an attempt to ascertain the origins of an endless supply of stray dogs, they often overlook the vicissitudes of authorial adjectives, wielding them thoughtlessly (even if they do so productively). In his positioning of Beckettian aesthetics with a larger surrealist aesthetic, for example, Daniel Albright maintains that "Impudently Bretonesque counterfactualities are an enduring feature of Beckett's work, early and late."[37] Here, we are asked to concur that "counterfactualities" are equally recurrent in Beckett and André Breton. To take another example, David Lloyd brilliantly demonstrates that not only did Beckett's understanding of Jack B. Yeats's painting differ from that of his friend Thomas MacGreevy, but also that the "ultimate *inorganicism* of everything" in Yeats's art, the "post-Cartesian predicament of scission and disaggregation, between mind and matter, subject and object," finally and "notoriously" informs "*all*" of Beckett's work.[38] The positing of a thematic or Stanislavskian "through line," a spine that stabilizes an author through the entire corpus of his works, is so common in literary critical discourse as to be unexceptional. But it is hardly a Beckettian claim, as again *Proust* intimates: "Life is habit. Or rather life is a succession of habits, since the individual is a succession of individuals." Through the brokering of "countless treaties," habit operates between the "subjects that constitute the individual and their countless correlative objects" (p. 8). If individuals can be identified as a result of such treaties, so too can authors. This appears to be the best hope we have, remembering that the terms of treaties might occasionally be re-negotiated.

While some readers posit a unified author through time, others discern breaks in this temporal field. In Connors' more Derridean sense of repetition, something is always changing, if only slightly, but in this latter sense of a more decisive rupture, the change seems irrevocable. Intrigued by a postmodernist world in which distinctions between the imaginary and the real have collapsed, for instance, Richard Kearney regards the publication of *Imagination Dead Imagine* as a confirmation that by 1965 Beckett had "exhausted" the conventional resources of the novel; as a consequence, his writings may be read as "repeated attempts to bring imagination to an end."[39] Alain Badiou also regards the 1960s as marking a turn in Beckett's writing, but for very different reasons. For Badiou, a "transformation" occurred five years earlier in 1960:

> We can take *How It Is* ... as the mark of a major transformation in the way that Beckett fictionalises his thinking. This text breaks with the confrontation that opposed the suffering *cogito* to the grey black of being. It attempts to ground itself in completely different categories ... above all, the category of alterity, of the encounter and the figure of the Other, which fissures and displaces the solipsistic internment of the *cogito*. ("Writing of the Generic," pp. 15–16)

Like Kearney's thesis, Badiou's underscoring of encounters with an Other – a proposition consistent with the "wager" of his masterwork *Being and Event* (1988) that "*ontology is a situation*" [his emphasis] – bristles with potential for reading Beckett and contemporary Irish literature alike.[40] But is it consistent with Badiou's later designation of *Worstward Ho* as a "recapitulatory text" that "takes stock *of the whole* [my emphasis] of Samuel Beckett's intellectual enterprise" ("Being, Existence, Thought," p. 80)?[41] If that enterprise is fundamentally different after the publication of *How It Is* – and, published in 1983, *Worstward Ho* is squarely positioned as a later text – how can it truly summarize the entirety of Beckett's work?

These are the sorts of contradictions inherent to adjectives like "Beckettian," yet they hardly obviate our need, like that of Beckett's protagonists, to press on. The discussion that follows will do just that, advancing several definitions of the Beckettian salient not only for their exemplariness, but also for their applicability to reading recent Irish and Northern Irish writing. These definitions include a meditation on what, in the previous chapter, Marina Carr referred to as Beckett's "black humor," the almost magical functioning of both material objects and such immaterial entities as the voice in Beckett's work as psychically fecund "things," the sudden importance of events in the otherwise *un*eventful fictive worlds he creates, and the project of communicating by way of a language as deficient as the body itself.

BUOYANT FORM AND RIANT SPACIOUSNESS

> Live and invent. I have tried. I must have tried. Invent. It is not the word. Neither is live. No matter. I have tried. (Samuel Beckett, *Malone Dies* [1951])

Fortunately, critics of Beckett's writing tend to agree about a few things. One, to recall Richard Kearney's thesis, concerns the decline of imagination in the later texts; another is represented by Declan Kiberd's emphasis of the "discrepancy between buoyant form and depressive content" in Irish writing from the seventeenth century through the modern period (*Irish Classics*, p. 17). The most potentially depressive and paradoxical of these contents is not only the inevitability of death, but also the possibility that the dead may continue to speak from the grave. As a result, Kiberd promotes *Malone Dies* as a paradigmatic novel both in Beckett's canon and the history of Irish letters: "The attempt [of the dead to speak] has persisted ... in Irish culture, in the diaries of hunger strikers and the poems of condemned rebels on the eve of execution: those critics who have interpreted *Malone Dies* as a radically new narrative without precedent may have ignored these other examples" (*Irish Classics*, p. 43). Both theses inform understandings of the Beckettian. What hasn't been sufficiently troubled, however, is the relationship between these positions, a relationship that finally evolves into a question of incommensurability: How can buoyant form survive the death of imagination? That is, of the several proveniences of comic buoyancy in Beckett's work, memory and imagination must surely rank near the top. The assertion of formal buoyancy thus needs to be parsed more deliberately, enabling finer discriminations in Beckett's canon between a *faux* exhilaration or resilience based in habit or self-deception, and an unblinkered, even philosophical, humor in the faces of death and Time. For it is this latter variety that such writers as Brian Friel, Bernard MacLaverty, and Paul Muldoon use to such great effect in some of their most – and *least* – successful works.

Again, little critical disagreement exists about the preeminent contribution of laughter to Beckett's buoyant form. As a kind of counterbalance to Theodor Adorno's understanding of *Endgame* and its relation to a post-Holocaust metaphysics, for example, Stanley Cavell assesses the play's qualified "hilarity," paying invaluable attention to "repartée" and the play's "adjoining [of] the genres of Restoration comedy, Shakespearean clowning, and the vaudeville gag" to "the sound of philosophical argument and of minute theological debate."[42] Citing Nell's often-repeated line in *Endgame* that "Nothing is funnier than unhappiness," Daniel Albright remarks that "Beckett consciously blasphemes against the distinction between comedy and tragedy on which so much earlier drama is predicated" – the "more obviously wrenching and painful the theme, the airier and more acrobatic the treatment."[43] Contextualizing Beckett not with the surrealists, with whom Albright is concerned, but with late modernists like Wyndham Lewis, Tyrus Miller quotes the same line in arguing that a "peculiar type of laughter" emerges in Beckett's writing as the "zero degree of subjectivity," an "index of a minimal residue of humanness" and a "minimal trace of the instinct for self-preservation."[44] An often-cited encounter in *Watt* further anchors Miller's argument when Arsene, whom Watt displaces in the system of service at Mr Knott's house, gives an impromptu dissertation on three types of laughter – the bitter, the hollow, and the mirthless:

> [T]he mirthless laugh is the dianoetic laugh ... It is the laugh of laughs, the *risus purus*, the laugh laughing at the laugh, the beholding, the saluting of the highest joke, in a word the laugh that laughs – silence please – at that which is unhappy. (p. 48)

All three laughs respond to "successive excoriations of the understanding" and travel a circuit from the ethical to the intellectual to the dianoetic. Bitter and hollow laughs are essentially dianoetic insofar as they originate in the mind, involve the intellect, and, respectively, respond to "that which is not good" and "that which is not true." Indeed, the dianoetic, as the *Oxford English Dictionary* (*OED*) explains, denotes the "operations of the discursive, elaborative or comparative faculties," thereby confirming the existence of a larger intellection and ironic consciousness.

Certainly Beckett's thesis on laughter is not reducible to that of a minor character in a novel, and one might be especially wary of drawing inferences when that character's name shares an etymology with a highly toxic poison.[45] Still, Arsene's taxonomy might help us appreciate Miller's redaction of the Cartesian *cogito ergo sum* to a Beckettian *rideo ergo sum*, "I laugh, therefore I (still) am," and his claim that – borrowing from Julia Kristeva – this laughter opens up a "riant spaciousness": a "rhetorical, textual, and formal structure that occasions laughter."[46] There is more to be said, not so much about Beckett's delineation of an alternative space for laughter in the face of mortality – as Cavell reminds us, his appropriations of conventions from a variety of comic genres are well known – but rather about the quality and dimension of what Miller terms "spaciousness." Stated another way, it should be possible to distinguish those moments when comic business fills – or deadens – time from those in which a purer laughter, a *risus purus* achieved through comparative thought, expands the dimensions of a subject's being. At stake here, I think, is not only a discrimination between emotional resilience in the face of inevitability and a more critical "hilarity," but also a confirmation of the identity of the subject. Miller summarizes this distinction well: "This laughter, functioning to preserve and shore up – to 'stiffen' – a subjectivity at the risk of dissolution, constitutes the telos and minimum basis of formal unity for the late modernist work."[47] To this function of laughter, one might also add the observation Mladen Dolar makes in *A Voice and Nothing More* (2006): "Laughter is a cultural trait of which only humankind is possible."[48] In a novel like *Watt*, one replete with animal noises and interactions with animals – and one in which the title character purportedly suffers from a "loss of species" (p. 85) – Dolar's emphasis of laughter's human origin accrues greater significance.

Like laughter, subjective spaciousness is predicated upon a particularly human, active agency – and imagination. In *The Poetics of Space* (1958), Gaston Bachelard adumbrates an "intimate immensity" that emanates from "pure imagination" and, in so doing, seems to describe a character like Beckett's Hamm. "Immensity," Bachelard observes, "is the movement of a motionless man" and is "one of the dynamic characteristics of quiet day-dreaming."[49] Developing the example of the forest, Bachelard characterizes "immensity" in ways that underscore man's promotion to "the dignity of the admiring being," recalling inadvertently the opening scene of *Endgame* in which Hamm, awakening from a sleep, exclaims, "What dreams! What forests!" (p. 3). In Bachelard's reading, an understanding of this experience of immensity requires a "phenomenology of extension, expansion, and ecstasy." And, in a metaphor of imprisonment that will return at the end of this discussion of riantic spaciousness, Bachelard says this:

> When the dreamer really experiences the word immense, he sees himself liberated from his cares and thoughts, even from his dreams. He is no longer shut up in his weight, the prisoner of his own being.[50]

If this "increase in being" requires imagination or an oneiric faculty that in Beckett's later work is radically diminished, how can riantic spaciousness anchor a definition of the Beckettian?

A comparison, first, between *Endgame* and *Happy Days* might help answer this question. In the latter, Winnie, trapped in a scorched mound of earth, proves to be indefatigable, as her reveries from the past and reading of the present bolster her spirits throughout *Happy Days*. This buoyancy, it seems, oddly relates to both her fallible memory and to the mystery that every audience desires to see unraveled: namely, the past. How did Winnie get in this predicament? Why is her confinement made more extreme between the two acts of the play? Beckett withholds this information, the same knowledge, we later learn, that passers-by named Cooker or Shower have sought: "What's she doing [Mr. Cooker] says? – What's the idea? he says – stuck up to her diddies in the bleeding ground" (*Happy Days*, pp. 42–43). "Strange thing," Winnie says, "time like this, drift up into the mind" (p. 44), confirming both the role of memory in her daily life and our sense that an explanation must exist for her predicament. Yet Winnie, repulsed by the coarseness of the terms "diddies" and "bleeding ground," remains calm in recounting her story and is even amused by what she regards as a fatuous inquiry. She is neither traumatized by the event that led to her imprisonment nor oppressed by a past incrusted "at the heart of the present, which acts as a counterweight to the innocent habit-memory."[51] The topic, like her inventory of misquotations, surfaces to consciousness occasionally, a strange reflection in a place where everything, she concedes, is "strange."

In fact, memories from the past help catalyze Winnie's (and our) buoyancy, and here I am not referring to actions prompted by "habit-memory" – the automatic procedures associated with brushing one's teeth or hair, for instance – but to moments in the play that exemplify Habit's ability to facilitate a "perpetual adjustment and readjustment of our organic sensibility to the conditions of its worlds" (*Proust*, p. 16). As the Goddess who presides over voluntary memory, Habit presents the past through "images" that are "as arbitrary as those chosen by imagination" and "equally remote from reality" (p. 19). This last definition in particular captures Winnie's almost uncanny abilities both to quote (or misquote) literary or Biblical passages that are vastly inappropriate to her circumstances *and* to derive consolation from the practice. In the opening minutes of *Happy Days*, for example, she scours her memory for vaguely remembered "wonderful lines," muttering them as "woe woe is me ... to see what I see" (p. 10). A portion of the audience's bemusement at this point originates in a sight gag. Groping for her spectacles, which require polishing, Winnie quite literally does not see *anything*, as actresses usually signal through squinting eyes and general fumbling about. But the audience's intellectually deeper laughter is evoked by her (mis)quotation of Ophelia's speech in *Hamlet*, an instance, perhaps, of the noetic laughter summarized in *Watt*: "O, woe is me/ T' have seen what I have seen, see what I see" (3.1.160–61). Here, Ophelia is devastated at hearing evidence of a "great mind o'erthrown": by Hamlet's demand that she get to a nunnery, by his indictment of women cosmetically enhancing their faces and, most relevant, by his accusation that women make their "wantonness" their "ignorance." It is thus difficult to understand how the lines can be construed as "wonderful."

Preparing to make herself a new face a few minutes later, Winnie recites similarly incongruous lines from Book Ten of *Paradise Lost*. Running out of lipstick, Winnie bubbles with another "wonderful" passage she must at one time have learned by heart: "Oh fleeting joys – (lips) oh something lasting woe" (*Happy Days*, p. 14). Here, prelapserian innocence and the more serious matter of spiritual damnation are conflated with the momentary pleasures of applying a cosmetic in short supply. But however consolatory these lines may be, is Winnie or the audience moved to the more rarified "dianoetic" laughter of *Watt*? Do these moments add sumptuousness to Winnie's destitution? And, while they may reveal to us something of Winnie's past education and her present addled state, do they perform the work of shoring up – or expanding – her subjectivity? To recall Bachelard's metaphor, do they momentarily liberate Winnie, releasing her from the imprisonment of her being?

Perhaps, though I do not want to suggest that literary allusion comprises the sole or even primary source of riantic spaciousness in Beckett's earlier plays. Examples of physical comedy in *Endgame* and *Waiting for Godot*, and other vaudevillian strategies like "capping the gag," are more crucial and contribute to his greatest theatrical achievements. But not always in the same ways. Consider Hamm's echo of *The Tempest* near the conclusion of *Endgame*: "Our revels now are ended." In Shakespeare's play, Prospero is referring specifically to the pageant of Spirits he produced for Ferdinand and Miranda's spectation – "These our actors/As I foretold you, were all spirits, and/Are melted into air ..." (4.148–50). This echo in *Endgame* has motivated some postcolonial critics to adduce parallels between Shakespeare's play and Beckett's: their abusive master-slave relationships, Caliban's similarity to Clov as a colonized subject, and so on.[52] Hamm's declaration nonetheless implies a dénouement that never occurs in a play so resistant to closure as *Endgame* (Clov is probably still preparing to leave Hamm). Further, Prospero the magician wields the power to summon airy players; Hamm enjoys no such prerogative, and here remarks only on Nagg's retreat into his dustbin after unsuccessfully attempting to rouse Nell from hers.

But more than adding depth to Hamm's character – a clue, perhaps, of his educational background – this reference to *The Tempest* underscores what Connor regards as the embodied reality of Beckett's theatre. There are no spirits in attendance here, no pageants or goddesses, only declining bodies and the haggard "pageant" of the quotidian. If Miller is right to link comic moments in Beckett to the creation of space or the addition of a sumptuousness to the destitution of Hamm's shelter, then perhaps it is also the case that such wry laughter corroborates or "shores up" subjectivity. In describing the poetic word in *Writing Degree Zero*, Roland Barthes characterizes zero degree as a moment in poetry when the Word is "pregnant with all past and future specifications. The word here has a generic form ..."[53] In this instance, "revels" serves as the Pandora's box Barthes describes, from which "fly out all the potentialities of language" and a more dianoetic laughter as well. Killing fleas lodging in crotches, playing with stuffed animals, verbally abusing parents – all these activities qualify as "revels" in Hamm's self-reflexive use of the term. We have witnessed all past specifications of the word in *Endgame* and can predict future ones in the process of "leastening" that is taking its course in Hamm's world.[54]

Other moments of resiliency and comic buoyancy enliven both *Happy Days* and *Endgame*, but many of these originate in a different variety of memory from that sketched above. That is to say, while Winnie deliberately, almost obsessively, searches her internal archive for quotations from Shakespeare, Milton, and popular songs, Hamm's allusion to *The Tempest* seems to emerge from the same region into which Prospero's actors melt: "thin air." The difference, given distinctions Beckett draws in *Proust*, is between a kind of habitual, entirely voluntary process and the "miracle" of "involuntary" memory:

> Involuntary memory is an unruly magician and will not be importuned. It chooses its own time and place for the performance of its miracle. (*Proust*, pp. 20–21)

Involuntary memory is "explosive" not passive; its flame consumes Habit and "in its brightness" reveals "what the mock reality of experience can never reveal – the real" (*Proust*, p. 20). To be sure, Winnie's mangling of quotations, like her frequent appropriations from a linguistic register of "the old style," speaks volumes about her past and its presence in her daily routine, just as her costume and "pearl necklet," like the shabby gentility of the tramps in *Godot*, act as class-markers from her past before she utters a word. But there would seem nothing involuntary or illuminating about her misquotation. These definitions, moreover, prompt other questions about Hamm's echo of Prospero: Is it an example of involuntary memory? While it certainly differs from the imperfect grinding of Winnie's memory – as does her allusion to *Cymbeline* "Fear no more the heat o' the sun" when testing Willie's ability to hear her – does it achieve all the things Beckett attributes to involuntary memory? Does it enable a riantic spaciousness and a Beckettian buoyant form?

Not surprisingly, I would answer "yes" to these questions, in part by juxtaposing Hamm's allusion to *The Tempest* to others that offer ironic humor and supplement character in *Happy Days* and *Waiting for Godot*. Several examples in Beckett's earlier, most influential plays are well-described by what Ricoeur – after Frances Yates – describes as "artificial memory":

> "The artificial (*artificiosa*) memory is established from places and images." As for the "things" that are depicted by the images and the places, these are objects, persons, events, relating to a cause to be argued. What matters is that the ideas be attached to images and that the items be stored in places. We thus meet up again here with the old metaphor of inscription, with places now in the role of the wax tablet and images in that of the letters inscribed on it.[55]

Beckett's plays of the 1950s and 60s contain numerous traces of this kind of memory, one in which a past episode redolent with meaning is metonymically replaced by a location or image. Estragon's cryptic comment in *Waiting for Godot* about once wanting to go to the Dead Sea for his honeymoon; Nell's association of Nagg's story about the tailor with Lake Como and its "white," clean water; and Winnie's reminiscence about sitting on Charlie Hunter's knees, which quickly turns into a memory of her first kiss in the "back garden at Borough Green, under the horse-beech" – all serve as examples of this process. Like Miller's conception of laughter, such memories "shore up" subjectivity, but almost as soon as they are evoked their veracity is challenged or undermined. Nagg remembers that he and Nell almost capsized on Lake Como, not because of Nell's happiness, as she recalls, but because of his comic story; and Winnie quickly adds a toolshed to her reverie of the garden at Borough Green, complete with piles of pots and deepening shadows in the rafters, although "We had no toolshed and he most certainly had no toolshed" (*Happy Days*, p. 16).

Although they might appear spontaneous and uncontrived, all of these recollections border on the factitious, on the artificial; audiences, after all, have no way of confirming these details, as "Nothing is certain" when Beckett's about. Gogo's memory of the map of the Dead Sea, unlike the other two, is neither directly rebutted by Didi nor undercut by his own uncertainty, yet no corroboration guarantees the accuracy of any of his wistful memories, particularly of his honeymoon. All of these examples of artificial memory, then, may produce artifice as a result, though this hardly matters to audiences so desperate for verifiable fact in Beckett's exposition that they eagerly snatch up any shard of information they can find. As such, these scenes on stage form a complement to the tactic so common in Beckett's fiction of what might be termed – after Derrida's grammatology – sentences "under erasure." Such sentences conclude *Molloy*: "It is midnight. The rain is beating on the windows. It was not midnight. It was not raining" (*Three Novels*, p. 176). Both devices, on the stage and on the page, proffer information – and with it, convey some sense of narrative certainty – then withdraw it.[56] But an important difference also obtains: Winnie describes her first kiss with excitement; Nell seems enraptured by her memories of Lake Como; and, to take another example from *Waiting from Godot*, Vladimir dispels his "gloom" by "cheerfully" recalling the days when he and Estragon were "respectable" – "hand in hand from the top of the Eiffel Tower, among the first" (p. 3). The operations of memory and imagination thus sustain Beckett's buoyant form, although not necessarily through an intellectual, self-reflexive laughter or the exposition of the larger story behind the dramatic narrative. Such laughter is far rarer because moments of involuntary memory in Beckett are far rarer. Routine, Habit, and voluntary memory predominate.

Perhaps too influenced by Beckett's *Proust*, I want to distinguish then between moments of riant spaciousness created either by habit or artificial memory and those instances in which involuntary memory flashes with both realism and ironic hilarity, for the latter case yields more momentary liberation from imprisonment. It offers progress, even if the advance seems minimal. As Cavell so convincingly explains, Beckett's unfixing of clichés and defeat of the "implications of ordinary language" create comedy in *Endgame*, provoking laughter in the audience, if not in the characters as well:

HAMM:	I've made you suffer too much.	
	(*Pause*)	
	Haven't I?	
CLOV:	It's not that.	
HAMM (*shocked*):	I haven't made you suffer too much?	
CLOV:	Yes!	
HAMM (*relieved*):	Ah you gave me a fright!	(pp. 6–7)[57]

Other comic devices in these plays, however diverting, are not the provenience of such laughter: broad physical comedy like the shaking of powdery insecticide down Clov's pants, for instance, or the nimble use of double entendres, like Didi's witticism while buttoning his fly in *Waiting for Godot*: "Never neglect the little things of life" (p. 4). Involuntary memory creates another kind of humor that at times may reach the dianoetic laughter described in *Watt*. When, for example, Vladimir tells Estragon that he should have been a poet, the latter responds, "I was. (*Gesture toward his rags*.) Isn't that obvious?" (p. 6). Here, the destitution signaled by their shabby attire becomes a symbol of artistry, but the joke wouldn't work if the poverty of struggling artists weren't a truism shared by Beckett's characters and his audience. Clov's response to Hamm's question, "Do you believe in the life to come?" – itself laughable given their circumstances – is both self-reflexive and pregnant with the future and present Barthes locates at the zero-point: "Mine was always that" (*Endgame*, p. 49). More seriously, we recognize that his life conveys a kind of unrequited potential – a *real* life of fulfillment has not yet existed for Clov. Here comic invention and an involuntary memory of unhappiness produce riantic space *and* the kind of intellection implied by the notion of dianoetic laughter; mere "revels," by contrast, only render the moment more endurable.

For the most part and with the exception of *Company* (1980), Beckett's later texts contain fewer of these moments because in them memory either wounds, as it does in *That Time* (1976) and *Footfalls* (1976), or it, along with imagination, has withered to near extinction. As such, Winnie's reflection on the past differs in kind, *not degree*, from the pain associated with the past in *Footfalls* and *That Time*, where laughter exists in short supply. In the latter, C remarks, "never the same after that never quite the same but that was nothing new if it wasn't this it was that common occurrence something you could never be the same after."[58] With a scintilla of irony, C observes that "turning-point ... was a great word with you," yet however fashionable the term or eccentric his use of it, in this instance the notion of a single event was also an accurate descriptor as opposed to the specious notion of multiple turning *points*: "always having turning points and never but the one the first and last" (*Shorter Plays*, p. 230).

This notion of a single episode from the past haunting the present, however, does not consistently emerge in Beckett's later work. At the close of *Footfalls*, Beckett muddles not only the identity of the characters – Is the Mother talking to May or Amy, or are they one and the same person? – but also the distinction between one and multiple sources of the past's traumatic effects:

> Will you never have done? (*Pause.*) Will you never have done ... revolving it all? (*Pause.*) It? (*Pause*) It all. (*Pause.*) In your poor mind. (*Pause.*) It all. (*Pause.*) It all. (*Shorter Plays*, p. 243)

"It" can only be followed by "all." It *is* all. More important, while the past might be turned to emotional advantage in earlier plays, in *Happy Days* for instance, such emotional spaciousness seems unavailable after *Not I* (1972);[59] thus, the revolutions of May's poor mind are projected onto and confined to the thin nine-step "strip" created by her incessant pacing.

Equally damaging, when not moribund, memory can become just the opposite, unrelenting and uncontrollable, much like the breathless pace of Mouth's lines in *Not I*. Mouth recalls her belief in a "merciful ... (*brief laugh*) ... God (*good laugh*) ... first thought was ... oh long after ... sudden flash ... she was being punished" (*Shorter Plays*, p. 217). She repeats the refrain about a merciful God, as her brain rages uncontrollably "trying to make sense of it ... or make it stop ... dragging up the past ... flashes from all over ..." (p. 220). Once, Mouth's brain was "in control," but by the end of *Not I* it flickers away "like mad" (p. 222). Such laughter scarcely expands space, riantic or otherwise, or supplements an identity verging on dissolution – on the contrary. Further, if laughter *were* to function in this way in the later plays, it would do so in a theatrical space inimical to such an expansive subjectivity. As Stanton B. Garner, Jr. observes, the "strictly aesthetic value of shape" Beckett privileges in his later plays – in *Not I*, Mouth's lips – is largely determined by stage lighting, which "dominates the human figure itself, modifying – even deforming – the body's own shape ..."[60] Moreover, the dazzling brightness of Beckett's earlier plays cannot withstand the encroaching darkness of the later plays – or the grayness of a mise-en-scène in which the "anthropomorphic signatures of 'inhabited space'" have been relinquished for "the aesthetic surface of visual abstraction."[61] Consequently, even when the possibilities of brightness and emotional buoyancy arise in later Beckett, they seem marked as fatuous, as in the first story in *Fizzles* (1976):

> For he might well have succeeded, in the end, up to a point, which would have brightened things up for him, nothing like a ray of light, from time to time, to brighten things up for one. (*Short Prose*, p. 225)

Here, the *faux* buoyancy and cheerfulness of Winnie's misquotation are exceeded by the mocking tone of Beckett's narrator, as rays of light obviously *do* cheer characters like Winnie in his earlier works. Nothing like a ray of light!

Not surprisingly, then, "Fizzle 1" begins with a critical forgetting: "To this vaguely prison garb none of these memories answer, so far, but all are of heaviness ... The great head where he toils is all mockery" (*Short Prose*, p. 224). To Kearney's thesis about the death of imagination in later Beckett, therefore, I would add the decline of both memory and Fancy, sources of riantic spaciousness in his earlier plays. Indeed, "Fancy," construed in vaguely Coleridgian fashion as an intellection different in kind from Imagination, emerges in Beckett's later texts. In *Footfalls*, Amy's Mother asks if she observed anything strange at Evensong, and Amy, who saw nothing, responds, "Just what exactly, Mother, did you perhaps fancy it was? ... Just what exactly, Mother, did you perhaps fancy this ... strange thing was you observed?" (*Shorter Plays*, p. 243). Here, fancy, as it often does, connotes defective perception, false imagining, and a false memory. In *All Strange Away* (1976), however, memory and a slightly different capital "F" Fancy are all interrogated more thoroughly. The story begins with a mocking of narrative convention:

> IMAGINATION DEAD IMAGINE. A place, that again. Never another question. A place, then someone in it, that again. Crawl out of the frowsy deathbed and drag it to a place to die in. Out of the door and down the road in the old hat and coat like after the war, no, not that again. (*Short Prose*, p. 169)

Laughter here, assuming that most readers would find this mocking recapitulation of narrative conventions amusing, depends again upon a kind of dianoesis: an implicit comparison of this introductory paragraph with those of other novels and short stories.

For the central character of *All Strange Away*, however, the consolation of even this self-parodic laughter lies beyond reach, and after the demise of Imagination is announced in the story's opening line, the refrain "Fancy is his only hope" begins. Similarly, for Emma, who later metamorphoses into Emmo and whose pictures in the nude decorate the walls, "Fancy is her only hope" (*Short Prose*, p. 174). We are asked first to "imagine" the protagonist "kissing, caressing, licking, sucking, fucking, and buggering" atomized close-ups of her breasts, anus, and so on, then to "imagine lifetime, gems, evenings with Emma" (p. 171). The narrator then asks us to "fancy" her being "all kissed, licked, sucked, fucked and so on" (p. 172), but shortly thereafter, there is "no image" or sound – "Fancy dead" (p. 173). Here, the drift toward the concerns of traditional literary criticism is clear, as we might recall that the Coleridgian Imagination repeats the "eternal act of creation in the infinite I AM," dissolving, dissipating, and then recreating realities in all of its unfettered power.[62] *Fancy*, by contrast, is relegated to play with "fixities and definites" and for Coleridge is actually a mode of memory; thus, the relationship it would be capable of producing is constrained by the excessive behaviors the narrator delineates. No matter, finally, as Imagination and Fancy are wiped away at the story's conclusion.

By the end of *All Strange Away*, memory joins both as a final victim – "Memories of past felicity no save one faint with faint ripple of sorrow of a lying side by side ..." (*Short Prose*, p. 179) – with the last sentence confirming this loss: "faint sighing sound for tremor of sorrow at faint memory of lying side by side and fancy murmured dead" (p. 181). By the end, Imagination is dead; Fancy lies mortally wounded; and memory languishes doubly faint, tinctured with sorrow at the lack of communion with the Other, only a laying side by side. The narrator's witticism "Fancy dead, to which now add for old mind's sake" (p. 181) thus amounts to little more than an irrelevant quip or a kind of truism: "old time's sake" *does* equate to "old mind's sake." As important as the Other is to the possibility of buoyant form and the creation of a rianic spaciousness – a topic to which I shall turn momentarily – the operations of not only imagination, but also of a more limited Fancy and memory are perhaps even more important.

Company, as I have mentioned, stands paradoxically as both a corroboration of this hypothesis and an exception to much of the later prose – to *All Strange Away* and *Imagination Dead Imagine*, for example, and to those greater achievements, *Ill Seen Ill Said* and *Worstward Ho*.[63] For from its first sentence – "A voice comes to one in the dark. Imagine" (*Nohow On*,

p. 3) – *Company* foregrounds an active imagination, rather than laments its passing, even as it pronounces the domination of the subject by an unidentified, or what Mladen Dolar terms an "acousmatic" voice: a voice whose origin cannot be identified or seen.[64] This voice instantiates memory and provides company "but not enough" (p. 5). In his isolation, Beckett's protagonist resembles all of us: "In isolation, in solitude, in complete loneliness, away from the madding crowd, we are not simply free of the voice," because, as the "very epitome of the society that we carry with us," it cannot be silenced.[65] This internal voice also resembles that of the dead, demanding our remembrance of an old beggar woman's blessing or a father's gentle command, all without revealing its own identity. Yet, by the end of *Company*, "you find yourself imagining you are not alone while knowing full well that nothing has occurred to make this possible" (*Nohow On*, p. 45).

In so doing, *Company* could be viewed in the way *Worstward Ho* is privileged by Badiou: as a "recapitulative" work and "short philosophical treatise ... of the question of Being" ("Being, Existence, Thought," p. 80). But in my reading of *Company*, the "event" and the imperative to speak – two highly valorized concepts in Badiou's understanding of *Worstward Ho* – are replaced by, or bracketed momentarily for, imagination, memory, and subjective expansiveness. In fact, memory in *Company* hearkens back not only to Beckett's earliest writing, but also to his biography, as Anthony Cronin has explained. The memory in *Company* of a young boy who asks his mother about the proximity of the sky, for example, parallels a question in *Malone Dies* and one Beckett, growing up in Foxrock, posed to his own mother. Similarly, the protagonist's recollection of meeting an old woman on the road who calls him "little master" mirrors an experience Beckett most likely had with the tinkers who wandered the roads south of Dublin during his childhood.[66] In these ways, *Company* recapitulates concerns evident in Beckett's writing from the time of "Dante and the Lobster" in *More Pricks than Kicks* and makes available *non*exorbitant readings based on biography and influence, two traditional "little spheres" for literary critical contestation and the marshaling of "trivial arcana."

Company never descends to preciosity, however. Juxtaposed to Mouth's frantic histrionics in *Not I* and the relative absence of memory in *Worstward Ho*, the narrator's intellection in *Company* seems exquisite in calibration:

> In order to be company he must display a certain mental activity. But it need not be of a high order. Indeed it might be argued the lower the better. Up to a point. The lower the order of mental activity the better the company. Up to a point. (*Nohow On*, p. 7)

A "certain activity of mind however slight is a necessary adjunct of company" (*Nohow On*, p. 5), the narrator of *Company* observes earlier, and the oxymoronic "necessary adjunct," much like "sumptuous destitution," hints at the heuristic potential of the term. We know from *Footfalls* and *That Time* that in Beckett unrelenting mental activity tortures rather than heals and that the low cognitive output of a "necessary adjunct" is required. So, when the narrator of *Company* remarks that after the protagonist, as a small boy, asked his mother about the distance of the sky from the earth, the sharp response he received – "For she shook off your little hand and made you a cutting retort you have never forgotten" (p. 6) – does not identify a turning point or trauma. Neither does the shock of discovering a decomposed hedgehog the boy had hoped to rescue: "You are on your back in the dark and have never forgotten what you found then. The mush. The stench" (p. 22). Such memories, horrific and reeking of the bodily, oddly constitute a kind of company, although they hardly generate comic buoyancy. Instead, humor in *Company* is produced by the kind of double entendres and language games common to Beckett's earlier plays, such as the narrator's witticism about an expectant father retiring to the garage during his wife's labor: "You may imagine his thoughts as he sat there in the dark not knowing what to think" (p. 8). So, while *Company* concludes with the all-too-familiar word "Alone," its foregrounding of imagination and memory – the former represented by the emergence and narrative dominance of the terms "devise" and "figment" – is both anomalous in the canon of Beckett's later works and not so productive of the riantic spaciousness of his earlier period.

To conclude this definition, the melding of comic buoyancy and depressive content – again, a supposition that informs many understandings of the Beckettian – more accurately describes his earlier work in which comedic effect is produced by a variety of textual features including both artificial memory and the more illuminating involuntary memory. Such consolation in the face of death or entombment remains in shorter supply for characters in Beckett's later works. Yet even this definition has its limitations. One of these limitations concerns the premise that Beckett's work grows increasingly depressive, as his longtime friend Anne Atik describes in Newtonian terms: "One notices how gravity – in various senses – stripped back his work over time: in the sense of terrestrial gravitation as defined by physics, in the tragic serious sense, and in the literal sense of the weight of words – fewer and fewer at the end of his life ..." While this assessment may seem accurate, Badiou by contrast maintains that "It is not true that Beckett's enterprise develops in a linear fashion ... It is also utterly wrong to maintain, as much critical opinion would have it, that his work drove itself ever deeper into 'despair', 'nihilism', or the defeat of meaning" ("Writing of the

Generic," p. 15). Badiou's animadversion, in my view, is worth heeding: the essential does not change in Beckett, only his characters' ability to transform it in response to their own "organic sensibilities," as Beckett describes the operations of Habit and memory in *Proust*. Importantly, in almost the same breath as she offers her Newtonian reading of later Beckett, Atik recounts Beckett's impatience with the "juvenile" literary allusions "very densely embedded in his early work" and his sense that they "overloaded" some of them.[67] Perhaps. But, tied to memory in *Happy Days*, *Waiting for Godot*, and *Endgame*, such allusions also defined his comic form in a way that the "vile jelly" of *Ill Seen Ill Said* does not. Gags cannot be "capped" without memory and imagination and as *Company* – in which a narrator "Devised deviser devising" figments "all for company" (*Nohow On*, p. 33) – suggests a figment lacks the expansive, dianoetic potential of involuntary memory.

This assertion might be tested against a perhaps unusual counter-example. Recall that in connecting *Malone Dies* to Irish literature's persistent depiction of the dead attempting to speak, Declan Kiberd gently upbraids critics who have ignored the trope in the earlier diaries of hunger strikers or condemned rebels, thus making *Malone Dies* not so much a revolutionary text, but rather one instance in a distinguished line of precedents. The observation seems equally apposite when juxtaposing Beckett's earlier writing to that of a later condemned man, Bobby Sands. In much of his writing from Long Kesh prison in the later 1970s, Sands frequently regarded himself as already dead. In his essay "I Fought A Monster Today" (1978), for example, he complains of being confined to a "dark smelly tomb"; his later poem "A Tribute to Screws" begins, "In the blackness I awoke like a corpse in the grave,/ Engulfed by the fear of a ghostly wave"; and the short prose piece "I Am Sir, You are 1066!" (1978) starts, "I must have died last night, because when I awoke this morning I was in hell. … I think I am in some sort of tomb."[68] Occasionally, Sands' self-described "battle for survival" is relieved by memories of his family or by the "entertainment" of heaving maggots out of the window of his cell for hungry birds to devour, a pastime later denied him after his jailers covered his windows with riveted sheets of steel. For the most part, far too little comic exhilaration brightens and no riantic spaciousness expands the coffin-like dimensions of the Blanket Men's cells, nor is Sands afforded any sudden insight analogous to that Watt and the narrator experience after feeding tiny frogs, a baby thrush, and young rats to the aggregation of rats waiting by a stream in Knott's garden: "It was on these occasions, we agreed … that we came nearest to God" (*Watt*, p. 156). There is, finally, only human misery. By comparison, even the later Beckett of the 1970s and 80s seems fundamentally different. Characteristic of late modernism or not, less available in later Beckett or not, riantic spaciousness and its catalyst buoyant form, as we become aware after juxtaposing Sands' prison writing to even the bleakest of Beckett's work (the "dramaticule" *Catastrophe* might provide the test case for this assertion), are irreplaceable. And, as these are connected to the inevitability of death, they inform one definition of the Beckettian.

ENCOUNTERS AND EVENTS, OBJECTS AND THINGS

Action – social being – kills Death.
(Henry Glassie, *All Silver and No Brass: An Irish Christmas Mumming* [1975])

And things, what is the correct attitude to adopt toward things? ... If a thing turns up, for some reason or another, take it into consideration. Where there are people, it is said, there are things ... The thing to avoid, I don't know why, is the spirit of system. (Samuel Beckett, *The Unnamable* [1953])

Intrigued by Irish mumming and eager to learn more about its performance history, folklorist Henry Glassie arrived in County Fermanagh in the summer of 1972. There, in the village of Ballymenone, he listened to stories about this popular entertainment traditionally associated with the Christmas season and, though this was hardly part of his agenda, discovered one parallel between the Beckettian and the socius produced by the Troubles. As older villagers recalled, mummers' plays were performed by mostly amateur actors, young men who traveled from village to village for a week or two, even a month, in December and January. Knocking on the door of a house, an actor playing Captain Mummer would request permission for the troupe to enter and, after a successful performance, they could expect to receive drinks or cups of tea for their efforts, along with a modest payment. Many plays in fact threatened their audiences with the playful admonition Glassie adapts for the title of his book: "All silver, no brass/If you don't give me money, I'll steal your ass."[69] Some of Ballymenone's oldest residents noted that mumming was suspended during the turbulence of 1916 and the early 1920s; similarly, in 1972, as the Troubles were spreading to rural communities, as one villager remarked, the actors "daren't go out now ... No indeed ... For since the Troubles they wouldn't be allowed out atall [sic]. Masked men in the dark. Not this [sic] years."[70] One result of the Troubles, therefore, was a perhaps subtle, but nonetheless real, assault on "the spirit of community", which in 1972, Glassie observed, "has not passed entirely. But groups of young men no longer walk to every house to act out the Christmas drama."[71] At such moments, many of the practices that bind societies together – and proclaim the metaphorical victory of collective life over Death – are displaced by sudden incidents, by a more monadic existence, and in the most extremes cases by an incipient sense of a profound inorganicism in which "nothing can be taken or given and there is no possibility of change or exchange."[72]

In this environment, "social action" is diminished, pushing the community toward an inorganic, solitary world defined by "the isolation of man from nature and man from man; with a reduction in the role of human will; and with solitude, illness, and death."[73] Referring specifically to the 1930s and Beckett's interest in Jack B. Yeats and Schopenhauer, James Knowlson adds that Beckett's "obsessions" with such a lived reality "prefigure the concerns of his later writings." If so, what replaces the human interaction and social ritual so prevalent in his earlier drama? Other "Beckettian" devices, I think, including incidents and things, but not just any kind of activity or thing. This connotation of the "Beckettian" relies upon several premises, none more important than Badiou's insistence, alluded to earlier – and opposed to Adorno's understanding of *Endgame* as involving characters who are no more than "flies that twitch after the swatter has half smashed them ..." – that Beckett is hardly a nihilist.[74] Quite to the contrary, as Jean-Michel Rabaté explains:

> In fact, what Badiou finds in Beckett is a lesson in affirmation, a lesson made more poignant and powerful as one has multiplied all the reasons that show how impossible any affirmation is.[75]

Consistent with this thesis and equally useful for my purposes here, another of Badiou's insights concerns the relationship between love and sudden action in Beckett:

> Beckett never reduces love to the amalgam of sentimentality and sexuality endorsed by common opinion. Love as a matter of *truth* (and not of opinion) depends upon a pure event: an encounter whose strength radically exceeds both sentimentality and sexuality. ("Writing of the Generic," p. 28)

Again, ontology is here understood as a situation, and an event either is "in the situation ... by interposing itself between itself and the void; or, it is not in the situation, and its power of nomination is solely addressed, if it is addressed to 'something,' to the void itself" (*Being and Event*, p. 182).

Framed by what Badiou terms the "grey black of being" – "Little by little, Beckett's poetics will fuse the closed and open into the grey black" ("Writing of the Generic," p. 6) – the "event-incident" contains the capacity for both "isolation and surprise" (p. 21). The result?

> This is the source of the subject's dis-closure, whereby it incurs the risk of the Other, of its figures and occurrences. It does so under the sign of the hope opened up by ontological alterity – the breach in being which is crystallised both by the suddenness of the event and by the brilliance of the ill seen.
>
> ("Writing of the Generic," p. 22)

"Hope," "suddenness," "surprise" – the "event" is vitally connected to affirmation and, at times, to the experience of love. In a passage of unexpected beauty in *Krapp's Last Tape*, Krapp relives the time he and his beloved drifted luxuriantly in a punt among the flags, yet this rare moment concludes almost as quickly as it began. In *First Love* where "What goes by the name of love is banishment" (*Short Prose*, p. 31), the narrator meets a woman on a bench and suffers the confusions of "love" before she magically reappears to summon him to her home and bed: "She wasn't there, then suddenly she was, I don't know how, I didn't see her come, nor hear her …" (p. 38). In this way, the term "love" implies a temporal dimension distinctly different from the one it possesses in most everyday usage, with its connotations of endurance, long-standing fidelity, and devotion. Beckettian love appears to possess the opposite temporal valence as something sudden and unexpected; and, as such, for Badiou it remains part of an "affirmationist" art that is "delocalized" and "impersonal," a "production of a truth that is addressed to all."[76]

What Badiou refers to as the "risk of the Other" might be transposed into a more overtly psychoanalytic register, as John Robert Keller outlines in *Samuel Beckett and the Primacy of Love* (2002). For Keller, Beckett's "fictional/dramatic universe is organized by an emerging-self attempting to maintain an enduring contact with a good primary object/mother and thus his writing explores the experience of this self, its genesis, defences, and reactions to failures of such contact."[77] Not surprisingly, the Mother looms large in Keller's reading, as does the process of introjection in which the subject models relationships with objects on the oral-incorporative mode of early infancy. Importantly, Keller excludes from consideration the transitional objects of an infant's attachment – blankies, stuffed animals, and so on – focusing instead on the concept of another person as he or she exists in "an internal world of objects."[78] From this conjunction of incident, space, and object – construed not only as a person but more precisely as a "thing" – I would like to hazard another connotation of the Beckettian as an economy in which the subject's being is occasionally relieved by meaningful encounters – many of which are sudden or accidental – with objects describable as *things* that frequently achieve the ends both Badiou and Keller outline.

Objects and things, of course, are not always identical in Beckett's writing. One of the most quoted lines in Beckett in regard to the former comes from *Molloy*, "To restore silence is the role of objects" (*Three Novels*, p. 13), a sentiment that emerges as Molloy vents his frustration with a "rigmarole" of questions about a dog-owner out for an evening walk. For Molloy, objects provide blessed relief from a language pockmarked with holes and from words "buzzing" like insects. In both the "trilogy" and *Watt*, objects also facilitate a desirable ataraxy or state of contentment akin to that Watt experiences in Mr. Knott's service: "Watt suffered neither from the presence of Mr. Knott, nor from his absence ... This ataraxy covered the entire house-room, the pleasure-garden, the vegetable-garden, and of course Arthur" (pp. 207–08). Perhaps more famous examples of object-gratifications are Malone's stones: "I loved to finger and caress the hard shapely objects that were there in my deep pockets ..." If not for them, Malone confides, he "might have been reduced to the society of nice people or to the consolations of some religion or another" (*Three Novels*, p. 248). Like some objects, things can be adequated to "company," but they often cause more than a contented silence, sparking excitement, analysis, even rebuke. As Winnie exclaims in *Happy Days*, "Things have a life." Later, referring to her mirror, she gushes, "That is what I find so wonderful things, the way things ... (*voice breaks, head down*) ... things ... so wonderful" (p. 39). Like Anna's almost magical appearance in *First Love*, Winnie's mirror mysteriously finds its way back to her handbag, and like objects, things are superior to the "empty words" Winnie feels compelled to use. And most "things" in *Happy Days* – the pornographic card she reviles posing a curious exception – elicit a refulgence she reserves for her happiest memories: "... that is what I find so wonderful, all comes back. (*Pause.*) All? (*Pause.*) No, not all ... Floats up one fine day, out of the blue. (*Pause.*) That is what I find so wonderful" (p. 20). "Things and imaginings," as Beckett's narrator observes in *Ill Seen Ill Said*, "As of always. Confusion amounting to nothing" (*Nohow On*, p. 58). Thus, although Imagination may very well be dead in Beckett's later work, things seem to "have lives" in the "farrago" of perception "from eye to mind" (p. 72), all of which recalls the question posed near the beginning of *The Unnamable*: "And things, what is the correct attitude to adopt toward things?" (*Three Novels*, p. 292). And what, too, of the stance of Beckett's narrator toward "the spirit of system" as something to be avoided in forming a "correct attitude" toward things?

To address this last question, Beckett's writing seldom engages the most obvious "system" within which objects are valued: that of economic exchange and the resultant social significance attached to the consumption of commodities. In Jean Baudrillard's "system of objects," for example, and in consumption more generally, "economic exchange value (money) is converted into sign exchange value (prestige, etc.)"; thus, as Baudrillard stresses, "it is not the psychological relation of the individual to the object that gives birth to fetishism ... but the *social principle of exchange* [that] *supports the fetishized value of the object*" [Baudrillard's emphasis].[79] Further, commodities "can usefully be regarded as having life histories," one chapter of which concerns the moments in which they are exchanged,[80] and the study of such moments can be enormously instructive when examining the society or societies in which the object is exchanged. But such a system, following the suggestion of *The Unnamable*, might just as well be ignored, because commodity exchange contributes little to definitions of the Beckettian. In fact, Beckett's texts typically parody the relationship between objects and such social values as prestige, undercutting the status that seems implicit in, say, Winnie and Willie's formal attire in *Happy Days*. Near the opening of *Mercier and Camier*, for example, when an overly proprietary ranger in military uniform, complete with a chestful of medals, confronts the pair about an abandoned bicycle, Mercier asks his companion, "Will you look at the clatter of decorations ... Do you realize the gallons of diarrhoea that represents?" (p. 16). In the Beckettian, objects seldom function as commodities.

Instead, objects, typically alloyed with imaginings, function more resonantly as "things," a term almost as elusive as the "Beckettian." For as Bill Brown, a scrupulous student of things concedes, "[E]ven the most coarse and commonsensical things ... perpetually pose a problem because of the specific unspecificity that 'things' denotes."[81] A cursory review of the catalogue of "things" in the *Oxford English Dictionary* (*OED*) confirms Brown's point. "Thing" at one time referred to a legal issue or proceeding; it serves as a term dividing the steps in a sequence (the "first thing," "second thing," and so on); and it can even refer euphemistically to the male sexual organ, as in Molly Bloom's fantasy of being a man "for a change just to try with that thing they have swelling up on you" (James Joyce, *Ulysses*, Chapter 18, pp. 1381–82), or in J. P. Donleavy's *The Ginger Man* (1955) when Sebastian Dangerfield's haughty British wife finds life to be intolerable in a "vulgar, filthy" post-war Ireland: "Children running barefoot in the streets in the middle of winter and men wagging their things at you from the doorways."[82] "Thing" can also denote the monstrous or alien, as in the 1950s science fiction film *The Thing* (remade in the 1980s); or in Prospero's deprecation of Caliban in *The Tempest*: "[T]his thing of darkness I/Acknowledge mine" (5.1.275–76); and Marina Carr's *Woman and Scarecrow*, in which a bird-like figure of Death perched in the wardrobe of a dying patient looms as a "thing" that is the "opposite of time."[83]

As the *OED* notes, "thing" can also convey the opposite connotation, as in Aufidius's commendation of Coriolanus as a "noble thing" (*Coriolanus*, 4.5.117). It can refer to a notion or idea, as in Hamm's question to Clov in *Endgame*, "Did you ever think of one thing?" (p. 39); or to a process or act to be completed. Hamm later asks Clov, "Do you not think that this has gone on long enough?" And after Clov asks "What?", Hamm responds, "This ... this ... thing" (p. 45). Beckett seems acutely aware of the versatility of "thing" in describing both material entities and acts to be undertaken, as in Malone's announcement that he will compile an inventory: "For then I shall speak of the *things* that remain in my possession, that is a *thing* I have always wanted to do [my emphasis]" (p. 181). Of course, the most common "things" in Beckett have little to do with taking stock: they are objects occupying space (material entities without life or consciousness) or non-sentient entities like insects. Some can be valuable and, precisely as they are *valued* by a person, such objects approach the definitions to be developed here, as in the admission of Banville's spy Victor Maskell in *The Untouchable* (1997): "Things, for me, have always been of more import than people."[84] At times, characters are unable to rationalize this import, adding ineffably to a thing's significance, as in a brief exchange from *Rough for the Theatre I* (1972):

A: I can't go without my things.
B: What good are they to you?
A: None.
B: And you can't go without them?
A: No. (*Shorter Plays*, pp. 70–71)

Apparently lacking both exchange value *and* obvious use value, things nonetheless have a life, as Winnie reminds us; and for many of Beckett's characters things prove more indispensable than people. Commodities, for our purposes and theirs, have a markedly less important "biography."

Most compatible with Badiou's and Keller's emphases of the search for love in Beckett are those "things" that blur not only divisions between subject and object, as the exchange from *Rough for the Theatre I* implies, but also distinctions between the material and the immaterial: the thing as encounter or incident. Given Beckett's interest in perception, in the writings of George Berkeley and others, this assertion may seem inevitable, as it collapses the doctrine of so-called "natural dualism" in which a subject's consciousness as a perceiver is rivaled by the subject's conscious awareness of the external nature of the reality or object perceived. Aesthetician Leo Stein, as Brown notes, maintains that "Things are what we encounter," intimating the "suddenness with which things seem to assert their presence and power" ("Thing Theory," p. 3), and one might expand upon the examples Brown outlines. A can opener is a mere can opener or functional object until the blade slips off the lid and cuts your hand; then, it becomes an assailant, an agent of action, *and* an object to be cursed or hurled against the wall on those "occasions of contingency – the chance interruption – that disclose the physicality of things" and their potential to effect a "changed relation to the human subject." In this way, "thing" denotes not just an object, but "a particular subject-object relation" (p. 4). As Brown extrapolates, the subjective force exerted by things can evolve into a more metaphysical, religious, or psychological presence in the form of a fetish, value, idol, or totem (p. 5). Within such definitions, he unwittingly parallels the kinds of uses to which things are put in Beckett. In one instance, this is hardly surprising, for as Badiou emphasizes in a "severe principle of economy" Beckett relentlessly strips his texts of ornamentation, reducing the "complexity of experience to a few principle functions" ("Writing of the Generic," p. 3). A similar economy obtains in much recent Irish writing, where "things" accrue added significance, often paralleling the importance of an encounter with a person in Beckett.

A few examples of the homology between incidents and things, Others and transformative objects, might help illuminate the boundaries of this conception of the Beckettian. I want to begin by juxtaposing Malone's stones (and Molloy's as well) with the living things that lack discernible consciousness and populate Beckett's texts early and late: namely flies, fleas, maggots, termites, emmets, and such creatures as worms, hedgehogs, and rats. Malone carefully registers the power of his stones to produce a contentment which supplants that associated with social interaction – with other people or within the congregation of a Church. At the same time, Beckett emphasizes throughout the "trilogy" and his later works alike that all narrative "action" occurs within the larger domain of a slaughterhouse; thus, the "embodied thought" Connor describes could be redacted as a specifically animalized thought insofar as Beckett creates a homology between human death and animal slaughter. (As we shall see in later chapters, this metaphor informs representations of the Troubles as well.) In *Ill Seen Ill Said*, for example, a lamb "Reared for slaughter like the others" follows the old woman home, halting at the same instant she does (*Nohow On*, p. 69). The growing number of critics interested in animal rights and the discourse of species might also point to Watt, who suffers from a "loss of species" and enjoys a peculiar relationship with rats. But in a world in which animals and men are "reared for slaughter," the quotidian often leads to encounters with things, sudden incidents that parallel interactions with people, even those people who become love-objects.

Objects become *things*, in other words, when they suddenly trouble the calm and engender a character's cathexis or, as in *Company*, an "abrupt saltation." Some things, of course, seem more replete than others with catalytic potential, like the explicit pictures of Emma in *All Strange Away* – always available for licking, kissing, and more. Yet insofar as these pictures elicit such routinized effects, they might be said not to incite desire, but inaugurate a kind of perverse daily routine. Not so with the flea or crablouse that has taken residence in Clov's crotch or the emmet Winnie spies in *Happy Days*. The flea provides both an occasion for baggy pants' comedy and verbal innuendo about "laying doggo" and "being bitched," and the emmet first produces Winnie's "recoil" and excited "shrill," then her contemplation of the technical term "formication." Such "things" are also connected to perhaps the most famous appearance of insects in Beckett, the termite in *Watt*:

> For the only way one can speak of nothing is to speak of it as though it were something, just as the only way one can speak of God is to speak of him as though he were a man ... and as the only way one can speak of man, even our anthropologists have realised that, is to speak of him as though he were a termite. (*Watt*, p. 77)

For Badiou, this passage contributes to an "as if" schema of representation, indeed of thought more generally, in Beckett,[85] one evident in Lucky's monologue in *Waiting for Godot* about a "personal God quaquaquaqua with white beard quaquaquaqua outside time" (p. 45). At the same time, in Beckett a comparative *no-thing* evolves into a *some-thing* to be examined, remarked upon, even exterminated. An insect becomes a thing as it becomes an incident in the sumptuous destitution and increasing monadicism of Beckettian space, but can the appearances of insects be described as *events*?

Would it be too precious to mention the putative fly in *Company*? The possibility of the fly's existence is preceded by the narrator's positing of the necessity of "Conation of some kind however feeble. A trace of emotion" (*Nohow On*, p. 19). Perhaps the supine protagonist clenches or unclenches his fists, perhaps he would raise his hand to ward off a pesky fly, and by doing so verify the existence of his will or volition. If so, the narrator of *Company* seems to ask, why not produce the fly? But the text retracts this possibility, as its protagonist's torpor would not allow him to respond to it. The fly *could* provoke an incident, suggesting that virtually any entity or object – an insect, a can of baked beans, a stuffed dog, a rocking chair – *could* become a thing in Beckett. Or not. And, following Casanova's reading of *Worstward Ho*, a text that she, much like Badiou, regards as a "virtually explicit synthesis of Beckett's formal questions and uncertainties," "Somehow" and "Nohow" might also be regarded as things: "[Beckett] substantivizes them and represents them as two points on a line, given as a beginning and an end between which the book will be written."[86]

I am reluctant to hazard distinctions between encounters, incidents, and events, in part because this last term is so heavily theorized by Badiou, but there is little choice. For Badiou, an *event "interrupts the law, the rules, the structure of the situation, and creates a new possibility"* [my emphasis]. The event creates something that did not exist before – possibility. He is careful to emphasize that an event does not alter a situation, yet it does have the potential to transpose the situation *within* the new possibility.[87] So, for example, of the three sudden appearances of creatures in *Endgame* that rupture the ordinary – the crablouse in Clov's crotch, the rat in the kitchen, and the boy spied on the horizon – only the sighting of the boy could qualify as an event that creates a new possibility. Because Clov attempts to kill both the louse and the rat, and because there is no reason to doubt his skills at extermination, no possibility of a new subjectivity can be attributed to their appearances, nor can any amelioration of the situation of the play be effected: all is, as Clov says, "Corpsed." The boy is another matter. He represents the possibility of a new Truth, a new subjectivity, or, as Nancy Levene has put it in conversation with Badiou, in the event "difference is encountered as value," and the boy's difference from the others suggests this valuation. For his part, in the same exchange with Levene, Badiou returned again and again to the metaphor of the "cut," the sudden possibility which characterizes the event.[88]

Especially in the later texts, Beckett poses the possibility of an inverse operation whereby an incident also becomes a thing, if indeed it is possible to forge distinctions between "things and imaginings." In *Ill Seen Ill Said*, for example, "Riveted to some detail of the desert the eye fills with tears. Imagination at wit's end spreads its sad wings" (*Nohow On*, p. 56). To "rivet," to fix intently upon something, also connotes a fastening or securing to an object, frustrating finally any attempt to discern the precise cause of the tears: Does the detail or imagination induce their flow? What "thing" can be blamed? Or praised, as later in *Ill Seen Ill Said* an "event" comes "to the rescue":

> Startling without consequence for the gaze the mind awake. How explain it? And without going so far how say it? Far behind the eye the quest begins. What time the event recedes. When suddenly to the rescue it comes again. (*Nohow On*, p. 83)

The problem of how to "say it" leads to the "uncommon common noun collapsion," and what Beckett's narrator finally terms a "slumbrous collapsion," a phrase which, after it is uttered, "then and only then," produces "'a gleam of hope'" ("Writing of the Generic," p. 22). Such a naming, Badiou speculates, "guards the trace of an Other-than-being, which is also an Other-than-self," while it is also a "breach in being ... crystallised both by the suddenness of the event and by the brilliance of the ill seen" (p. 22). The keywords of this reading merit attention: suddenness, breach in being, naming – and the production of life. In the Beckettian, for better or worse, incidents and things suddenly rise to consciousness, hence alterity does as well. Things bring fear and relief, sadness and hope. They undermine, if only for a brief moment, David Lloyd's trenchant observation about the inorganicism and post-Cartesian scission of the Beckettian. They seize attention and induce words, however inadequate, precisely because they function like events in proclaiming a victory over the inorganic and the routine, the monadic and the dim.

METAPHOR, EXHAUSTION, AND GANTELOPES OF SENSE AND NONSENSE

Every sentence is a death sentence, in the sense that every statement is no sooner begun that it is already starting to die on an exhalation of breath. No writer has understood this better than Samuel Beckett ...

(Declan Kiberd, *Irish Classics* (2001))

asylum under my tread all this day
their muffled revels as the flesh falls
breaking without fear or favour wind
the gantelope of sense and nonsense run
taken by the maggots for what they are

(Samuel Beckett, "Echo's Bones" [1935])

No effort to define the Beckettian can ignore language, and for this reason it would be unwise to quibble *too* much with John Banville's synopsis, alluded to earlier but here rendered more fully: "Beckett's artistic venture, from his first, exuberant volume of stories, *More Pricks Than Kicks*, published in 1934, to his last published writing ... was unequalled [sic] in its dedicated single-mindedness and unrelenting ideological rigour. That venture was always and only a struggle with language ..."[89] Earlier, I responded to Banville's thesis with approbation, but here I want to disagree mildly with two points: first, Beckett clearly waged other struggles as well, hence the notion that language was his "only" adversary seems overstated; and second, Beckett was mired in these struggles several years before 1934, as much of his earliest poetry suggests. This poetry constitutes an important starting-point for this last connotation of the Beckettian. For as Deirdre Bair cautions readers of *Echo's Bones and*

Other Precipitates, Beckett's poetry should not be dismissed "lightly." Like his more celebrated novels and plays, several poems in this volume depict language in ways developed in his more mature work.[90] In particular, several early poems deploy now familiar metaphors to represent language as so riddled with deficiencies that far more than the "missaying" Badiou privileges as the "essence" of the Beckettian critique is involved ("Writing of the Generic," p. 8). In this regard, however much the Beckett of the 1930s was not the same Beckett of the 1980s – and however prescient Steven Connor's asseveration of the difficulty of assigning a "finality" or "separative integrity" to his oeuvre – Beckett's "struggles" with language and the metaphors he devises to describe them remain more or less constant throughout his career.

My brief consideration of Beckettian language is driven by two premises, the first of which animates Badiou's thesis in "Tireless Desire": "The lesson of Beckett is a lesson in measure, exactitude, and courage" (p. 40). Badiou's second tribute, his praise of Beckett's attention to the minutiae of syntax, diction, and phrasing, is of particular relevance, as it illuminates one key paradox of the Beckettian: because of the inadequacy of words, all saying is missaying, an inescapable catachresis, yet at the same time Beckett's language is so meticulously crafted, so uncommonly precise. The second premise concerns metaphor construed not as an isolated figure of speech, but rather as the mode of conceptualization George Lakoff and Mark Johnson define: "*The essence of metaphor is understanding and experiencing one kind of thing in terms of another.*"[91] In *Metaphors We Live By* (1980) Lakoff and Johnson foreground such everyday examples as "Argument Is War" and "Time Is Money" – in the latter metaphor, for example, this new gadget will *save* hours, that interruption *wasted* my time, one *spends* his or her time *investing* in this or that activity, and so on. Yet the "very systematicity that allows us to comprehend one aspect of a concept in terms of another," they caution, will "necessarily hide other aspects of the concept."[92]

This danger aside, it is nonetheless the case that Beckettian language, as Connor characterizes Beckettian thought, is irreducibly embodied language. As lively and playful as this language can be, however productive of riantic spaciousness it might be, words in particular frequently mirror the declining condition of Beckettian bodies: they are diseased, or ridden with parasites, or – especially in the later works – the sources of painful "secretions." Nonetheless, Beckettian language is precise, even though he deploys metaphors that disparage words as just the opposite, as inexact or imprecise, or as sources of annoyance or pain. In *Molloy*, "when the icy words hail down upon me, the icy meanings, and the world dies too, foully named" (*Three Novels*,

p. 31). Shortly thereafter, as I have mentioned, in a metaphor Hamlet employs to deride Polonius's babbling, Molloy is plagued by words that "were often to me as the buzzing of an insect" (p. 50). It is also the case that in novels like *Molloy*, Beckett's characters take great delight in obscure words connected to bodily productions and (mis)functioning. One night Moran suffers a "fulgurating pain" in his knee, yet the next morning he is elated to discover that the "anchylosis" of his knee "was not total!" (pp. 138–39). Later in his final report, he asks, "Does it really matter which hand is employed to absterge the podex?" (p. 167). Bodily functions, imperfections, and basic anatomy thus provide Beckett and his characters with a rich thesaurus of terms and euphemisms and, occasionally, a source of humor "laying doggo" in their connotations or "obnubilated" by the clouding of common usage.

One dominant metaphor throughout Beckett's writing, therefore, implies that words are more like failing bodies or bodily functions. Yet, just as bodies, albeit defective and vulnerable, are necessary for being, words are equally indispensable; and like the Unnamable, most of Beckett's characters cannot remain silent. At times words, like those in Lucky's monologue, spew from mouths like blood or pus from a wound, a trope that underlies the titles of two poems written in the later 1920s, "Sanies I" and "Sanies II" ("sanies" refers to pus secreted by a wound or ulcer).[93] In the opening pages of *Dream of Fair to Middling Women*, thought for Belaqua – in "the mizzle of love" with Smeraldina-Rima – leads to sorrow and a "gush" of tears at her departure from him. This "gush" parallels the "gush" of mard exuded from under a horse's arched tail in the novel's opening paragraph, and just a few pages later becomes figuratively associated with language as Smeraldina-Rima regales her family with a story:

> When she was in form, launched, she could be extremely amusing, with a strange feverish eloquence, the words flooding and streaming out like a conjuror's coloured paper. She could keep a whole group, even her family, convulsed with the ropes and ropes of logorrhoea streaming out in a gush.[94]

In this latter trope, words are not akin to a magician's tools, but more like tears, pus, and mard – a necessary evacuation. At other times, the flow is reduced to a painful secretion, drop by burning drop.

In the "Trilogy," Beckett develops another metaphor for language as words are infested with parasites or other contaminants, causing holes or infection. In *The Unnamable* the relationship between language and parasitism is made explicit when Beckett's narrator complains, "Having nothing to say, no words but the words of others, I have to speak" (*Three Novels*, p. 314). Here the echo of the pensum resonates, one that is connected later to the death of his "kith and kin" by the bacillus botulinus and his near obsession with relating the details of their fatal poisoning to anyone who will listen: "I shall never weary of repeating this" (p. 322). Soon after, speaking of his possible social assimilation, he implies that language works much like a toxic agent: "What I speak of, what I speak with, all comes from them … Not to be able to open my mouth without proclaiming them … that's what they imagine they'll have me reduced to" (p. 324). A reduction of self induced by the imposition of language thus parallels a physical decline caused by a parasite that gradually overwhelms its host organism. And this homology between toxins or parasites, the infectious social system of assimilation, and the incursions of education represented by the pensum recall the question Michel Serres poses in *The Parasite* (1982): "Who will ever know if parasitism is an obstacle to [a specific system's] proper functioning, or if it is its very dynamics?"[95] Beckett, in effect, answers Serres's query: contamination *is* the dynamic of thought, socialization, and perhaps language.

So, too, is deterioration. *Worstward Ho* in this regard becomes the recapitulative text both Badiou and Casanova deem it to be, for here words ooze and are analogous not so much to typical bodily products – tears and mard, for example – but to mysterious secretions: "Says? Secretes. Say better worse secretes. What it is the words it secretes say" (*Nohow On*, pp. 104–05). In a double-entendre in *Worstward Ho*, these emanate from the head, the "Seat of all. Germ of all" (p. 91). The germ, the rudiment of a new organism and the seed of disease, originates in the sunken head and the contaminated word. Further, words aren't so much oozed or gushed as they are excreted in a kind of pinched lexical evacuation, as in *Ill Seen Ill Said*: "See now how words too. A few drops mishaphazard. Then strangury. To say the least" (p. 81). If ill-seeing is attributable to the "vile jelly" of the eye, an echo of the plucking out of Gloucester's eyes in *King Lear* (p. 81), then ill-saying is akin to a difficult urination – the "least" effective evacuation of the bladder one can imagine and a far cry from the almost enviable gushing of *Dream of Fair to Middling Women*. In this earlier work, words flow more freely, as when Belaqua is "raped" by his beloved, putting an end to his desire to keep their relationship "pewer and above-bawd" (p. 18). But in *Ill Seen Ill Said* words are either parasitic invasions or secretions; and insofar as seeing is also connected to eating and parasitism emerges from an etymology of eating and a guest's siphoning of sustenance from its host, vision too is related to the metaphor of parasitism: "Quick enlarge and devour [the fading light] before night falls" (*Nohow On*, p. 60), and "So the unreasoning goes. While the eye digests its pittance" (p. 61).[96] Yet, for all of this,

Beckettian words are also comic – "to say the least." The more "depressive" the content, the more comically buoyant the plays on words, as in the pun in *Ill Seen Ill Said*: "The eye glued to one or the other window has nothing but black drapes for its pains" (p. 53). Or in *Worstward Ho*: "From bad to worsen. Try worsen. From merely bad. Add–. Add? Never. The boots. Better worse bootless" (*Nohow On*, p. 100). One might go so far as to say that such tropes – "pains" for "panes" or the double meaning of "bootless" – almost operate like "things" in the Beckett text.

This is not to say that words are not, in the final analysis, inadequate. "Bad" and "Worsen," to name two, can never convey the real in Beckett, because neither can be adequated to the quotidian process of decline, the inevitable reductions of self. For this reason, neologisms like "leastening" need to be invented – and "unlessenable," "unworsenable," "ununsaid," and one of Badiou's favorites, "slumberous collapsion," to name just a few. Earlier in his career, in poems like "Home Olga" (1932), Beckett followed Joyce's lead by supplementing English with appropriations from other languages – Latin, French, Italian – and even added an occasional Irishism, as he does in "Home Olga": "Yesterday shall be tomorrow, riddle me that my rapparee" (*Poems, 1930–1989*, p. 10). The early poems, much like Joyce's work, also feature portmanteau words ("pickthank" in "Home Olga"), mild vulgarities ("for the love of Jesus" in "Eneug II"), and varied, at times punning, deprecations ("the churn of stale words" and "the unalterable/whey of words" in "Cascando"). But while puns remain and words still ooze in Beckett's later texts, dense allusions and borrowing from other languages largely disappear, precisely because such devices lack the precision of "leastening" and "collapsion." If the Beckettian finally communicates anything, it is that "At bounds of boundless void. Whence no farther. Best worse no farther. Nohow less. Nohow worse. Nohow naught. Nohow On." One is still compelled, as Badiou properly insists, to speak: "Said Nohow on" (*Nohow On*, p. 116), even if the language is the "best worse" one can manage.

Which leaves, at this point, only exhaustion: yours, mine, and Beckett's. The term acquires clarity in Deleuze's "The Exhausted," which distinguishes physical fatigue from a more debilitating metaphysical exhaustion: "The tired person has merely exhausted the realization, whereas the exhausted person exhausts the whole of the possible. The tired person can no longer realize, but the exhausted person can no longer possibilize."[97] Among Beckett's protagonists, Watt, that inveterate contemplator of all possible permutations in Knott's navigation of the furniture in his room, or the order in which a chorus of frogs produces its croaks, provides Deleuze with abundant examples to support such distinctions. Moreover, the project of exhaustion can only be undertaken by the exhausted. Although Deleuze does not employ these terms, causally connected to exhaustion is a character's "velleity" or lack of "conation" (both terms appear in *Company*, for example). And this lack of conation admits to a Deleuzean explanation.

> [O]nly an exhausted person can exhaust the possible, because he has renounced all need, preference, goal, or signification. Only the exhausted person is sufficiently disinterested, sufficiently scrupulous. Indeed, he is obliged to replace his plans with fables and programs that are devoid of meaning. For him, what matters is the order in which he does what he has to do ...[98]

Amplifying this point, Jean-Michel Rabaté argues that "Logical exhaustion leads to the hollowing out of meaning" and, further, that the "semantic vertigo" caused by the relentless accounting of all permutations of an operation "parallels the absurdly rational knowledge of theologians" in *Watt*.[99]

Rabaté's point about theologians in *Watt* is well taken, and there seems to me equally little question about the "hollowing out of meaning" generated by Watt's lists, given their minutely considered permutations, their exhaustivity in analyzing process or operationality. Deleuze's distinction between physical fatigue and a more metaphysical exhaustion seems equally compelling. But if we concede these points about exhaustion, must we also concur with Deleuze about the exhausted? Is the hard-fought affirmation Badiou finds in the dessicated environments of *Worstward Ho* and *Ill Seen Ill Said* recuperable from Deleuze's exhausted? Can the concepts of riantic spaciousness, buoyant form, the magical appearance of things, the sudden hope of event-incidents, and the impossible project of verbal exactitude accommodate the thoroughly exhausted Deleuzean subject? Is this all we mean when we say "Beckettian"?

No. Questions answered. On.

On to contemporary drama, fiction, and poetry, Northern Irish writing in particular, but not simply to enact a literary criticism that resembles an abbatoir by mechanically processing texts as if they were so many sides of beef. These ruminations about the "Beckettian" are not merely the gears of an intellectual meat-grinder; they neither constitute a "system" or master-code with which to read contemporary Irish literature, nor aspire to a statement of totality. Texts cannot simply be passed through these definitions and carved down to size. Rather, these definitional categories are intended to initiate a conversation about Beckett's centrality to recent Irish writing and to Irish culture more generally without, one hopes, replicating the excesses and trivialities, the jousting and intellectual mud wrestling, of the "dead dog" discipline of orthodox literary criticism.

NOTES

1. Steven Connor, "Over Samuel Beckett's Dead Body," in *Beckett in Dublin*, ed. S. E. Wilmer (Dublin: The Lilliput Press, 1992), p. 107.
2. Joe Cleary, "The World Literary System: Atlas and Epitaph," *Field Day Review* 2 (2006), p. 197.
3. Cleary, "The World Literary System," p. 198.
4. Cleary, "The World Literary System," pp. 198, 218.
5. Cleary, "The World Literary System," p. 218. Here he is referring to Pascale Casanova's *The World Republic of Letters*, trans. M. B. DeBevoise (Cambridge, MA: Harvard University Press, 2004). In *Shroud* (2002, rpt. New York: Vintage, 2004), p. 97, Banville's protagonist is not describing literary criticism, but his own discipline of Philosophy.
6. Pascale Casanova, *The World Republic of Letters*, pp. 2–3. Casanova concludes this book with two valuable chapters on Ireland which students of Beckett will find of great interest.
7. Casanova, *The World Republic of Letters*, pp. 41–42.
8. Banville, *Shroud*, p. 97.
9. Terry Eagleton, *After Theory* (New York: Basic Books, 2003), p. 5.
10. Martin Esslin, "Introduction," in Jan Kott, *Shakespeare Our Contemporary*, p. xi.
11. Charles R. Lyons, "Beckett, Shakespeare, and the Making of Theory," in *Around the Absurd: Essays on Modern and Postmodern Drama*, eds. Enoch Brater and Ruby Cohn (Ann Arbor: University of Michigan Press, 1990), p. 103.
12. Bloom, *The Anxiety of Influence*, p. xxiii.
13. Connor, "Over Samuel Beckett's Dead Body," p. 101.
14. John Banville, *Athena* (New York: Vintage Books, 1995), p. 82.
15. Samuel Beckett, *Proust* (New York: Grove Press, 1957), p. 2. All quotations from this volume will be followed by page numbers in the text. For a psychoanalytic reading of this sentence, see John Robert Keller, *Samuel Beckett and the Primacy of Love* (Manchester: Manchester University Press, 2002). Keller's emphasis of this sentence's relationship to the "Paranoid Schizophrenic Position" is noteworthy: in this position, "change is felt as inherently dangerous, since self-integration has not been achieved" (p. 37). Keller quotes *Proust* as defining love as "our demand for a whole" (p. 44).
16. Casanova, *The World Republic of Letters*, p. 15; Kiberd, *Irish Classics*, p. ix. Further citations from *Irish Classics* will be followed by page numbers in the text.
17. Tropes of ghostliness are common in discussions of Beckett's characters and of his own uncanny presence in contemporary Irish literature. For example, Katharine Worth begins her essay "Beckett's Ghosts" in Wilmer (ed.), *Beckett in Dublin* with the observation that "Ghosts are a potent presence in Beckett's theatre" (p. 62). In "Banville's Other Ghost," Brian Duffy concludes that "the Beckettian traces in *Eclipse* suggest that he has not been immune from, nor insensitive to, his own visitations from the past" (p. 103).

18. Here Kiberd consciously echoes Deleuze and Guattari's *Kafka: Towards a Minor Literature* (1986), emphasizing "minoritarian" literature's agonistic relationship with the language of "masters." See Gilles Deleuze and Félix Guattari, *Kafka: Toward a Minor Literature*, trans. Dana Polan (Minneapolis: University of Minnesota Press, 1986), p. 19.
19. Robert Scholes, *Protocols of Reading* (New Haven: Yale University Press, 1989), p. 78.
20. I am borrowing the term "read across" from Shaun Richards' excellent comparison of Martin McDonagh and John Millington Synge in "'The Outpouring of a Morbid, Unhealthy Mind': The Critical Condition of Synge and McDonagh," in Chambers and Jordan (eds.), *The Theatre of Martin McDonagh*, p. 259.
21. A. Alvarez, *Samuel Beckett* (New York: Viking Press, 1973), p. 5.
22. Aaron Jaffe, *Modernism and the Culture of Celebrity* (Cambridge: Cambridge University Press, 2005), p. 61.
23. Jaffe, *Modernism*, p. 60.
24. Simon Dentith, *Bakhtinian Thought: An Introductory Reader* (London: Routledge, 1995), p. 88.
25. Dentith, *Bakhtinian Thought*, p. 90.
26. "Dante ... Bruno . Vico .. Joyce," in *Disjecta: Miscellaneous Writings and a Dramatic Fragment*, ed. Ruby Cohn (New York: Grove Press, 1995), p. 19. A generation of Joyce scholars might be fairly accused of both worship and idolatry, as the religious connotations of their study of *Ulysses* and *Finnegans Wake* are often quite conspicuous. In *The Books at the Wake: A Study of Allusions in James Joyce's Finnegans Wake* (New York: Viking Press, 1960), for example, James S. Atherton, with admirable self-consciousness, argues that the "basis" for Joyce's book is "that the artist is God-like in his task of creation" (p. 27).
27. On the latter topic, see, for example, Joseph S. O'Leary, "Beckett's Intertextual Power," *Journal of Irish Studies* 18 (2003), pp. 87–101.
28. Samuel Beckett, Three Novels (New York: Grove Press, 1955), pp. 31–32. All quotations from *Molloy*, *Malone Dies*, and *The Unnamable* come from *Three Novels* (New York: Grove Press, 1955) and will be followed by page numbers in the text.
29. See Keller, *Samuel Beckett* p. 11. He adds that "this notion seems central to Beckett: his work struggles to have part of itself (the primary mother/auditor) hear the infantile self."
30. Paul Ricoeur, *Memory, History, Forgetting*, trans. Kathleen Blamey and David Pellauer (Chicago: University of Chicago Press, 2004), p. 60.
31. Ricoeur, *Memory*, p. 58.
32. John Banville, "Beckett's Last Words," in Murray (ed.), *Samuel Beckett 100 Years*, pp. 130–31.
33. I am indebted to Nicholas Zurbrugg, "*Ill Seen Ill Said* and the Sense of an Ending," in *Beckett's Later Fiction and Drama: Texts for Company*, ed. James Acheson and Kateryna Arthur (London: Macmillan, 1987), especially pp. 146–47.

34. Steven Connor, *Samuel Beckett: Repetition, Theory and Text* (Oxford: Basil Blackwell, 1988), p. 1.
35. Connor, *Samuel Beckett*, p. 7.
36. Connor, *Samuel Beckett*, p. 5.
37. Daniel Albright, *Beckett and Aesthetics* (Cambridge: Cambridge University Press, 2003), p. 12. For another important reading of Beckett and earlier twentieth-century visual art, see Stanton B. Garner, Jr., *Bodied Spaces: Phenomenology and Performance in Contemporary Drama* (Ithaca: Cornell University Press, 1994), especially pp. 52–86.
38. David Lloyd, "Republics of Difference: Yeats, MacGreevy, Beckett," *Field Day Review* 1 (2005), pp. 47, 46.
39. Richard Kearney, *The Wake of Imagination: Toward a Postmodern Culture* (Minneapolis: University of Minnesota Press, 1988), p. 308.
40. Alain Badiou, *Being and Event*, trans. Oliver Feltham (New York: Continuum, 2005), p. 27. All quotations from this volume will be followed by page numbers in the text.
41. Pascale Casanova makes a similar claim in *Samuel Beckett: Anatomy of a Literary Revolution*, trans. Gregory Elliott (London: Verso, 2006), when describing *Worstward Ho* as a "virtually explicit synthesis of Beckett's formal questions and uncertainties" (p. 21).
42. Stanley Cavell, "Ending the Waiting Game: A Reading of Beckett's *Endgame*," in *Must We Mean What We Say?* (Cambridge: Cambridge University Press, 1976), p. 127. In a telling qualification, Cavell terms this "hilarity, but with all the passion spent." The adversion to Theodor Adorno is not only to his essay "Trying to Understand *Endgame*," trans. Michael T. Jones, *New German Critique* (Spring Summer 1982), but also to the section "Meditations on Metaphysics" in *Negative Dialectics*, trans. E. B. Ashton (New York: Continuum, 1973), pp. 361–408, which emphasizes a very different reading of *Endgame*.
43. Albright, *Beckett and Aesthetics*, p. 6.
44. Tyrus Miller, *Late Modernism: Politics, Fiction, and the Arts Between the World Wars* (Berkeley: University of California Press, 1999), p. 49, 58.
45. In *Change All the Names: A Samuel Beckett Onomasticon* (Szeged, Hungary: The Kakapo Press, 2004), Jeremy Parrott notes that Arsene derives from the Greek *arsēn* or "male," implying that the character is, first, an "emblematic male, like most of Beckett's protagonists." Arsenic was once regarded as both a highly toxic and irreducibly male element; Beckett took small quantities of the substance while recuperating from a "botched operation" in 1932 (p. 106).
46. Miller, *Late Modernism*, p. 49.
47. Miller, *Late Modernism*, p. 63.
48. Mladen Dolar, *A Voice and Nothing More* (Cambridge, MA: MIT Press, 2006), p. 29.
49. Gaston Bachelard, *The Poetics of Space*, trans. Maria Jolas (Boston: Beacon Press, 1964), p. 184.
50. Bachelard, *Poetics of Space*, p. 195.

51. Ricoeur, *Memory*, p. 54.
52. See, for example, Nels C. Pearson, "'Outside of Here It's Death': Co-dependency and the Ghosts of Decolonization in Beckett's *Endgame*," *ELH* 68.1 (2001), pp. 215–39.
53. Roland Barthes, *Writing Degree Zero*, trans. Annette Lavers and Colin Smith (New York: Hill & Wang, 1968), p. 48.
54. Badiou describes this process in *Worstward Ho* in "Being, Existence, Thought," pp. 83–86. See also Badiou, "The Writing of the Generic," pp. 1–5.
55. Ricoeur, *Memory*, p. 62.
56. This same device appears at the beginning of Vincent Woods' *At the Black Pig's Dyke* (1992) when Lizzie Boles begins a story with "It was a long time ago, Elizabeth, and it was not a long time ago ... It was a time when to go east was to go west, when to go south was to go north ..." (p. 3). See Woods' play in *Far from the Land: Contemporary Irish Plays*, ed. John Fairleigh (London: Methuen, 1998), pp. 1–60.
57. See Cavell, "Ending the Waiting Game," pp. 119–27.
58. Samuel Beckett, *The Collected Shorter Plays of Samuel Beckett* (New York: Grove Press, 1984), p. 230. All quotations from Beckett's shorter work come from this volume and *The Complete Short Prose*, 1929–1989 (New York: Grove Press, 1995), and will be followed by page numbers in the text.
59. For quite different reasons related to stage-picture, including the body as an image often deformed by light in Beckett's mise-en-scène, Garner categorizes the "later plays" as spanning *Not I* (1972) through *What Where* (1983). I will return to this distinction later in the chapter.
60. Garner, *Bodied Spaces*, pp. 63, 65.
61. Garner, *Bodied Spaces*, p. 63. Garner's emphasis of the visual qualities of Beckett's later plays is echoed by Beckett's friend Anne Atik, wife of painter Avigdor Arikha. See her *How It Was: A Memoir of Samuel Beckett* (2001, rpt. New York: Shoemaker & Hoard, 2005), pp. 4–7.
62. Samuel Taylor Coleridge, *The Complete Works, vol. 3, Biographia Literaria*, ed. W. T. G. Shedd (New York: Harper, 1860), pp. 363–64.
63. *Stirrings Still* (1988), the title of which comes from a phrase in *Company*, also is somewhat exceptional in Beckett's later work, but a full discussion of it will not be possible here.
64. Dolar, *A Voice*, p. 60. He borrows this term from Michael Chion's *La voix au cinéma* (1982).
65. Dolar, *A Voice*, p. 14.
66. Cronin, *Samuel Beckett*, pp. 25–26.
67. Atik, *How It Was*, p. 52.
68. Bobby Sands, *Writings from Prison* (Dublin: Mercier Press, 1998), pp. 159, 163, 171. Many selections in this volume were first published in 1978 or 1979 in *An Phoblacht/Republican News*.
69. Quoted in Henry Glassie, *All Silver and No Brass: An Irish Christmas Mumming* (1975, rpt. Philadelphia: University of Pennsylvania Press, 1983), p. 33.

70. Quoted in Glassie, *All Silver*, p. 8.
71. Glassie, *All Silver*, p. 19.
72. Quoted in Lloyd, "Republics of Difference," p. 47. Here Lloyd alludes several times to Knowlson's *Damned to Fame*, especially pp. 247–51.
73. Knowlson, *Damned to Fame*, p. 250.
74. Adorno, "Trying to Understand *Endgame*," p. 128. See also Lambert Zuidervaart, *Adorno's Aesthetic Theory: The Redemption of Illusion* (Cambridge, MA: MIT Press, 1991), pp. 150–77, who summarizes Adorno's reading of *Endgame*: "Metaphysical meaninglessness becomes the meaning of *Endgame* because its aesthetic meaninglessness acquires meaning as a determinate negation of the dramatic forms that used to *affirm* metaphysical meaning" (p. 155).
75. Jean-Michel Rabaté, "The Unbreakable B's: From Beckett to Badiou to the Bitter End of Affirmative Ethics," in *Alain Badiou: Philosophy and Its Conditions*, ed. Gabriel Riera (Albany: State University of New York Press, 2005), p. 89.
76. Alain Badiou, *Polemics*, trans. Steve Corcoran (London: Verso, 2006), pp. 142, 43.
77. Keller, *Samuel Beckett*, p. 33.
78. Keller, *Samuel Beckett*, p. 5. Keller discusses Winnicott and transitional space on pp. 32–33.
79. Jean Baudrillard, *For a Critique of the Political Economy of the Sign*, trans. Charles Levin (St. Louis: Telos Press, 1981), pp. 112, 118.
80. Arjun Appadurai, "Introduction: Commodities and the Politics of Value," in *The Social Life of Things: Commodities in Cultural Perspective*, ed. Arjun Appadurai (Cambridge: Cambridge University Press, 1986), p. 17.
81. Bill Brown, "Thing Theory," *Critical Inquiry* 28 (Autumn 2001), p. 3. Further references to Brown's article will be followed in the text by page numbers.
82. J. P. Donleavy, *The Ginger Man* (1955, rpt. New York: The Atlantic Monthly Press, 1988), p. 53. The *OED* uses this passage to illustrate the definition, but neglects to include the anti-Irish bias of this use of "things," which is consistent with Prospero's in terms of its stereotyping of the colonized as monstrously sexual or dirty.
83. Marina Carr, *Woman and Scarecrow* (London: Faber and Faber, 2006), p. 63.
84. John Banville, *The Untouchable* (New York: Vintage International, 1998), p. 200.
85. In "Tireless Desire" Badiou poses the "philosophical construction of the question" in Beckett in this way: "what can be pronounced about the 'there is' *qua* 'there is' from the vantage point of thought, in which the imperative of saying and the modification of the shades (i.e. the circulation of visible humanity) are given simultaneously?" (Power and Toscano (eds.), *On Beckett*, p. 85).
86. Casanova, *Samuel Beckett*, pp. 21, 17.
87. Max Blechman, Anita Chari, and Rafeeq Hasan, "Human Rights Are the Rights of the Infinite: An Interview with Alain Badiou," unpublished interview (2005), pp. 1–3.
88. Nancy Levene and Badiou appeared in a "Roundtable Discussion" held at Indiana University-Bloomington on November 9, 2007. These remarks come from that discussion.

89. Banville, "Beckett's Last Words," p. 123.
90. For a helpful discussion, see Deirdre Bair, *Samuel Beckett: A Biography* (London: Jonathan Cape, 1978), pp. 185–88. Here Bair is quoting self-critical comments Beckett made to Lawrence Harvey. Of the major biographies, Bair's gives the fullest attention to Beckett's poems of the 1930s.
91. George Lakoff and Mark Johnson, *Metaphors We Live By* (Chicago: University of Chicago Press, 1980), p. 5.
92. Lakoff and Johnson, *Metaphors*, p. 10.
93. All quotations from Beckett's poems come from *Poems, 1930–1989* (London: Calder Publications, 2002). Page numbers will follow quotations in the text.
94. Samuel Beckett, *Dream of Fair to Middling Women*, eds. Eoin O'Brien and Edith Fournier (New York: Arcade Publishing, 1992), p. 14.
95. Michel Serres, *The Parasite*, trans. Lawrence R. Schehr (Baltimore: Johns Hopkins University Press, 1982), p. 27.
96. The metaphor surfaces in later Beckett. W in *Rockaby* (1980), for example, suffers from "famished eyes" in her longing to see and be seen.
97. Gilles Deleuze, "The Exhausted," in *Essays Critical and Clinical*, trans. Daniel W. Smith and Michael A. Greco (Minneapolis: University of Minnesota Press, 1997), p. 152.
98. Deleuze, "The Exhausted," p. 154.
99. Rabaté, "The Unbreakable B's," p. 98.

CHAPTER 2

The Northern Ireland "Troubles" Play and Brian Friel's Beckettian turn

> Since the fateful year of 1968, everything [Friel] has written has been imbued, however obliquely or indirectly, with the events of the Northern crisis.
>
> –Fintan O'Toole, *The Irish Times*, January 7, 1989

Seldom in my experience has a topic such as the one to be addressed here been, at the same time, both so straightforward and so mired in complexity. Even if Fintan O'Toole had qualified his assertion about the Northern crisis inflecting *everything* Brian Friel has written since the later 1960s to include only the two plays to be discussed here – *The Freedom of the City* (1973) and *Volunteers* (1975) – the matter would be far from settled.[1] One might even marvel at O'Toole's restraint in making this point, for at about the same time Richard Kearney more ominously diagnosed Friel as tormented by an "amputated Ulster" that "acts as a phantom limb haunting his work."[2] Of course, both O'Toole and Kearney offered these analyses some years ago, well before the productions of such plays as *The Yalta Game* (2001) and *The Home Front* (2006), which in their respective ways reconfirm the long-standing influence of Chekhov so evident in *The Aristocrats* (1979), Friel's adaptations of *Three Sisters* (1981) and *Uncle Vanya* (1998).[3] Still, O'Toole's and Kearney's underscoring of the Troubles' effect on Friel's writing remains incisive, and the effect is far from simple. Indeed, the phrasing of this chapter's title, with its implications of relationships between two very different writers, contemporary history, and dramatic form, intimates both the complexity of the enterprise and the trajectory of my argument which, simply put, is this: of the many strategies writers have employed to represent the Troubles, the most salient – as seen in *The Freedom of the City* and *Volunteers* – and, arguably, those responsible for prompting the harsh reaction both plays initially elicited, are Beckettian.

I am aware that this contention may seem unlikely given Friel's stated antipathy toward Beckett. Isn't it too great a counterintuitive leap to urge Friel's affinity with a writer about whom he harbored such ambivalence? In a 1970 interview, for example, while expressing his affection for the plays of Henrik Ibsen, Eugene O'Neill, John Osborne, John Arden, and others, Friel announced his quite pointed view of Harold Pinter, leading him to an all-too-familiar aspersion of nihilism in Beckett's plays:

> What I dislike about [Pinter] is the complete dehydration of humanity in him. This is also something I don't like in Beckett. There is a complete abnegation of life in both these men. They're really bleak.[4]

Ironically, this same interview begins with Friel's admission that he, too, is "a bleak sort of person" and that his tastes in comedy frequently veer toward the "absurd sort" (*Brian Friel*, p. 25). His earlier 1967 lecture "The Theatre of Hope and Despair" betrays a similarly wary, if more generous view. In an unlikely juxtaposition of Beckett with Neil Simon – an odd couple indeed – whose commercial success with *Barefoot in the Park* (1963), *The Odd Couple* (1965), and *Plaza Suite* (1968) made him Broadway's most visible playwright of the 1960s, Friel argued, "I believe that Neil Simon and Sam Beckett both have their place in the scale of things. And I am equally opposed to an exclusive diet of one or the other" (*Brian Friel*, p. 23). In this lecture and consistent with his later assertion of Beckett's bleakness, Friel identifies him – along with Pinter, Jean Genet, and Jack Gelber – as a practitioner of a "theatre of despair," and so the question arises: If, in representing the Troubles just a few years later, Friel makes a "Beckettian turn," does it necessarily follow that this self-described "bleak" playwright has succumbed to the despair of the moment? Or might *The Freedom of the City* and *Volunteers*, irrespective of hostile reviews to the contrary after their initial productions, be regarded as contributing to what near the end of his lecture Friel characterized as a "Theatre of Hope" in which playwrights enable their audiences "to recognize that even in confusion and disillusion, strength and courage can exist, and that out of them can come a redemption of the human spirit" (*Brian Friel*, p. 24)?

Holding these questions in abeyance, I want to turn to a potentially more troublesome obstruction to the project of this chapter: namely, that however they might be defined, few instances of a dramatic genre known as the "Troubles play" graced Irish stages prior to the productions of Friel's two controversial works in the early and mid 1970s. In his history of modern Irish drama, Christopher Morash addresses this paradox:

> In many ways ... the importance of the classic Troubles play is that it provides a set of rules to be broken in the search for a more meaningful response to an increasingly extreme reality. And this is precisely what happened less than two years after the première of [John Boyd's] *The Flats*, when Brian Friel's *The Freedom of the City* opened at the Abbey on 20 February 1973.[5]

Morash's hypothesis is too tempting to resist, as it begs the question of what constitutes a "classic Troubles play" and implies that one of its features is a voracious iconoclasm. Given this definition, how could *The Freedom of the City* and *Volunteers* subvert the conventions of a genre barely in its infancy when they were written? What "set of rules" did Friel undermine?

Answers to such questions might be marshaled by employing my title as a rubric, especially its two principal halves separated by a puny "and": What counts as a Northern Irish "Troubles" play, classic or otherwise? And how might we identify Friel's turn to Beckett in his two most significant contributions to the genre? One implication of my thesis, again, is that both plays' Beckettian qualities are largely responsible for the critical failure of their first productions – by contrast, later revivals, such as the 1998 production of *Volunteers* at London's Gate Theatre, have fared much better. And another is that while historical events, especially those nearly coterminous with their aestheticization, might be fictionalized in any number of ways, those bearing resemblance to Beckett's drama are almost always susceptible to being read as originating in a Theatre of Despair. In what I hope to show are their Beckettian qualities, *The Freedom of the City* and *Volunteers*, however fumigated of romance and however subversive, demonstrate just the opposite: that they are more accurately situated in a Theatre of Hope, if we understand such a theatre – as Friel did some forty years ago – as representing courage in the midst of sociopolitical confusion and, in so doing, offering to its audiences a redemption of the human spirit.

THE NORTHERN IRELAND TROUBLES PLAY

What you must remember is that our particular generation of Irish folk were born into all that crap. We knew nothing else. Think about it. Picture it. The mid-sixties … There aren't actually very many bombs and guns around as yet – just a lot of jobless Catholics getting the shit kicked out of them and having their homes burnt down … What chance did we ever have? For a piece of normality. Not much.

(Robert McLiam Wilson, *Ripley Bogle* [1989])

The phrase "Northern Ireland 'Troubles' Play" is problematic in at least two ways, striated as it is, on the one hand, with political nuance and, on the other, with the vicissitudes of literary – in this instance, genre – theory. For Elmer Kennedy-Andrews in *Fiction and the Northern Irish Troubles Since 1969* (2003), difficulties with the "intensely problematic" phrase "Northern Ireland 'Troubles'" begin with the term "Northern Ireland," which signals "some recognition of constitutionalized partition and is thus an unacceptable designation to Nationalists," yet redacting Northern Ireland simply as "the North" would seem too mindlessly geographic to satisfy many Unionists.[6] This isn't all. Following David Lloyd's lead, Kennedy-Andrews recognizes that the term "Troubles" distorts a nationalist view of resistance to British domination by appearing to regard violence as a "spasmodic" and disruptive "outrage" that, at its foundation, lacks a "legitimating teleology."[7] Much as it mismanages the motives behind an organized resistance to social marginalization, discrimination, and economic inequity, "Troubles" equally fails to communicate a sense of Unionist outrage over civic unrest, chaos, and the acts of violence that claimed so many innocent lives. It is thus difficult to take up the challenge Robert McLiam Wilson's brilliantly irreverent tramp Ripley Bogle issues to "picture" Belfast and the North as he experienced them.[8] From either side of the sectarian divide, then, "Troubles" is an abject failure, an instance of recourse to a "least worst" oozing of terminology, though lacking a better alternative I will employ it throughout in an unavoidable "missaying."

Then, there is the matter of dramatic genre; the notion that a variety of performance text definable as a "Troubles" play exists. Of course, on one level of abstraction there is no such dramatic form, any more than such a distinct dramatic kind as the Elizabethan revenge tragedy exists. But doesn't it also matter in this phrasing what connotations inhere in the word "exists"? The Elizabethan revenge tragedy *exists* in the academy and in theatre history – and has for some time – even if the term was unavailable to Shakespeare's audiences for the inaugural productions of *Titus Andronicus* and *Hamlet*. And for very good intellectual reasons, as Jacques Derrida underscores in "The Law of Genre": "Can one identify a work of art, of whatever sort, but especially a work of discursive art, if it does not bear the mark of genre, if it does not signal or mention it or make it remarkable in any way"?[9] In the cases of *Hamlet*, Thomas Kyd's *The Spanish Tragedy*, and the revenge tragedies of John Webster and Cyril Tourneur on the early seventeenth-century stage, several features might qualify as distinguishing "marks": the burden of wergeld on an individual to exact revenge, the attendant madness if not psychosis inherent to the avenger's dilemma, the gory excesses demanded by *lex talionis*, and so on. As Derrida maintains, the mark of genre cannot be construed as infiltrating and overwhelming authorial consciousness – if it could, how could a playwright add unique qualities to a genre or subvert it? – and membership in one genre does not preclude affiliation with others. For Derrida, even the metaphor of membership fails to express this sense of genre: "I would speak of a sort of participation without belonging – a taking part in without being part of, without having membership in a set." Rather, at stake in the individual texts that comprise a genre is "exemplarity," and the "*récit* which works through the logic of the example."[10] Here, *récit* means literally "re-cite," to repeat or summon again, hence the question of what recurring mark of genre identifies a text – dramatic, filmic, novelistic – as a "Troubles" narrative or, more specifically, a "Troubles Play."

Such an inquiry is pertinent only if it enhances our understanding of *The Freedom of the City* and *Volunteers*, and an ever-expanding canon of contemporary drama, fiction, and film based on the conflict in Northern Ireland – and its expansion into the Republic, Great Britain, and even America – provides a context within which we might reread Friel's plays. Novels like Bernard MacLaverty's *Cal* (1983) and Jennifer Johnston's *The Railway Station Man* (1984), and thrillers like Jack Higgins' *A Prayer for the Dying* (1976) and Tom Clancy's *Patriot Games* (1987), all of which have been adapted for film, indicate two directions in which narratives depicting Northern violence often move: toward a tragic love story or spectacular confrontation between good and evil not unlike the so-called "sensation scenes" of nineteenth-century melodramas by Dion Boucicault and a host of imitators. In the former variety, as in *Romeo and Juliet*, lovers from warring tribes struggle to prise happiness from an impasse inhospitable to its creation; in the latter, domestic heroes like Clancy's Jack Ryan (Harrison Ford in the 1992 movie) combat adversaries like Sean Miller who transport political violence to America (a formula repeated in such later films as *Blown Away*, 1994, and *The Devil's Own*, 1997). Catholic, Protestant, or British, member of the Provos, UVF, INLA, or other groups, the "villains" in such melodramas ruthlessly slaughter their enemies and innocent bystanders alike or, as in the case of Victor Kelly in Eoin McNamee's *Resurrection Man* (1994), embark upon a psychotic project of emulating the gangsters in films they have idolized. In addition to examining these novels, Kennedy-Andrews also identifies as a "Troubles" text a form of contemporary fiction like *The Railway Station Man* or Edna O'Brien's *The House of Splendid Isolation* (1994), in which the protagonist attempts a solipsistic project of escaping Northern cities and retreating to the country, an exodus which seldom proves sufficiently removed from the turmoil to produce the desired immunity.[11]

To whatever telos such narratives progress, "Troubles" texts purport to represent conditions in the six counties of Ulster, the activities of one or more parties embroiled in this conflict, the British response to them, or aspects of all of these. Some texts, as I have mentioned, focus on a pair of lovers; others depict the concerns of political prisoners (*In the Name of the*

Father, 1993), their mothers (*Some Mother's Son*, 1996), or their wives (*The Boxer*, 1997). And all offer, if at times too predictably, a view of historical processes that supplements our presumptions or knowledge about life in Northern Ireland, usually at specific moments when sectarian tensions were the most extreme or the intransigence of the Thatcherite government most pronounced, as in the Gerry Conlon case and the hunger strikes of the Blanket Men. Importantly, however, given the imaginative license the commercial cinema necessarily takes, a license historical dramatists from Shakespeare to Bernard Shaw have nearly always embraced, such filmic treatments do *not* constitute a history per se, as Hayden White insists:

> Because history, unlike fiction, is supposed to represent real events and therefore contribute to knowledge of the real world, imagination ... is a faculty particularly in need of disciplinization in historical studies.[12]

In this instance, "discipline consists less of prescriptions of what *must be done* than *exclusions* or proscriptions of certain ways of imagining historical reality."[13]

If White *were* in the business of prescription, one would surely demand that politically motivated incidents be represented in their particularity, a desideratum undermined by media coverage of events in the North. In villages like Ballymenone in County Fermanagh, as Henry Glassie reports, residents followed events in the cities on the wireless: "In silence we listen to the news from Dublin and Derry, Belfast and Washington. Bad news as usual."[14] But whether the violence occurred in Belfast or Ballymenone, as it unfortunately did, newspaper readers and radio audiences alike became conditioned by coverage prone to homogenize sectarian violence. Ryan and Coppinger, two journalists reporting on Victor Kelly's crimes in *Resurrection Man*, dissect this tendency:

> Ryan noticed how newspapers and television were developing a familiar and comforting vocabulary to deal with violence. Sentences which could be read easily off the page. It involved repetition of key phrases ... Coppinger pointed out how the essential details of an attack, the things which differentiated one incident from another, were missing ... They agreed that the reporting of violent incident was beginning to diverge from events ...[15]

In *Passing the Time in Ballymenone* (1982), Glassie describes the "workaday reality" of villagers who agreed about one all-too-common motif of the "bad news" on the radio: "The death of 'innocent people' is universally cited as the worst aspect of the current 'Trouble,'" in part because when an innocent person is "prematurely stolen from the community, energy is robbed from the little commonwealth. All are harmed."[16] No routinization, no palliative vocabulary can numb this collective pain.

Most examples of the Northern Ireland Troubles play similarly avoid soothing analgesics, thus revealing another proscription: few are "emplotted" as melodramas.[17] That is to say, recent Troubles plays seldom center around the sacrifices of patriotic heroes in the melodramatic tradition of Michael Dwyer or Robert Emmet, or upon the Judas-like villains who betray them. Morash's emphasis of the genre's subversive tendency thus seems apt, as contemporary writers search for "suitable means to engage with the civic strife around them" without lapsing into cliché.[18] A partial list of instances of the genre includes Patrick Galvin's *We Do It for Love* (1975), Graham Reid's *The Death of Humpty Dumpty* (1979), Martin Lynch's *The Interrogation of Ambrose Fogarty* (1982), Anne Devlin's *Ourselves Alone* (1986), Christina Reid's *The Belle of Belfast City* (1989), Robin Glendinning's *Donny Boy* (1990), Vincent Woods' *At the Black Pig's Dyke* (1992), Marie Jones' *A Night in November* (1994), Conall Morrison's *Hard to Believe* (1995), Martin McDonagh's *The Lieutenant of Inishmore* (2001), Owen McCafferty's *Mojo Mickybo* (2002), and *The History of the Troubles (accordin' to my Da)* (2002) by Martin Lynch and the comedy team of Conor Grimes and Alan McKee. Perhaps the most radical in form, Jones' and Morrison's plays are written for one actor; the seventeen roles in McCafferty's *Mojo Mickybo* are played by two. While the majority of these plays are set in urban locations, Woods' *At the Black Pig's Dyke* takes place in rural Leitrim. Reid's play concerns itself with the lives of a working-class Protestant family; Devlin's *Ourselves Alone* focuses on Catholic sisters whose father, brother, and lovers are actively involved in the struggle, imprisoned, or – in one case – acting as an undercover operative for the British government. McDonagh's notorious "Lieutenant" is a one-man terrorist gang who tortures his enemies even more savagely than the hoodlums do in Quentin Tarantino's *Reservoir Dogs* or Martin Scorsese's *Casino*, obvious influences on McDonagh; while Devlin's women seek a respite from violence: a place to be themselves. And, more than avoiding clichés, Troubles plays also interrogate other forms of consolation, including contrived romantic endings and more institutional forms of apotheosis.

Arguably the most controversial Troubles play since *The Freedom of the City*, *The Lieutenant of Inishmore*, purportedly motivated by McDonagh's outrage at the IRA's murder of two boys in Warrington,[19] assails its audience with killings and gore with little time for consolation or meaningful critique. As Ashley Taggart reports, London's Garrick Theatre production of *The Lieutenant of Inishmore* in the summer of 2002 – its premiere was at the RSC's Other Place in Stratford in 2001 – elicited an uneasy response from its audience, as during the production's last fifteen minutes while two blood-spattered characters hack away at the limbs of corpses, "the dam finally, belatedly, burst and the auditorium exploded with laughter."[20] This minor consolation aside and, perhaps, that afforded London audiences of watching "psychotic morons" confirm long-standing stereotypes of Irishness, as Mary Luckhurst charges, McDonagh's "black satire" offers little comfort.[21] Defenders of McDonagh like Catherine Rees contextualize *The Lieutenant of Inishmore* with the contemporary "in yer face" school of dramas like Sarah Kane's *Blasted* (1995), or rationalize its violence by comparing it to notorious scenes in earlier political drama such as the stoning of a baby in Edward Bond's *Saved* (1964). (This latter analogy seems unconvincing, as it overlooks Bond's meticulous staging in such plays as *Saved* and *Bingo* that strategically links such atrocity to its origins in capital and class consciousness.[22]) As unconstrained verbally as McDonagh's play is visually, Morrison's *Hard to Believe* (1995) indicts religion with particular ferocity, and in this regard bears resemblance to Friel's Troubles plays. As a devastated John Foster returns from his mother's funeral, he recalls the murder of his brother and relives the outrage of "Some bloody priest, his hands warm from an altar boy's balls, spouting crap" over his brother's coffin. He also remembers why the last mass he deigned to attend was at his father's funeral: "And when I heard some white-haired old duffer try to transfigure my grief through his childish images, I said, that's it, from now on, Ah'm livin' on Reality Row."[23] Sadly, the final destination on "Reality Row" is Foster's suicide by electrocution. In the play's closing moments, he shaves his wrists, tapes wires to them, and connects them to a light socket. As the lights lower on the play's final tableau, he pulls the fatal cord.

Formal experiments like Morrison's monologue or McDonagh's Tarentino-like blood orgy, however much they subdue the melodramatic or provoke an alienated laughter, should not suggest that Troubles plays are devoid of emotion. The violent summer of 1970 intrudes upon the psyches and friendship of two Belfast kids in *Mojo Mickybo*, leading, sadly, to a reprise of the ending of their favorite film, *Butch Cassidy and the Sundance Kid*. The action of Glendinning's *Donny Boy* also concludes with the rattle of automatic gunfire, the origin of which is uncertain – British or IRA – as a former "tout" driven by unemployment and desperation to complicity with the army races out of a tenement into certain death. The most shocking element in this final scene, though, is not the sound of violence, but the response of Donny's Ma to the shooting. Reacting in a fashion exactly opposite that of Sean O'Casey's Juno Boyle when she mourns the murder of her son Johnny, Glendinning's Ma, who moments before feels "thirty years younger" after kissing the doomed Cahill passionately, prays that he has been shot by soldiers: "God grant that if there's a bullet in him it's a British bullet and not one of our own. Killed in action, a loaded revolver in one hand, what better way to go?"[24] The more open-ended conclusion of *Ourselves Alone* requires two sisters and their sister-in-law to plot different courses, none of them certain, in an effort to survive the traumas they have suffered. One fears that she "may have lost the capacity for happiness"; another, preparing to emigrate to England, declares that she would rather "be lonely" there than "suffocate" in Andersontown.[25] In Marie Jones' *A Night in November* Northern protestant Kenneth McCallister follows the Republic's soccer team to the World Cup in New York, where his growing sense of estrangement from the biases with which he was raised leads to an exuberant epiphany: "I am free of it, I am a free man ... I am a Protestant man, I'm an Irish man."[26] Whether offering pathos or perversity, tragic catharsis or comic refulgence, as in the rare case of Jones' soccer fan,[27] most Troubles plays nevertheless originate in a dramaturgy of sentiment in which dramatic action both assures narrative closure and engages audiences' emotions.

The forms of Troubles plays are thus extraordinarily varied. Some, like *Ourselves Alone* and *Donny Boy*, can be located within a tradition of urban realism, the latter in particular evoking comparison with O'Casey's "Dublin Trilogy" of the 1920s. Yet neither Devlin nor Glendinning counterbalances the tragic valences of their plays with the antics of the knockabout comedians which O'Casey was so adept at creating (and which Beckett so much admired).[28] When playwrights adapt comedy to represent the Troubles – as in *A Night in November* or *The History of the Troubles (accordin' to my Da)* – they generally exclude the marriage(s) and transformed socius conventional to romantic comedy, and instead conclude with a birth (real or symbolic) that restores hope to a character or group of characters akin to Mary's celebration of Dolly's pregnancy at the end of Tom Murphy's *Bailegangaire* (1985). In *At the Black Pig's Dyke*, Vincent Woods revives the folk tradition of mummers' plays, while in *Summerhouse* (1994) Glendinning creates Chekhovian melancholy in portraying the decline of Protestant hegemony through the travails of an upper middle-class family. Others borrow from cinematic genres – the buddy film (*Mojo Mickybo*) or the gangster film (*The Lieutenant of Inishmore*) – or from popular performance genres like the review sketch. And while in *The Freedom of the City* and *Volunteers* Friel appropriates conventions from reviews, news broadcasts, academic lectures, and nationalist ballads, neither play bears strong resemblance to those that followed them; instead, they approach a Beckettian theatre that, for many critics, failed to represent the enormity of "Bloody Sunday," internment, or the Troubles more generally.

FRIEL'S BECKETTIAN TURN

MARY: What was that topic again that kept them on laughing?
MOMMO: Misfortunes. (Tom Murphy, *Bailegangaire* [1985])

The Freedom of the City, which Friel himself once disparaged as an "ill-considered play" written "out of a kind of anger at the Bloody Sunday events in Derry," concerns the killing of three civil rights marchers by British paratroopers and the latter's exculpation by a judicial inquiry, a scenario that parallels the events of 30 January 1972 when thirteen civilians were shot by soldiers who, in hearings conducted by Lord Widgery in February and March of that year, were acquitted of wrongdoing.[29] The similarly doomed protagonists of *Volunteers* are five internees for whom the term "volunteer" possesses a double resonance in recalling the commitment of patriots in Ireland's past and commenting ironically on the prisoners' decision to work on an archaeological excavation in the center of an Irish city, an unpopular decision that has motivated fellow detainees to plot their murders when they return to prison. Like "Bloody Sunday," internment resided in the forefront of political consciousness after the Special Powers Act was enforced in 1971, leading in August to the arrests of several hundred men suspected of involvement with the IRA.[30] Within six months this number rose to over 2,300, with some 1,600 detainees eventually released in a "revolving door" campaign destined to fuel the resentment of Northern Catholics.[31] In part because of these extratextual realities, these unvarnished relationships to real historical tensions, *The Freedom of the City* and *Volunteers* seemed to elicit greater critical scrutiny – and, at the times of their inaugural productions, sharper detraction – than other plays by Friel, and they are often linked together, as they will be here.

Even though both works found champions in the 1970s and have attracted even more admirers today, it was "still surprising," as Seamus Deane recalls, "to see the ferocity and the blindness with which critics, especially in London and New York, reacted to them."[32] While in Morash's view critical response to *The Freedom of the City* in Dublin was "muted and uncertain," it still played to 86 percent capacity at the Abbey[33]; produced in London and New York in 1974, however, it closed in the latter after only nine performances, in part because Clive Barnes, the influential theatre reviewer of *The New York Times*, condemned the play as "luridly fictionalized," "far-fetched," and "impossible." No viewer could ever believe, he demurred, that the British army would mobilize against just three protestors "22 tanks, two dozen armored cars, four water cannons," and more.[34] (Some years later, Lionel Pilkington defended Friel's representation of Britain's military operations, noting that with a few minor exceptions, descriptions in the play bear "close similarity" to the personnel and equipment deployed on Bloody Sunday.[35]) Although producer Joseph Papp at the New York Shakespeare Festival Theatre and Richard Watts of the *New York Post* countered such charges, the latter hailing the play a "genuine masterpiece," its New York run could not be saved.[36]

Volunteers fared no better after the Abbey Theatre's 1975 production. Gus Smith of the *Sunday Independent*, who had earlier leveled a negative judgment on *The Freedom of the City*, was similarly harsh in his verdict on *Volunteers*, published under the headline "Friel Must Dig Deeper."[37] Responding in the *Times Literary Supplement* in a rejoinder entitled "Digging Deeper," a "dig" aimed squarely at this review, Seamus Heaney compared Smith's allusion to the "great dramatic subject of internment" with the "pieties and patriotism implicit in another phrase, now heard less ... but once almost de rigueur when speaking of the Catholic minority in Ulster, who were 'our people in the North.'" In *Volunteers*, Heaney concluded, Friel finds a "form that allows his gifts freer expression," and reviewers like Smith "simply refused to accept the dramatic *kind* that Friel has broken into, a kind that involves an alienation effect but eschews didactic address."[38]

Two points merit brief comment here. The first is Smith's premise that "great" subjects like internment *demand* "great" theatrical treatment, a thesis that suggests, as O'Casey painfully learned a half century earlier with *The Plough and the Stars*, that some critics and audiences will countenance only a drama bordering on hagiography or heroic tragedy in the representation of the "Troubles." No ironic undercutting or character idiosyncrasy, no suspicions about the motives of those who lost their lives. Some reviewers of McDonagh's *The Lieutenant of Inishmore*, to take another example, betrayed a similar bias, objecting in one case that "the net result of the characters' trivial obsessions is to make *Lieutenant* feel like a small play about a big subject."[39] But Friel, who in his "Self Portrait" (1972) recalled the numerous encouragements he had been given to address contemporary Northern politics, rejected the notion that play writing involves taking a "do-it-yourself kit up to your study [to] assemble the [historical] pieces according to the enclosed leaflet."[40] On the contrary, often in contemporary Irish writing "big" subjects like internment are comically, even grotesquely, whittled down to size, as in Ripley Bogle's memory of four young British soldiers on "Internment Night" kicking down the door of his house in working-class Belfast. As army jeeps and Saracens waited on the street for soldiers and the suspects they dragged out of their homes, young Ripley noticed that Muire Ginchy, the girl who lived next door, had been mistakenly identified by a nervous soldier as a suspect with a gun. Ripley informed the soldier of his mistake just as the latter was poised to shoot, and when the frightened girl became aware of the danger she faced, she fell from the fence upon which she was balanced, "her open legs straddling the barbed wire."[41] Such horrific images can hardly be reduced to ready-to-assemble parts produced for use by historical dramatists, as one terrified and bloodied "wee girl" serves as a synecdochical figure for the outrages wrought by internment.

The second point concerns Heaney's insight that *Volunteers* produces an "alienation effect that eschews didactic address." Lionel Pilkington similarly discerns a "neo-Brechtian" strategy and effect in *The Freedom of the City* when Friel's three doomed marchers address the audience and recount their final moments together before being gunned down.[42] Both Heaney and Pilkington therefore imply a subtle political intention to Friel – Bertolt Brecht, after all, theorized the alienation effect – that has been distorted by opponents of these plays. That is to say, several American and British reviewers regarded *The Freedom of the City* as stridently anti-British, a charge both Seamus Deane and Pilkington after him refute. The play "does not simply attack the fact-finding objectivity upon which Widgery's *Report of the Tribunal* and the play's fictional inquiry both claim to be based," Pilkington asserts, nor given Friel's irony here and elsewhere is there any sure way of detecting in his play a "recognizable or political engagement" beyond the commitment of any "political" interpreter of events to bring to light the public conditions of his or her text.[43] In a 1973 interview with Eavan Boland, Friel concedes the difficulty of "writing about events which are still happening," regarding *The Freedom of the City* not as a thesis on recent history, but rather as a "study of poverty." Agreeing with him, Boland observes that the play "provides the scenario of a political" work, yet determines that it would be "surprising if it was" as "its author seems uninterested in polemics or propaganda."[44] Hence the formal conundrum arises: to what end can such tactics of the Brechtian epic theatre as the "A-effect" lead if not to a dismantling of capitalism, class consciousness, and the apparatuses – repressive and ideological – that enforce and rationalize social inequality?

Responding to the question of Friel's politics, Fintan O'Toole observes that while *The Freedom of the City* "seems to be 'about' Bloody Sunday ... it is much more about the impossibility of writing about Bloody Sunday,"[45] something borne out in the play by the shallow or flatly inaccurate analysis of events proffered in monologues by an American sociologist (Professor Dodds), a television reporter, and a priest; a patriotic song written by a nationalist balladeer; and the testimony of policemen, British officers, and a forensic scientist in the play's several scenes of legal proceeding. This "impossibility" includes the incomprehensible conclusions Lord Widgery reached in the judicial inquiry, some of which are summarized in the play's final scene. The tribunal, as is well known, ascribed culpability for the murders to just about everyone save the soldiers who pulled the triggers. In fact, the first of the Report's eleven conclusions – which is echoed in Friel's closing scene as the first of four findings read by the Judge – blames the deaths on the Northern Ireland Civil Rights Association: "There would have been no deaths in Londonderry on 30 January if those who organised the illegal march had not thereby created a highly dangerous situation in which a clash between demonstrators and the security forces was almost inevitable." Seemingly groping for some counterbalance to this accusation, the report also alleged that if the army had maintained a "low key attitude" and not attempted to arrest "hooligans," the "day might have passed off without serious incident." Still, as the tenth conclusion confirms, although "none of the deceased or wounded" was "proved to have been shot whilst handling a firearm or bomb" – and while no British soldier is known to have been killed or even wounded during the march and ensuing mêlée – the tribunal nonetheless found, in a sentence Friel quotes, "no reason to suppose that the soldiers would have opened fire if they had not been fired upon first."[46] How does one respond to such a decision? As Brian Lynch summarizes in *Pity for the Wicked* (2005), the decision is as outrageous as it is ironic: "His lordship … blamed the murdered for being dead."[47]

If nearly thirty-five years after the event, Bloody Sunday remains a kind of "mystic writing pad" upon which later outrages are inscribed, one can only imagine how the murders haunt dramatic representations like Friel's. I employ the trope "haunt" quite deliberately, in part to recall Marvin Carlson's work on the myriad "ghostings" invariably present in theatrical productions, visitations especially evident in the representation of well-known historical events where spectators experience both "a different example of a type of artistic product they have encountered before" *and* the identical thing – or *seemingly* identical thing – they have experienced outside of the theatre or in the media.[48] By the time of the inaugural production of *The Freedom of the City*, for example, the names "Derry" and "Belfast" evoked strong images for audiences who followed breaking news on the radio or watched reports daily on television. Television coverage of violence in Northern cities and towns, as Robert McLiam Wilson relates in *Eureka Street* (1996), create expectations simply by identifying the scene of the action. For Wilson's Jake Jackson, Belfast and Derry are identical in this respect:

> When you considered that [Belfast] was the underpopulated capital of a minor province, the world seemed to know it excessively well. Nobody needed to be told the reasons for this needless fame. I didn't know much about Beirut until the artillery moved in. Who'd heard of Saigon before it blew its lid? Was Anzio a town, a village or just a stretch of beach? Where was Agincourt exactly? Belfast shared the status of a battlefield.[49]

The very names Belfast and Derry instantiate expectations in theatre audiences – and, for that matter, in visitors to these cities, too, as Colin Bateman's protagonist in *Divorcing Jack* (1995) recognizes when taking an American acquaintance on the "usual terrorist tour" of locales seen on CNN: Stormont, the Falls Road, and Shankhill. And, as Friel once emphasized to an interviewer shortly after cofounding the Field Day Theatre Company, Derry, like Belfast, is "an important psychic town on this island,"[50] hence its larger-than-life image as a battlefield – or specter. Friel's television commentator in *The Freedom of the City* reinforces this notion in his coverage of the funeral of the three victims near the end of the play: "This is surely the most impressive gathering of church and state dignitaries that this humble parish of the Long Tower has ever seen."[51]

Of the congeries of expectations Friel confronted in writing these plays, then, a constrained understanding of dramatic form as a shape that matches both the magnitude of the historical event *and* the larger-than-life image created by the media loom as two of the most significant. In the latter case, one doesn't require Jean Baudrillard's dissertations on the image or Guy Debord's deconstruction of the "society of the spectacle" to appreciate the obstacles Friel confronted.[52] The narrative intrusions in *The Freedom of the City* produce history as image or spectacle only to discredit it. That is to say, Professor Dodds' calm, yet wildly inaccurate and condescending lectures on the subculture of poverty supplant the sounds of rumbling tanks, exploding gas canisters, and a fleeing mob heard offstage. The effect of his appearances rivals that created by the newscaster's reports during the play which, in resembling a documentary's voice-over narration, transform the events of Bloody Sunday into so much television footage – in short, into an image. Friel's greatest challenge, therefore, was neither to represent the highly mediated, hence distorted, ways in which contemporary historical events reach consumers, nor to critique the findings of the Widgery Tribunal, although he accomplishes both objectives. Rather, as in *Volunteeers*, the challenge was to excavate human realities from these all-too-public events, ones more resistant to the manipulations of the media or the judiciary, and these perforce were smaller, everyday realities that transcend the historical moment or its portrayal in the media. And, although highly-charged emotion could be expected to accompany any representation of Bloody Sunday or the effects of internment, Friel also sought to produce a measure of detachment. In short, he needed Beckett or, rather, the Beckettian.

Perhaps the most obvious Beckettian trace in *The Freedom of the City* and *Volunteers*, to recall Seamus Heaney's defense of the latter, pertains to a distinctly Irish "alienation effect" reminiscent not so much of the Brechtian epic theatre, but of the tradition of Irish writing as a "cult of last words" that Declan Kiberd outlines in *Irish Classics*:

> In his later, more anorexic writings, Beckett would develop a voice very close to that of the Gaelic bards: his protagonist would lie on his back in the dark, summoning voices, working on a set exercise. Invariably, he would offer to do something rather strange: both to die and in the very act of dying narrate an account of his own passing. *Malone Dies* is the classic text.[53]

Indeed, *Malone Dies* begins with the sentence "I shall soon be quite dead in spite of all" (*Three Novels*, p. 179), and within the first paragraph of *Molloy* Beckett's narrator admits, "What I'd like now is to speak of the things that are left, say my goodbyes, finish dying" (Three Novels, p. 7). In the opening stage directions of *The Freedom of the City*, Friel similarly foregrounds the status of its central characters: "*The stage is in darkness except for the apron which is lit in cold blue. Three bodies lie grotesquely across the front of the stage*" (p. 107). This direction clarifies that, excluding the scenes of judicial inquiry and the intrusions of expert commentators, what follows are the words and actions of three people who have already died, thereby – in a fashion compatible with alienation in epic theatre – blunting our emotional engagement with their fates. The tactic also helps produce the detachment necessary for comedy more generally, as Friel's later play *Performances* (2003) confirms. Stage directions for this play, like those in *The Freedom of the City*, underline the status of its protagonist from the outset – "*It becomes apparent very early that Janáček is long dead. It is important that he is played by an actor in his fifties or energetic sixties*"[54] – a status that is crucial to the ironically comic potential of later dialogue. So, when a musician flatters Janáček by saying, "You're looking energetic today, Maestro" (p. 35), or even when the latter asks the graduate student who is interviewing him, "Sure you're not cold?" and offers to light a fire, it is almost impossible for us not to be amused. Even Janáček's analysis of his own funeral service and his cause of death grows mildly – if rather oddly – diverting, as do several scenes in *Freedom of the City* which would function differently if any doubt remained about the status of the play's three principals.

Friel creates a similar effect in some of his greatest achievements, including *Volunteers*. In *Faith Healer* (1979), for example, audiences become aware from Grace Hardy's monologue in Part Two that her husband Frank is already dead, and from Teddy's following monologue that Grace died from an overdose of sleeping pills. Some memory plays, Peter Gill's *Small Change* (1976) and Marina Carr's *The Mai* (1994), for instance, present the death of a major character in the opening act, only to have her return after the interval. The narrators of other memory plays like Michael Mundy in Friel's *Dancing at Lughnasa* (1990) reveal much later that some characters are dead or will die, although the report of their passings does not prevent Agnes and Rose from appearing in the closing scene. Although *Volunteers* announces the death of its pricipals somewhat differently, the effect is similar. Instead of carrying a body on stage immediately before the First Act curtain descends – as Robert does in *The Mai* holding his wife in the "ghostly light" and pausing for what Carr describes as a "ghostly effect"[55] – in the waning moments of Act One Keeney, one of the five internees who has agreed to work on the excavation that will eventually be the site of a luxury hotel, informs his compatriots of what awaits them at prison:

> Our fellow detainees held a meeting the night before last – no, not really a meeting – a sort of kangaroo court. And they discussed again our defection in volunteering for this job ... And the assembled brethren decided that the only fit punishment would be ... capital. (*Volunteers*, p. 44)

Because earlier exposition confirms that the play's action occurs on the final day of the "dig," the hotel's developers being anxious to begin construction, it becomes apparent that this will also most likely be the last day of these mens' lives. As in *The Freedom of the City*, and much like *Malone Dies* and *Molloy*, *Volunteers* concerns the last words and actions of characters approaching the bourne of death. And, unlike the ghostly effect of the Mai's drowning in Carr's play, or the bittersweet nostalgia of Michael's penultimate report in *Dancing at Lughnasa*, Keeney's announcement is both direct and ironic, as the kind of justice meted out by another kangaroo court had ordered the mens' incarceration in the first place.[56]

Volunteers communicates the presence of death – and the dehiscence Beckett so much enjoyed in O'Casey's one-act farce *The End of the Beginning* – from its opening stage picture. Much of the play's action takes place in a "huge crater" which, as Friel's stage directions relate, functions as both a "womb" and a "prison yard" (*Volunteers*, p. 11). Recalling Pozzo's line in *Waiting for Godot*, "They give birth astride of a grave" (p. 103), this crater qua womb also serves as a grave housing bones which, after being reassembled, form a skeleton displayed right of stage center and nicknamed Leif by the inmates. Offstage left is a smaller excavation, the cesspit, a reminder of the material realities of bodies that await final judgment. This setting, as realized to great effect in the play's revival by London's Gate Theatre in 1998, overwhelmed the reviewer for the *Financial Times*, who lavished praise on the production:

> Never have I seen quite such a reinvention of the Gate Theatre's space ... Liz Cooke's archaeological-dig set is so irregular and seemingly ramshackle that the warning signs outside the theatre turn out to be more than mere effect. We are informed that we may "sit anywhere where there are white tags," and find ourselves surrounding the bulk of the play's action in a hole in the ground ... [a] dimension not unlike a prison cell.[57]

In the *Times*, Jeremy Kingston describes much of the audience sitting in niches against the side walls, "peering down at sifted earth, ancient posts, and the crumpled skeleton of, maybe, a Viking." Spotting the leather noose around the skeleton's neck and the hole in its skull, Kingston wonders if the fates of the workers will be any different, and remarks that the play's closing moments are "steeped in the bitterly humorous fatalism of First World War drama."[58] And writing a feature on the Peter Brook/Empty Space award given to studio theatres receiving little or no subsidies, Paul Taylor recounts Brook's enthusiasm for the Gate production, which converts a tiny space into a "boggy architectural burrow."[59] A "ramshackle" burrow littered with timbers, plastic, and other debris, including bones and the crumbled clay-and-wattle walls of an ancient house; a womb-like hole in the ground that is the site of a bitterly humorous fatalism; a dramatic moment capturing the endgame of a five-month process – all of these suggest a kind of Beckettian mise-en-scène and "emplotment." As in *Endgame*, "Something is taking its course," and it is irrevocable.

Dramatic action in *Volunteers* is comprised mostly of the prisoners' stories, limericks, skits, displays of wit, and minor schemes either to get out of duty in the cesspit or cadge a needed cup of tea. To be sure, dramatic tension is created in Act One when Desmond, a post-graduate student working on the site who befriends the prisoners, is informed by George, the project manager, that their labors will cease at the end of the present work day. They argue briefly, Des insists that the prisoners be told the bad news, and then rushes off to make an ultimately futile effort to save the project by appealing to the museum board. Before his exit, he vows to support whatever protest the men deem appropriate. But, true to their origins in knockabout comedy, Friel's Keeney and Pyne undertake no protest other than comic deflation of the bad news:

PYNE: God, that's heartbreaking. I mean to say, this is the first time in my life I've ever felt – you know what I mean like – fulfilled in my work.
KEENEY: As the actress said to the bishop. (*Volunteers*, p. 40)

Soon after, another internee named Butt takes exception to Keeney's inexhaustible supply of quips and jokes, threatening to close his mouth "for good." But this friction leads nowhere, largely because at this moment, near the end of the First Act, the men discover a potentially more serious problem: their friend Smiler, beaten senseless before the play begins and exhibiting a markedly diminished intellectual capacity as a result, has escaped. The men debate the possibility that it might be better for Smiler if his absence was reported to the authorities, but eventually decide to prevent George from doing so. No matter, as Smiler is returned safely later in Act Two.

The inevitable sense of a world winding down pervades the second act. One reviewer of the Gate production even characterized Keeney, so exuberant in earlier scenes, as sinking into a "mire of despair" (which contradicts Friel's stage direction that he seems "even more assured, more relaxed, than in Act One" [*Volunteers*, p. 45]). The set design of the second act reflects a sense of decline, for when the lights come up work-related materials have already been cleared away and George is seen packing books and papers in the site's makeshift office. The dialogue begins in serious fashion as well, as Keeney tells George how the internees came to be detained and how Smiler, a shop steward from the west of Donegal, angered by the internment of a friend, led a small group of stonemasons in a protest march, for which he was arrested and given a savage beating. Moments later, Keeney discusses Smiler with his fellow inmates, one of whom, fearful that Smiler will be killed when he is apprehended, regrets not allowing George to report the escape. Keeney then underscores the inevitable end for all of them:

Yes, they'll [the police] kill [Smiler] this time. Or his own mates'll kill him – or kill you or me or Pyne or Knox. Yes, one way or the other there's going to be a blood-letting. (*Volunteers*, p. 48)

To borrow a metaphor from *Sir Thomas More*, parts of which have been ascribed to Shakespeare and from which Ciaran Carson borrows for *Belfast*

Confetti (1989), Friel's internees, like the "vanished public houses" and disappearing shops on the Falls Road Carson remembers, will all be "swallowed in the maw of time and trouble."[60] In this figure, the Troubles, like the word "maw," signifies a voracious appetite and powerful jaws; it will swallow and digest them all, "blood-letting" one way or the other. MacLaverty's *Cal* employs the same metaphor, as the people of Ulster find themselves "caught between the jaws of two opposing ideals."[61] The mise-en-scène of *Volunteers*, with its skeleton, debris, and womb/grave/excavation pit, communicates this eventuality just as surely as the corpses of Lily, Michael, and Skinner do in the opening tableau of *The Freedom of the City*. All that remains is for the "sheeted dead" to "squeak and gibber."[62]

This reading of Friel's theatre of alienation, to reiterate, owes more to Kiberd's sense of the irreducibly Beckettian quality of Irish "classics," and, as I have suggested, to Shakespeare and even James Joyce, than to Brecht's epic theatre. Friel underscores the "membership" of both plays in an Irish "cult of last words" through means other than the composition of striking or disturbing stage pictures. One strategy, as Richard Pine contends, is reflected in the names of both plays' central characters, as "naming, for Friel, as for Beckett is the key to identity."[63] If a proper name in a literary text is truly the "prince of signifiers," as Roland Barthes claims,[64] then both *Volunteers* and *The Freedom of the City* might be understood, at least in part, by the names Friel creates. Much like the pairs of names in Beckett's plays – Hamm and Clov in *Endgame*, Didi and Gogo in *Waiting for Godot*, Winnie and Willie in *Happy Days* – several in *Volunteers* designate one-half of a meaningful pair. The two detainees Smiler and Butt come to mind, but more important are the comic duo Keeney and Pyne, whose names both resemble those of a comedy team – a clever or "keen" one perhaps – and advert to types of mourning or longing: to keen (from the Irish *caoine*, to wail) and to pine.

In a more subtle allusion, in *The Freedom of the City* Michael and Lily bear the names of characters in Joyce's "The Dead." At seventeen, Michael Furey, whose health had declined after he took a job in the gasworks, died out of love for Gretta Conroy; while at twenty-two, Friel's Michael Hegarty is engaged to be married and may find a job in the gasworks nearby. Like Michael Furey, Hegarty is an "evocation" of "a figure from the dead," the figure of a young man ironically embarking upon a course of self-improvement (Michael Furey aspires to be a singer, Michael Hegarty is enrolled in business courses) who dies far too early. Joyce's Lily, "literally run off her feet" in the first sentence of "The Dead," views men cynically as "only palaver and what they can get out of you,"[65] while Friel's haggard, middle-aged Lily Doherty, an impoverished cleaning woman and mother of eleven, has given all she can to an unemployed and idle husband. Like Joyce's housekeeper, Friel's Lily is exhausted from the outset, gasping for breath in an effort to recover from the gas deployed by the soldiers. Soon after entering the Mayoral office, she drops into a chair and covers her face with her hands.

More significantly, lilies are traditionally symbols of peace, while Casimir–Skinner's real name is Adrian Casimir Fitgerald – literally "to destroy" (*kazic*) "peace" (*mir*). "Adrian" is a form of Hadrian, recalling Hadrian's wall, and Adrian IV (1154–1159) was the only English pope. And while it would be grossly inaccurate to place guilt for their deaths on one of the victims themselves – this would reproduce the Widgery tribunal's principal finding – it is also true that Skinner understood the likely consequence of their occupation of Guildhall much earlier than the others and explains this directly to the audience in Act Two: "A short time after I realized we were in the Mayor's parlour I knew that a price would be exacted ... So I died, as I lived, in defensive flippancy" (*Selected Plays*, p. 150). Thus, if Seamus Deane is correct that "recurrent elements" in Friel's plays include "a closed community, a hidden story, a gifted outsider with an antic intelligence, [and] a drastic revelation leading to violence,"[66] then the "hidden" story of *The Freedom of the City* does not so much concern the inadequacy of language or the failure of the court to uncover the truth. These inadequacies are scarcely hidden. Rather, the inevitability of death and its haunting of the living, the sense of something taking its inexorable course, subtends this play as much as it does *Rockaby* or *Footfalls*. We might see this as a Beckettian haunting, not merely a hidden story.

The "gifted" outsiders with the "antic intelligence" are, of course, Skinner in *The Freedom of the City* and Keeney in *Volunteers*, the latter supported by his sidekick, Pyne. Like Didi and Gogo, or O'Casey's Darry Berrill and Barry Derrill in *The End of the Beginning*, Friel's pair in *Volunteers* entertains the audience as the internees move inexorably to the beginning of their end. Less given to physical comedy than O'Casey or Beckett's pairs – a tactic implied by the combination of thick and slender body types in O'Casey and demanded by the dexterity required for the comic (mis)performance of calisthenics to music or the exchange of bowlers in comic rhythm – Keeney and Pyne create a riantic spaciousness through a series of limericks, anecdotes, and short skits in which quips about death and mortality function as punch lines almost as often as those about sex and the body do. During one interchange rife with sexual innuendo, for example, Keeney impersonates an academic while Pyne plays a female schoolteacher nicknamed "Tits" leading schoolchildren on a tour. Upon his entrance in Act One, Keeney recites a limerick about Charles Stewart Parnell's mistress, Kitty O'Shea, "Who was known as a fabulous lay" (*Volunteers*, p. 18); moments later, in a more archaeological mood, he entertains his colleagues with another limerick about a "randy young buck from Kilgarvan" who "On a girl tried out radiocarbon" (p. 20). Death equally becomes fodder for Keeney's antic sensibility. So, as the men leave the stage at the end of the play, he attempts to transpose the precariousness of their return to prison into a low comic register:

> On an archaeological site
> Five diggers examined their plight
> But a kangaroo court
> Gave the final report– [...]
> They were only a parcel of ... (*Volunteers*, p. 70)

"Shite," the last word of the limerick, metaphorically combines the site's two excavations, tomb and cesspit; at the same time, the verdict of imminent death is undercut by comedy. Much the same thing happens earlier in *Volunteers* when Keeney reports that Des had been rushed to the hospital to have his stomach pumped. Apparently, he had mistaken a recently delivered urn containing the ashes of his dead aunt Coco for a "swanky jar of American coffee" and made himself a hot cup – of ashes. To ratchet up the story's grotesquely comic potential, Keeney adds one more "disquieting" aspect to his report: "Wilson says he loved the taste" (*Volunteers*, p. 27).

Death and the body, then, in all of its inadequacies, so much a concern of the Beckettian and so often a source of comic invention, function similarly in Friel's play. So, too, do literary allusions. *Endgame* and *Happy Days*, as I have discussed in the previous chapter, contain numerous literary and Biblical allusions; references that, in Winnie's case, provide consolation yet often seem drastically incongruous to her predicament. At the same time, allusions to Shakespeare in Beckett seem almost always ironically appropriate: "Fear no more the heat o' the sun" in *Happy Days*, "Our revels now are ended" in *Endgame*, the eye as "vile jelly" in *Ill Seen Ill Said*, and so on. After concluding his last limerick in *Volunteers*, Keeney adds "Good night, sweet prince," one of several echoes of *Hamlet* in the play, resulting in what might initially appear to be an irreverent joining of forms – profane limerick and "classic" tragedy. Scholars have long recognized the influence of *Hamlet* on *Volunteers*: the presence of a Yorick-like skeleton "*banked slightly*" on stage "*so that it can be seen fully and clearly*" (*Volunteers*, p. 9), the parallels between Des and Laertes, Keeney's question to George, "Was

Hamlet really mad?" (p. 21), and so on. Yet, while the center of dramatic focus in most scenes, Keeney scarcely qualifies as a tragic hero; he is a self-described "Friday-night man" whom Patrick Burke terms an "emblem of celebratory individuality and joyous anarchy,"[67] a working man who, after receiving his pay packet, goes home, cleans up, and heads out for a night on the town. Ironically, on those Friday nights Keeney, like many working men, experiences an "almost overwhelming sense of power and control and generosity and liberation" (p. 47); on *this* Friday, by stark contrast, Keeney and his friends are little more than "spancelled goats" (p. 57). We sympathize, of course, with the men's diminished lives, and we worry that, upon their return to prison, Keeney, whose wit and inventiveness have entertained us, will be "the one they'll go for first" (p. 75). But Friel never shows us this closing spectacle conventional to revenge tragedy. Instead, all the audience is afforded of *Hamlet* at the curtain is Keeney's "Good night, sweet prince" and the actions of another character tidying up the now abandoned work site.

Allusions to Shakespeare, in this instance *King Lear*, work similarly in *Freedom of the City*, producing consolation, even entertainment, for the characters, and foreshadowing both their ends and the likely conclusions of the Widgery hearings. They also provide evidence of the educational backgrounds of and intellectual differences between the three "terrorists,"serving therefore as both an antidote to homogenizing media constructions of the Troubles and a rebuttal of several of Professor Dodds' hypotheses about the "subculture" of poverty. Contrary to Dodds' assertions that the poor possess "very little sense of history" (*Selected Plays*, p. 111) and that they are "present-time orientated" and seldom plan for the future (p. 133), Michael recalls the origins of the civil rights movement and is enrolled in school to study business administration and computer science. Lily endures a life of grinding poverty with an infirm husband and eleven children. And Skinner, less idealistic and committed than Michael, enjoys betting on horses and drinking, but he is hardly provincial, another of Dodds' hypotheses. As the action shifts from Dodds' lecture to the inside of Guildhall in Act One, Skinner emerges from a dressing room "*dressed in splendid mayoral robe and chain and wears an enormous ceremonial hat jauntily on his head*" quoting from Act Four of *King Lear*: "You're much deceived: in nothing am I chang'd/But in my garments" (4.6.9–10), and "Through tattered clothes small vices do appear;/Robes and furred gowns hide all" (4.6.164–65). As Skinner distributes mayoral finery to Michael and Lily, both lines appropriately accompany the trio's impromptu costume party, and the latter passage in particular ironically prepares us for the tribunal's conclusion that the shootings were justified. For as Lear advises Gloucester in *King Lear*, when sin is plated with gold, the "strong lance of justice breaks"; in other words, when the powerful control the courts, justice cannot be rendered.

This allusion, more so than Dodds' sociological babble about poverty, the priest's unfounded suggestion that Marxian radicalism has misled the three, and the Balladeer's inclusion of them in a long procession of nationalist martyrs, illuminates the trajectory of the plot in *The Freedom of the City*. Like Gloucester and Lear, or like Winnie and Willie, Hamm and Clov, Friel's characters are the victims of History and the cruel maw of Time. Like flies killed by "wanton boys" in *King Lear* – like Lear himself – Skinner, Michael, and Lily never really have a chance.

But, as prescient as these allusions to *King Lear* are, as predictive as they are of the injustice that will follow, they also provide moments of pleasure. In the liminal space of Guildhall – not long after entering the space and being informed of precisely where they were, Lily exclaims, "We shouldn't be here" and "No place for us" (*Selected Plays*, p. 119) – Friel's ill-fated marchers deploy what they can to live, to *be*, and this includes adversions to the bleak reality of injustice in Shakespeare. Fortunately for Friel's three marchers, however, the Mayor's office also furnishes them with costumes, paintings and stained-glass windows to admire, even sherry to drink before they march into a cascade of bullets. As is typical of the Beckettian, then, objects, even the simplest of objects, become *things* and thus constitute resources for enduring the quotidian. The convention is much stronger and more apparent, however, in the sumptuous destitution of *Volunteers* where, to recall Bill Brown's point, "The story of objects asserting themselves as things ... is the story of a changed relation to the human subject." One can imagine a thing as connoting what is "excessive in objects," a quotient that exceeds their materiality and utility. In the most pronounced cases of objects becoming fetishes, values, idols, or totems, things exert their "force as sensuous presence or as a metaphysical presence" almost as if by magic.[68] In the previous chapter, I mentioned some of the more extreme instances of magical objects in Beckett, but numerous objects from stuffed animals to Winnie's looking glass confirm that, indeed, "*things* have a life" in Beckett (*Happy Days*, p. 54). They cannot be ignored.

The use of objects as *things* or, more precisely, their transformation into things, is perhaps most apparent in *Volunteers*. In an amusing way, the ashes of Des' Aunt Coco constitute a thing, as the urn containing them metamorphoses into a coffee tin and, finally, into the punch line of a joke. But the most significant object, the most polysemous object, is the antique jug reassembled from 593 pieces uncovered in this archaeological dig. In a manner paralleling the set composed of a large hole and a smaller cesspit offstage, the jug and the skeleton of Leif create a kind of visual balance of overdetermined things. Leif is an antique as well, but also an echo of Shakespeare's Yorick *and*, more important, a victim of violence with a leather rope around his neck and a hole in his skull. Like the internees, he may have been a victim of religious violence, as one of Pyne's limericks proposes:

> There once was a Norseman called Leif
> Whose visit to Ireland was brief
> He was caught in a war
> Between Jesus and Thor
> And came to a permanent grief. (*Volunteers*, p. 19)

Leif was caught, in other words, in an ideological battle analogous to that in which Friel's internees are ensnared, and through this object – this thing – audiences during the Troubles can see themselves as potential victims of History and religion. In this regard, the skeleton and limerick substitute for the lectures, homilies, and news reports in *The Freedom of the City*, and for the similar indictments in such Troubles texts as Benedict Kiely's *Proxopera* (1980), in which a retired teacher delivers a feisty diatribe to his IRA captors indicting King William, the Pope, Ian Paisley, and a long Irish history for misleading youth and catalyzing sectarian fanaticism.[69] Jesus and Thor, Paisley and the Pope, nooses and smashed skulls.

The antique jug is equally demonstrative of the elision of boundaries between subject and object that Brown theorizes. In the beginning of the play, the reassembled object represents a valuable antique, a find of inestimable cultural and, possibly, monetary value. In Act Two, as the office is being disassembled, Keeney seizes the jug and at first, predictably enough, uses it as a prop in a joke. First, he pretends it's a valuable item on sale at an auction and formally reviews its provenance before the imagined bidding commences: "Lot 142 – the unique Burgundy jug discovered in Ireland in the 1970s by Professor Smiler! ... Gentlemen, what am I offered for Smiler's jug?" (*Volunteers*, p. 48). Then, he quickly improvises a close reading of the jug comparable to that in Keats's "Ode on a Grecian Urn," from which he quotes: "To what green altar, O mysterious priest,/ Lead'est thou that heifer lowing at the skies" (p. 49). George, concerned about the jug's safety, inserts himself between Keeney and Pyne, who threaten to toss it back and forth in a childish game of keep-away, and finally Keeney positions the jug at Leif's feet and poses a series of searching questions: "Where does it belong? Is it Smiler's – finders keepers? Or is it the Professor's? Or does in belong to the nation? Or does it belong to – Brother Leif?" (p. 50). Near the end of the play, Butt picks up the jug just as George has elevated it to a symbol of the now completed excavation: "I was just saying to Dr. King last night: if we'd got nothing else here, the dig would have been worth it for [the jug] alone" (p. 63). Hearing this, Butt pretends that he will return it to George for safekeeping, but instead deliberately allows it to fall out of his hands and shatter on the ground. As a relic to be excavated and reassembled – as a thing to labor over and care for – the jug had great value for all the men, great personal meaning; absent that, it means little to the interns. And, as a totalizing emblem of a troubled Irish history, the assembled object is misleading in its unity. The seemingly endless turmoil defining this history is more accurately represented as shards of debris still awaiting coherent organization and explanation. Readings of this history, of the mens' internment, like the shattered jug in *Volunteers*, will have to be patiently assembled and reassembled from the bits of evidence that can be uncovered. For like the jug, Friel's plays offer death and destruction as the only certainties.

POSTSCRIPT: THE TROUBLES, *HAMLET*, AND AFFECTIVE TIME

"As usual, the clock in The Clock Bar was a good few minutes fast:
A fiction no one really bothered to maintain, unlike the story
The comrade on my left was telling, which no one knew for certain truth."
(Ciaran Carson, "Hamlet" in *Belfast Confetti* [1989])

Set in the Clock Bar, the final poem in Ciaran Carson's *Belfast Confetti* uses *Hamlet*, much as Friel employs Shakespeare, as an analogue to the Troubles. In "Hamlet" Carson borrows phrases from Shakespeare's play, emphasizing that the name of the Falls Road where the bar is located comes from the Irish *fál* which means "*frontier, boundary*, as in *the undiscovered country/ From whose bourne no traveller returns*, the illegible, thorny hedge of time itself [emphasis in original]" (*Belfast Confetti*, p. 106). The Falls Road thus serves as a synecdochical figure of the "*strange eruption to our state*," signifying also the liminality of no-go areas where the boundary between life and death was beaten into airy thinness. As Carson explains, this area was once patrolled by a bomb-disposal expert in a knightly "suit of salamander-cloth/ Shielded against the blast of time by a strangely-mediaeval visor," a vestige of the ghost of King Hamlet. But this workaday "knight," like Shakespeare's king, has been deposed, symbolically killed, in this instance by a "jerky robot" with metallic hooks for turning over "*corpses that may be booby-trapped*" (p. 106). Technology and the passage of time have reduced the armored expert to a specter, a "tin ghost" whose voice can be heard among other sounds reverberating "from the grave" (p. 107). The visitations of ghosts, the reverberation of the voices of the dead, the disjointing of time – all of these tropes link the Troubles not only with Shakespeare, but with Friel and Beckett as well.

Perhaps the strongest commonality between all of these writers concerns The Clock and the kind of time it signifies. As "Hamlet" begins in the lines rendered above, the inaccuracy of the pub's actual clock is yoked to yet another imprecision: that of representing historical events in an accurate and coherent narrative. That is, the story the speaker's comrade tells about an episode from the earlier Troubles of the 1920s may or may not be accurate: "no one knew for certain truth." Here, then, as Linda Charnes discusses in connection to *Hamlet*, chronological or what Bruno Latour terms "calendar time" is juxtaposed to "another kind of time that 'situates the same events with respect to their intensity'":

> Thus we might say that in order to comprehend any history that approaches (rather than backs away from) "the truth", we must acknowledge that for every temporal chronicle there is an affective anti-chronicle, for every linear reconstruction of calendar events there is a constellation of significant intensities that are excluded from the story ... In *Hamlet*, the significant intensities of the play guarantee that an accurate calendar-history of what actually "happened" can never be produced.[70]

Like Charnes' *Hamlet*, neither *The Freedom of the City* nor *Volunteers* provides a linear chronology of events. The narrative of the former play conflates events without ever providing an unimpeachably accurate account of why the civil rights marchers were killed: Were the British paratroopers ordered to fire? Did they panic? Were they attempting to suppress the actions of "hooligans"? Similarly, in *Volunteers* chronologies of the men's arrests and of the processes of internment are not provided. What *is* clear, however, is that as the play progresses – while Keeney and Pyne entertain us – Smiler, an otherwise minor character, grows in affective importance: *his* fate as an escapee concerns us; *his* story of being beaten by police repulses us; *his* jug, a symbol of the project's success, explodes into pieces in the play's affective time.

Dramatic conflict in such narratives derives then not so much from any Aristotelian unity of action or chain of causality, but from periodic intensities. In some respects, like Beckett's dramas, Friel's plays provide exposition that allows only glimpses into characters, but not the foundations of a resolving or resolvable action. We know in general how the three dead marchers in *The Freedom of the City* were forced into the temporary shelter of Guildhall, and we have some sense of how the internees in *Volunteers* came to be arrested with, again, Smiler's chronicle meriting our most concerted attention. But we really aren't given many details. Similarly, we know very little about the circumstances that led Hamm and Clov in *Endgame* to their shelter, or the events that caused Winnie to be entombed in earth in *Happy Days*. In the latter play, Beckett strongly implies that such knowledge really doesn't matter, as Winnie ridicules passers-by who inquire as to her predicament: "What's it meant to mean – and so on – lot more stuff like that usual drivel." Why doesn't Willie "dig her out?" they ask – "usual tosh" (p. 43). As a result, time – chronicle time – is devalued. Time simply *is*, and as in the fecund refrain from *Rockaby*, in these plays – for these doomed characters – "*time she stopped.*" In *Rockaby*, "she," of course, is W, the old woman in the chair, but the pronoun also refers to time itself. The problem is, in such historical moments time cannot stop, though it can be rocked out of joint. As Pozzo screams furiously in *Waiting for Godot*, "Have you not done tormenting me with your accursed time?" (p. 103). Accursed time is intensive time, and in Beckettian representations of the Troubles like *Volunteers* and *The Freedom of the City*, "calendar" or chronological time withers into moribundity.

Affective time also encompasses more than Smiler's brutalization or Pozzo's torment, as Friel demonstrates in these plays. Commenting on Friel's early play *Lovers* (1967), Thomas Kilroy discusses "Losers," the second part of the diptych "Winners" and "Losers" that comprises *Lovers*. In his reading Kilroy remarks, "It is significant that this play … opens and closes with a man staring through binoculars at a blank wall, a very Beckettian image indeed."[71] Perhaps it is. As I have tried to show here, such an act is Beckettian insofar as it provides an expansiveness to the otherwise limiting space of the dramatic world such characters inhabit. The bare wall may be transformed into a "thing" of psychical importance, breaching the perimeter circumscribing its status as object and allowing for a relationship with the subject. The act of viewing the wall may also exert an alienating or haunting effect; it may be accompanied by the reverberating voices of the dead and located in an intertextual network of previous writing. There may be a broken and meaningless clock slightly above the wall in the distance. And the wall may also stand in the war zones of Derry or Belfast, in a liminal space above the ruins of Irish history and the horrific intensities of the Troubles.

NOTES

1. O'Toole's review is reprinted in *Critical Moments: Fintan O'Toole on Modern Irish Theatre*, eds. Julia Furay and Redmond O'Hanlon (Dublin: Carysfort Press, 2003), p. 302.
2. Richard Kearney, *Transitions: Narrative in Modern Irish Culture* (Dublin: Wolfhound Press, 1988), p. 125.
3. For an excellent review of Friel's interest in and indebtedness to Chekhov and Turgenev, see Richard Pine, "Friel's Irish Russia," in *The Cambridge Companion to Brian Friel*, ed. Anthony Roche (Cambridge: Cambridge University Press, 2006), pp. 104–116.
4. Brian Friel, "In Interview with Desmond Rushe," in *Brian Friel: Essays, Diaries, Interviews: 1964–1999*, ed. Christopher Murray (London: Faber and Faber, 1999), p. 31. Further references to Friel's interviews and to his lecture "The Theatre of Hope and Despair," a copy of which is included in this volume, will be followed by page numbers in the text.
5. Christopher Morash, *A History of Irish Theatre 1601–2000* (Cambridge: Cambridge University Press, 2002), p. 246.
6. Elmer Kennedy-Andrews, *Fiction and the Northern Irish Troubles Since 1969: (De)-Constructing the North* (Dublin: Four Courts Press, 2003), p. 10.
7. Kennedy-Andrews, *Fiction and the Northern Irish Troubles*, p. 11. Here he is quoting from David Lloyd's *Anomalous States: Irish Writing and the Post-Colonial Moment* (Dublin: Lilliput Press, 1993).
8. See Robert McLiam Wilson, *Ripley Bogle*. (1989; rpt. New York: Ballantine, 2000), pp. 111–115.
9. Jacques Derrida, "The Law of Genre," in *Glyph 7: Textual Studies*, ed. Samuel Weber (Baltimore: Johns Hopkins University Press, 1980), p. 211.
10. Derrida, "The Law of Genre," p. 206.
11. See Kennedy-Andrews, *Fiction and the Northern Irish Troubles*, for readings of these novels from a feminist perspective. See also his reading of Tom Clancy's unsympathetic portrayal of the Republican cause and dubious later claim to support reunification of Ireland, pp. 57–62.
12. Hayden White, "The Politics of Historical Interpretation: Discipline and De-Sublimation," in *The Politics of Interpretation*, ed. W. J. T. Mitchell (Chicago: University of Chicago Press, 1983), p. 129.
13. White, "The Politics of Historical Interpretation," p. 130.
14. Glassie, *All Silver and No Brass*, p. 12.
15. Eoin McNamee, *Resurrection Man* (London: Picador, 1994), p. 58.
16. Henry Glassie, *Passing the Time in Ballymenone* (1982, rpt. Bloomington: Indiana University Press, 1995), pp. xiv, 144–145. "Community" also possesses a strong resonance in urban locales. In his memoir *In the Name of the Father* (1990, rpt. New York: Plume Books, 1993), Gerry Conlon recalls that growing up "Nationalism meant nothing to me, because Irishness meant nothing … The world I lived in – those few street corners in the Lower Falls – was a very small one. What I felt was what absolutely everyone felt, a fierce loyalty to that community" (p. 24).

17. In *Meta-History: The Historical Imagination in Nineteenth-Century Europe* (Baltimore: Johns Hopkins University Press, 1973), pp. 7–11, Hayden White argues that because history comes to us fashioned into a story, its "mode of emplotment" implicitly offers an explanation of historical events.
18. Ronán McDonald, "Between Hope and History: The Drama of the Troubles," in *Druids, Dudes and Beauty Queens: The Changing Face of Irish Theatre*, ed. Dermot Bolger (Dublin: New Island, 2001), pp. 232–33.
19. For a discussion of McDonagh's "pacifism," see Catherine Rees, "The Politics of Morality: *The Lieutenant of Inishmore*," in Chambers and Jordan (eds.), *The Theatre of Martin McDonagh*, p. 131.
20. Ashley Taggart, "An Economy of Pity," 163. After being rejected by the National Theatre and the Royal Court in London, and by the Druid Theatre Company in Ireland, the play had its premiere at the Royal Shakespeare Company at the Other Place in Stratford, May, 2001 and transferred to the West End in June, 2002.
21. Mary Luckhurst, "Martin McDonagh's *The Lieutenant of Inishmore*: Selling (-Out) to the English," in Chambers and Jordan (eds.), *The Theatre of Martin McDonagh*, p. 119 and *passim*.
22. For a discussion of the dual stage-picture in Bond, see Malcolm Hay and Philip Roberts, *Bond: A Study of His Plays* (London: Eyre Methuen, 1980), pp. 189–93. Using the example of a young peasant woman being gibbetted in *Bingo* (1973), they observe that "The audience is shown a scene with two centres, the girl and Shakespeare sitting down stage … The two centres are visually set apart, but the link between them is unavoidable" (p. 190).
23. Conall Morrison, *Hard to Believe*, in Fairleigh (ed.), *Far From the Land*, p. 330.
24. Robin Glendinning, *Three Plays: Mumbo Jumbo, Donny Boy, Summerhouse* (Belfast: Lagan Press, 2004), p. 143.
25. Anne Devlin, *Ourselves Alone* (London: Faber and Faber, 1986), pp. 89–90.
26. Marie Jones, *A Night in November* (Dublin: New Island Books, 1995), p. 47.
27. The comic collaboration of Martin Lynch, Conor Grimes and Alan McKee, *The History of the Troubles (accordin' to my Da)* (Belfast: Lagan Press, 2005), which premiered in Belfast in 2002, concludes on an optimistic note similar to that of *A Night in November* with the birth of the protagonist's grandson.
28. Biographers underscore Beckett's admiration of *Juno and the Paycock*, which he saw as a young man at the Abbey Theatre. He regarded O'Casey as a "master of knockabout in this very serious and honorable sense – that he discerns the principle of disintegration in even the most complacent solidities" (Bair, *Samuel Beckett*, p. 183). Anthony Cronin emphasizes Beckett's fondness for O'Casey's one-act farce, *The End of the Beginning*, with its knockabout comedians, Darry Berrill and Barry Derrill (Cronin, *Samuel Beckett*, p. 58).
29. See his 1986 interview with Laurence Finnegan reprinted in Murray, *Brian Friel*, pp. 123–34.
30. Some 450 arrests were authorized on August 9 and 346 prisoners were apprehended. R. F. Foster regards the detainees as "rounded up on the basis of out-of-date police lists," and even though the Ulster Volunteer Force by this time

had grown to "grisly prominence," no Protestant paramilitaries were apprehended. See Foster's *Modern Ireland 1600–1972* (London: Penguin Books, 1988), pp. 590–91. Other commentators place the number of arrests on August 9 at 342.

31. See David R. Lowry, "Internment: Detention Without Trial in Northern Ireland," *Human Rights* 5 (1975–76), pp. 261–331. Lowry furnishes these data on p. 274.
32. Seamus Deane, "Introduction," in *Brian Friel: Selected Plays* (London: Faber and Faber, 1984), p. 19. Later productions like that at the Gate Theatre, London in October, 1998 have proven more successful.
33. Morash, *A History of Irish Theatre*, p. 247.
34. Quoted in Fachtna O'Kelly, "Can the Critics Kill a Play?" *Irish Press*, March 28, 1975, rpt. in *Brian Friel in Conversation*, ed. Paul Delaney (Ann Arbor: University of Michigan Press, 2000), p. 117.
35. See Lionel Pilkington, *Theatre and State in Twentieth-Century Ireland: Cultivating the People* (London and New York: Routledge, 2001), pp. 196–97. Pilkington's discussion of Troubles plays is excellent, see especially, pp. 196–209.
36. Papp and his New York Shakespeare Festival Theatre were no strangers to the issue of experimental theatrical treatments of controversial political realities. In 1971, Papp helped David Rabe develop *The Basic Training of Pavlo Hummel* and *Sticks and Bones*, two biting critiques of American involvement in Vietnam.
37. O'Kelly, "Can the Critics Killa Play?" p. 117.
38. Seamus Heaney, "Digging Deeper," *Times Literary Supplement* (January–March 1975), p. 306, rpt. in Heaney, *Preoccupations: Selected Prose 1968–1978* (London: Faber and Faber, 1980), pp. 214–20.
39. Dominic Cavendish, *The Daily Telegraph*, May 12, 2001, as quoted in Luckhurst, "*The Lieutenant of Inishmore*," p. 120.
40. Brian Friel, "Self Portrait," in Murray (ed.), *Brian Friel*, p. 46.
41. Wilson, *Ripley Bogle*, p. 36.
42. See Pilkington, *Theatre and State*, p. 199.
43. Pilkington, *Theatre and State*, pp. 198–99, who is echoing Seamus Deane, *Celtic Revivals: Essays in Modern Irish Literature, 1880–1980* (London: Faber and Faber, 1985), p. 168.
44. Eavan Boland, "Brian Friel: Derry's Playwright," *Hibernia*, February 16, 1973, rpt. in Delaney (ed.), *Brian Friel in Conversation*, p. 114.
45. Fintan O'Toole, *The Irish Times*, February 10, 1990, rpt. in Furay and O'Hanlon (eds.), *Critical Moments*, p. 220.
46. *Bloody Sunday, 1972: Lord Widgery's Report of Events in Londonderry, Northern Ireland, on 30 January 1972* (London: The Stationery Office, 2001), pp. 97, 98, 99, 100.
47. Brian Lynch, *Pity for the Wicked* (Dublin: The Duras Press, 2005), p. 21.
48. Marvin Carlson, *The Haunted Stage* (Ann Arbor: University of Michigan Press, 2001), p. 7.

49. Robert McLiam Wilson, *Eureka Street* (New York: Ballantine Books, 1996), p. 14.
50. "In Interview with Ray Comiskey," in Murray (ed.), *Brian Friel*, p. 101.
51. Brian Friel, *Selected Plays*, p. 167. All quotations from *The Freedom of the City* come from this edition and will be followed in the text by page numbers. All quotation from *Volunteers* come from the 1979 Faber edition and will be followed by page numbers in the text.
52. Guy Debord, *The Society of the Spectacle* (Detroit: Black and Red, 1983), paragraph 36 (this work is numbered by paragraph).
53. Kiberd, *Irish Classics*, p. 40.
54. Brian Friel, *Performances* (Oldcastle: Gallery Press, 2003), n.p.
55. Marina Carr, *The Mai* in *Plays: 1* (London: Faber and Faber, 1999), pp. 147–48.
56. See Lowry, "Internment," p. 261, who argues that "the essence of internment lies in incarceration without charge or trial." It is thus an "extrajudicial deprivation of liberty by executive action."
57. Ian Shuttleworth, "Review," *Financial Times*, October 27, 1998. For a brief discussion of responses to this production and to *Volunteers*, see Patrick Burke, "'Them Class of People's a Very Poor Judge of Character': Friel and the South," *Irish University Review* 29.1 (Spring/Summer 1999), pp. 42–47.
58. Jeremy Kingston, *Times*, October 26, 1998, p. 21.
59. Paul Taylor, "Theatre: Master of the Empty Space," *The Independent*, November 4, 1998, p. 7.
60. Ciaran Carson, *Belfast Confetti* (Winston-Salem, NC: Wake Forest University Press, 1989), p. 63. Quotations from this collection will be followed in the text by page number. *Sir Thomas More* is considered a collaboration between Anthony Munday, Henry Chettle, Shakespeare, and others; the "maw of Time" is not included in those sections thought to have been written by Shakespeare.
61. Bernard MacLaverty, *Cal* (London: Jonathan Cape, 1983), p. 92.
62. Horatio describes this graveyard uprising in the opening scene of *Hamlet*, proffering it as a portent of the fall of Julius Caesar. It is redacted in Muldoon's *Six Honest Serving Men*; here, the "sheeted dead" are prisoners in Long Kesh.
63. Richard Pine, *Brian Friel and Ireland's Drama* (London and New York: Routledge, 1990), p. 15.
64. Roland Barthes, as quoted in Jeremy Parrott, *Change All the Names*, p. 9.
65. James Joyce, *Dubliners* (1914, rpt. London: Penguin Books, 1976), pp. 175, 178, 219.
66. Seamus Deane, *Celtic Revivals*, p. 166.
67. Burke, "'Them Class of People's,'" p. 47.
68. Brown, "Thing Theory," pp. 4, 5.
69. Benedict Kiely, *Proxopera: A Tale of Modern Ireland* (Boston: David R. Godine, 1980), p. 84.
70. Linda Charnes, *Hamlet's Heirs: Shakespeare and the Politics of a New Millennium* (New York and London: Routledge, 2006), p. 46.
71. Thomas Kilroy, "The Early Plays," in Roche (ed.), *The Cambridge Companion to Brian Friel*, p. 16.

CHAPTER 3

Bernard MacLaverty: The "Troubles," late modernism, and the Beckettian

> We must not allow our justified loathing of the horrors and tragedies of the past to become a barrier to creating a better and more stable future for our children ... In looking to that future, we must never forget those who have suffered during the dark period from which we are, please God, now emerging.[1]
>
> –Ian Paisley, March 26, 2007

> But I was in Derry that day. They had us cowering behind a wall. There was an old man lying in the open. In the rush one of his shoes had come off and was lying on its side. There was a big hole in the heel of his sock. Can you believe that? Will that be recorded in history books?
>
> –Bernard MacLaverty, *Cal* (1983)

At the end of March 2007, television and print media around the world trumpeted the unprecedented news that, after decades of bitter enmity, Ian Paisley and Gerry Adams had met at the same table to discuss the formation of a new government in Northern Ireland. In a more philosophical register, the pair's announcement to set aside their differences constitutes an *evental* proclamation, for much like the example Alain Badiou offers of one person saying to another "I love you," these two longtime rivals pledged their fidelity to a "new singularity." As is the case with Badiou's lovers who declare their commitment to each other, Paisley and Adams proclaimed that an "undecidable disjunctive synthesis" has been "decided," and "the inauguration of its [collective] subject is tied to the consequences of the evental statement."[2] That is to say, Paisley – at one time dubbed "Dr. No" because of his unwavering opposition to the Catholic civil rights movement (indeed, "Paisleyism" has been regarded as a "populist Protestant repudiation of any movement at all")[3] – and Adams pledged their allegiance to a new country, one that in its future synthesis will "disjoin" formations from the past. Not surprisingly, representatives of the British government were ebullient at the prospect: "Today the clouds have lifted," Britain's minister for Northern

Ireland remarked, "and people can see their future." Nearly a decade after the Good Friday peace accord of 1998, all sides struggling through the dark night of the Troubles – Protestant, Catholic, and British – vowed to come to terms with the past and welcome a brighter day for the long-suffering people of Northern Ireland.

As he has with so many similarly opaque matters, Theodor Adorno has considered the connotations of "coming to terms with the past," a deceptively simple phrase that is "highly suspect" in its tacit invitation *not* to undertake a "serious working through of the past" and a consequent "breaking of its spell." Nevertheless, like Ian Paisley and Gerry Adams, Adorno, in this instance alluding to survivors of the Holocaust, envisions a future that can transcend the past; importantly, though, the securing of this future involves complications that the phrase "coming to terms with the past" fails to capture:

> One wants to get free of the past: rightly so, since one cannot live in its shadow, and since there is no end to terror if guilt and violence are only repaid, again and again, with guilt and violence. But wrongly so, since the past one wishes to evade is still so intensely alive.[4]

From this perspective, although the Paisley-Adams rapprochement augurs a renewed Northern Ireland few would have predicted, their endorsements also raise questions which, among others, Northern writers have been asking for decades and, more broadly, Irish writers have contemplated for centuries: How can such an "intensely alive" past *ever* be accommodated? How do we prevent this past, a spectrality Paul Ricoeur so elegantly describes – "Hauntedness is to collective memory what hallucination is to private memory, a pathological modality of the incrustation of the past at the heart of the present" – from haunting the present?[5] Conversely, "coming to terms" with such events as the Great Famine or Bloody Sunday cannot also imply, as Adorno fears it might, an irrevocable "wiping it from memory." Yet, if we refuse to forget the past, or are simply unable to forget it, how do we prevent it from taking residence in – and overwhelming – the present? How do we work through its implications in ways that do not imperil that cloudless future which all parties seated together in Stormont on March 26, 2007 greeted with such optimism?

It is fair to say, I think, that of the many Northern Irish artists who have pondered such matters, few have been so persistent in their representation as Bernard MacLaverty, although it would be inaccurate to characterize him as a Troubles writer (though there are, of course, worse things to be) or to promote the "Troubles" as the sole focus of his work. Still, although

MacLaverty's first volume *Secrets and Other Stories* (1977) and his novel *Lamb* (1980) are ill-described as "Troubles" fiction, this history of sectarian tensions lurks ominously nearby.[6] "A Happy Birthday" from *Secrets*, for example, accrues irony not merely from the disparity between its title and the story's bathetic conclusion, but also from its setting during Ulster '71, a summer-long celebration of the fiftieth anniversary of the Northern state that in MacLaverty's story is complemented by student protestors and a phalanx of British soldiers poised to intervene. The demonstrators foist placards that redact "EXPO '71" as "EXPOSE '71" – one of their aims being to call attention to the country's high unemployment rate – and many reporters feared the event might devolve into "EXPLO '71" given the rise in violence that plagued Northern Ireland at the time.[7] This possibility is comically undercut by events in the story and, because it presages one strategy MacLaverty refines in his later work – a strategy grounded in several connotations of the Beckettian – "A Happy Birthday" deserves brief attention before moving on to more substantial texts.

On the morning of his fiftieth birthday, Sammy lifts two bob from his mother's purse before leaving home, promising to repay her after he walks to town and collects his dole. Stopping first at the library to read the newspapers, a point to which I shall return, he arrives at the bureau shortly before eleven, gathers his money, and proceeds to a pub to celebrate with "the boys." Emerging later into the bright afternoon sunlight, he veers uncertainly through the streets, catches a bus where he favors other passengers with a song, and arrives at a checkpoint outside the expo. Passing through the gates guarded by British military, Sammy mutters to a soldier, "Yis are doing a grand job." Unable to decipher the compliment even after it is repeated, the soldier can only mutter "Wot?" in response, but no matter, as there are noisy student protestors for Sammy to confront with taunts like "Yis have never done a day's work in your lives," and "You'll get no work coming to the country with the likes of you parading about making trouble."[8] (Here, the ironies of an unemployed alcoholic accusing a protestor of indolence and conflating military service with a "job" resound loudly.) There is no "trouble" made on this day, however, no "job" for soldiers to perform other than to stand and watch, for after hurling a few more jeers at the students, Sammy discovers the "blue igloo of the bar tent." There, he buys more stouts, chasing each down with a whiskey, and unwisely decides to board an amusement ride, the Hurricane Waltzer, which exerts a devastating effect on his stomach. As the machine gathers speed and hurls its thrill-seekers through its programmed loops and dips, and as Sammy's hand "tightened convulsively on the bar in front of him"

(*Secrets*, p. 29), his mouth fell open helplessly as he released an "emulsion of minestrone-stout" on observers below, sending them scurrying for cover. Perhaps the only person without "a spot of boke on him," or so the ride's operator speculates to his amazed friend, is Sammy himself, who moments later clambers out of his seat, inquires about other attractions at the exposition, and declares his intention to spend his last pound on yet another drink. After all, he announces in the story's final sentence, "It's my birthday" (p. 30).

"A Happy Birthday" is not only a grotesquely comic sliver of fiction, an oddly entertaining resuscitation of the irrepressible stage Irishman, but also an example of what will become a central, though not the only, mode of representing the historical past in MacLaverty's work. EXPO '71 or ULSTER '71 took place during a summer when the recession and discrimination protested by MacLaverty's students were all too real. While the investments of international or multinational businesses in Northern Ireland increased dramatically in the 1960s, and the government continued to fund a program of new capital development, by 1970 some 86 percent of the workforce was still employed outside these projects.[9] Moreover, evidence exists that "Orangeism was becoming absorbed into the new workplaces," as it had been for decades in more traditional industries.[10] At the same time, as R. F. Foster observes, the growth of Protestant unemployment and the criticism that the Unionist government was "truckling" to Catholics helped sustain the ferocity of Paisley's fundamentalism.[11] Seen in an allegorical vein, MacLaverty's feckless Sammy serves as an almost transparent stand-in both for the country and for Paisleyism, especially when he grabs a long-haired student protestor and assails him with, "Who do you think is paying your grants for you, eh?" And a moment later, continuing in his tirade: "So-called civil rights. Why don't yis go down south where yis belong?" (*Secrets*, p. 29). More to the point, however, the presence of British soldiers and the policies their presence signifies are rendered in "A Happy Birthday" in essentially ironic and comic ways.

For some historians, after Brian Faulkner became Prime Minister earlier in the spring of 1971, he "was given his head" and the opinions of army officers or the Ministry of Defence were "systematically overruled."[12] One result of such a shift, as Paul Bew, Peter Gibbon, and Henry Patterson describe, was the implementation of a "short-run policy of aggression," epitomized by the introduction of internment in early August of 1971. Sammy, no doubt, would have supported what turns out to have been a monumentally poor policy decision that contributed to Faulkner's eventual downfall. My prediction is based upon Sammy's response to the news stories he reads at the library, a response valorizing short-term solutions over longer term consequences: "The IRA was getting the run of the country without one to say boo to them … *Something* would have to be done" (*Secrets*, p. 28). This insight precedes the *something* Sammy actually does; emulating Belacqua in "A Wet Night," who "catted" with "demonstrative abundance" on a guard's shoes, he spews "boke" from atop an amusement park ride. As a political allegory, or travesty, "A Happy Birthday" reinscribes the Troubles and the social problems inherent to them within a grotesque, low-comic frame, as both a fifty-year-old state and fifty-year-old drunk stagger precariously into the future.

Volumes of "boke," however, cannot be adequated to volumes of books or historical reflection; and irony and physical humor don't always achieve the deliberate working through – the critical *remembering* – that Adorno calls for, a process ill-described by a phrase like "coming to terms with the past." And from the publication in 1983 of *Cal*, one of the most celebrated "Troubles" novels of the era, to the opening story of *Matters of Life & Death and Other Stories* (2006), MacLaverty's protagonists have undertaken projects of the will or heart that might qualify as a kind of working through of the Troubles. That is – as is the case with *Cal* and the inaugural stories in *A Time to Dance and Other Stories* (1982), *Walking the Dog and Other Stories* (1994), and *Matters of Life & Death and Other Stories* – MacLaverty eschews the physical comedy of "A Happy Birthday" and instead represents the violent, even tragic ramifications of the historical moment. As it does on the Classical and early modern stages, sectarian violence shatters families in *Cal* and "Father and Son," the opening story of *A Time to Dance* that concludes with a son dying in his father's arms after being shot in his own home. In both texts, the Troubles illuminate the disaffection between fathers and sons, as single fathers play the role typically assigned to mothers (Sean O'Casey's Juno Boyle) of worrying about their sons' potentially dangerous political involvements, and sons grow to question their fathers' courage and virility. At other times in MacLaverty's writing, citizens act with conspicuous bravery to save strangers. In "On the Roundabout" from *Matters of Life & Death*, the narrator recalls driving into Belfast and spotting a hitchhiker being bludgeoned by UDA toughs, one of whom wields a clawhammer to complete the assault. Without any hesitation, the narrator drives his car into the gang to scatter them, puts the "poor bastard onto the floor of the back seat," and rushes him to the hospital as he bleeds "all over the place."[13] Once at the hospital, however, MacLaverty's protagonist grows angry. He imagines testifying in court and facing the same thugs who attempt to intimidate him into silence; in a temporal ellipsis, he then reports that while his younger child could not remember this gruesome incident, his daughter Kate was "really scared and timid for a long time." But then, two months later, a long letter from the victim appears in the *Belfast Telegraph* thanking the good Samaritan who saved him that terrible night. "Wasn't that good of him?" the narrator reflects, "To tell the story" (*Matters of Life & Death* 4).

This act of testimony is crucial if more than a pallid "coming to terms" with the past is to be accomplished. For Adorno, again speaking of the Holocaust, we have an obligation not to cheat victims out of "the one thing that our powerlessness can grant them: remembrance."[14] The letter to the newspaper in "On the Roundabout" inventories this remembrance in a collective, not only a personal, archive or consciousness, and MacLaverty's fiction represents the complexity of both domains. In *Cal*, for example, violence destroys the calm of neighborhoods, as it does for Cal and his father Shamie when an illiterate threat denouncing them as "Fenyan scum" demands that they move or be burned out, both of which eventually occur. In "A Trusted Neighbor" from *Matters of Life & Death*, Catholics Ben and Maureen believe that "Explosions and petrol bombings, snipings, doorstep killings … All the trouble seemed to be happening on television" and not in their neighborhood, which is "utterly quiet" (*Matters of Life & Death*, p. 67). They didn't live in a "dodgy mixed area" like Ben's friend Paul, whose windows had been shattered twice and whose house had provided target practice for an aspiring gunman. But after their neighbor, an RUC policeman, moved away, Ben and Maureen discover that the odd practice he had adopted of parking his car askew in front of their house, not his own, might not have been the result of excessive drinking, as they had supposed. Rather, as they learn later, this "trusted" friend of the family feared that an IRA reprisal was imminent, and he had warned all his other Protestant neighbors to keep their children in the back rooms at night. He hadn't said a word about it to Ben or Maureen.

For Cal, memory calcifies into irremediable guilt. Manipulated into driving a getaway car for his "friend" Crilly – the manipulation originates both in intimidation and unemployment, familiar conventions in Troubles literature – Cal has participated in the murder of Robert Morton, an officer in the Royal Ulster Constabulary. Ironically, he later meets and falls in love with Morton's widow Marcella, gains employment on the Morton farm, and for the first time in his young life at least part of the novel's opening sentence has been rendered moot, and happily so: "He stood at the back gateway of the abattoir, his hands thrust into his pockets, his stomach rigid with the ache of want."[15] His brief intimacy with Marcella helps numb this ache; his stomach, empty for the lack of breakfast as the novel begins, is eventually filled by Marcella's own need, her food and drink, and her affection for him. *His* psychical need, unfortunately, grows as the novel progresses, for immediately after enjoying their first sexual encounter, Cal "wanted to share his guilt with the person he had wronged"; he longed to "commune with her and be forgiven" (*Cal*, p. 157). But this absolution so devoutly wished for can never occur. For Cal can never escape his past which, like the Grünewald picture of the crucified Christ Marcella shows him, has "become a permanent picture in his mind" (p. 169). The morning after his last, blissful assignation with her, he is arrested, "grateful that at last someone was going to beat him to within an inch of his life" (p. 170).

At this point, one wonders if Cal's gratitude isn't excessive: Hasn't he, as much as Marcella's dead husband, been a victim of the Troubles? Has the past become so pathologized by Cal as to constitute a kind of evasion of historical forces altogether on MacLaverty's part, as the narrative displaces their complexity onto one troubled psyche? Or, recalling the repellent images of the abattoir with which the novel begins – the hanging carcasses, the nauseatingly sweet smell, the workers' white coats "japped all over with blood and stiff with cold fat" (*Cal*, p. 8) – has the metaphor of the slaughterhouse finally grown to overwhelm the novel and the historic moment it represents? In this reading Cal is neither victim nor criminal, neither masochist nor guilt-obsessed Catholic but, quite literally, a kid led to slaughter.

Critical disagreement over this issue and MacLaverty's more recent representations of the Troubles occupy the focus of this essay. For as illuminating as it may be to privilege a "Catholic intertextual field" in *Cal*, constituted of references to Matt Talbot, Maria Goretti, and Grünewald's Christ,[16] I want here to develop another explanatory field that rises to prominence in much of MacLaverty's later fiction, an intertextual field of the "Beckettian." Perhaps the result of a confessional urge akin to Cal's, I also want to admit that my fascination with MacLaverty's writing, which began years ago with the publications of *Lamb* and *Cal*, was once connected, however obliquely, to a particular construction of the Beckettian informed by the "trilogy" – and, more directly, to Michael and Cal's commitments to live fully in the shadow of the abattoir with which *Cal* begins and *Lamb* metaphorically ends.

That is to say, the trope of the world as a slaughterhouse pervades Beckett's "trilogy" and informs MacLaverty's early novels. In *Molloy*, for instance, slaughterhouses are "not confined to towns, no, they are everywhere, the country is full of them" (*Three Novels*, p. 29); in *Malone Dies*, the patriarch of the Lambert family is introduced as a highly proficient butcher, a man possessed both of great knives – "so lovingly whetted before the fire the night before" a job (*Three Novels*, p. 200) – *and* an unusual "gift" when it came to "sticking pigs" (p. 201); and Worm in *The Unnamable* doesn't fear offending "hypersensitive" passers-by because such people avoid the neighborhood in which he resides "for fear of being overcome at the sight of the cattle, fat and fresh from their pastures, trooping towards the humane killer" (*Three Novels*, p. 327). Given this context, the facts that the narrative of *Cal* begins at the abattoir and that images of butchery surface throughout the novel recast the Troubles as a meat-processing plant which, in turn, reduces the population to so much doomed livestock. For example:

> People were dying every day, men and women were being crippled and turned into vegetables in the name of Ireland ... It was the people of Ulster who were heroic, caught between the jaws of two opposing ideals trying to grind each other out of existence. (*Cal*, p. 92)

This figure of a voracious consumption relates the Troubles to the "maw of Time" employed in the Shakespearean collaboration, *Sir Thomas More*, and, as have I mentioned previously, Ciaran Carson in *Belfast Confetti*. And the notion that, during the Troubles, Death resides nearby informs much contemporary Irish fiction, which is precisely why the women in Jennifer Johnston's *The Railway Station Man* (1984) and Edna O'Brien's *House of Splendid Isolation* (1994) can never move far enough away to escape it.[17] But the more horrific image of victims of the Troubles as animals awaiting slaughter emerges when Cal warns Crilly about shooting people with the dead bolt, as it will leave no exit wound and lead investigators back to the abattoir. In the final sentence of *Lamb*, Michael mourns the drowned Owen (meaning lamb) as three gulls hover menacingly above the boy's corpse, "their yellow beaks angled with screeching, descending slowly, with meticulous care" (p. 152). This lamb, too, has been led to slaughter and will be ruthlessly devoured.

An emphasis on these images and their connection to the ubiquity of slaughterhouses in Beckett's "trilogy" might motivate an interpretation of MacLaverty's fiction that, in one respect, echoes my reading of Brian Friel's plays: namely, that the protagonists of *Cal* and *Lamb* are dead before the action begins or well before it concludes, just as the bodies of the three demonstrators lie on display before the action of *The Freedom of the City* commences and the internees in *Volunteers* are doomed by the end of the opening act. Such a reading would draw MacLaverty's representation of the human subject living through the Troubles closer to the opening sentence of *Malone Dies* – "I shall soon be quite dead at last in spite of all" (*Three Novels*, p. 179) – or to the inhabitant-victims of the "corpsed" world Jan Kott describes in both *King Lear* and *Endgame*:

> In a tragic and grotesque world, situations are imposed, compulsory and inescapable. Freedom of choice and decision are part of this compulsory situation, in which both the tragic hero and the grotesque actor must always lose their struggle against the absolute … The absolute is transformed into a blind mechanism, a kind of automaton.[18]

Some years ago, I attempted to explain MacLaverty's representation of human agency in contemporary Northern Ireland. Then, thinking largely of *Cal* and the insinuation of Troubles into the idyllic landscape so beautifully created by Pat O'Connor's film adaptation, one of my conclusions was that although the fates of MacLaverty's protagonists "appear to result from choices they themselves make," he "*always* makes such a determination exceedingly difficult, because his characters' 'freedom of choice' is typically exercised within a narrowly circumscribed ambit of possibility."[19] Reading, among others, Michel de Certeau at the time, I was particularly intrigued by a derelict cottage in *Cal*, a site of relief from sectarian violence where Cal and Marcella can share a fleeting measure of bliss: "As Marcella's feeling for Cal evolves into sexual passion, the cottage itself is transformed, albeit … precariously, into an alternative space for both of them."[20] Now, these suppositions about subjectivity and resistance strike me not so much as indefensible, but as imprecise, as MacLaverty's more recent fiction, his enlarged *oeuvre*, demands reassessment.

Oeuvre in this context connotes yet another matter associated at times with Beckett and informs much of what follows. For, as H. Porter Abbott contends, in his later years Beckett began to respond to "the emergent familiarity of his own work" leading to an increasingly self-referential *oeuvre* in which he was "always writing about everything he has written."[21] With some skepticism, we might object that writers often return to their own earlier works, some obsessively so. Yet one might also regard such reprises as implicit refusals to "come to terms" with former intellectual positions one can no longer endorse or even countenance. Beckett's biographers and friends, for example, agree that he "grew impatient" with certain qualities of his earlier work,[22] and much the same might be said of MacLaverty's returns to the Troubles in his writing, particularly in his volume of short stories *Walking the Dog* and his novel *Grace Notes* (1997). Both works reveal his increasingly ironic understanding of subjectivity – one might push the matter a little further and say Northern Irish subjectivity – and, considered together, comprise a primer by which we might reread his earlier work. I do not intend, however, to revisit *Cal* or *Lamb* at any length here; instead, I want to focus on several stories in *Walking the Dog* and on Catherine McKenna, MacLaverty's depressed composer in *Grace Notes*. And on Samuel Beckett, who makes several cameo appearances in *Walking the Dog*, and whose presence in *Grace Notes*, albeit never made explicit, might lead us to a fuller sense of the relationship between ironic Beckettian laughter and subjectivity in MacLaverty's fiction. In the process, the concept "late modernism" will rear its helpful, yet inherently vexed head, as the aesthetic sensibility it connotes has often been employed to illuminate Beckett's writing. It is, in my view, similarly helpful in considering MacLaverty's recent work which, when added to his earlier writing, forms an *oeuvre* illuminating larger tensions within cultural memory of the Troubles. In particular, texts like *Walking the Dog* and *Grace Notes* outline for their readers the memorial parameters of obsession and erasure, tragedy and comedy, the annihilation of the subject and the subject's triumphant resurrection. In another register, MacLaverty's *oeuvre* might be said to stake out the terrain between Theodor Adorno's Beckett and Alain Badiou's, a terrain I will explore after summarizing what might be termed the "Beckettian intertext" in MacLaverty's writing.

THE BECKETTIAN INTERTEXT, THE BECKETTIAN COUNTER-TEXT

An intertext is a text lurking inside another, shaping meanings, whether the author is conscious of this or not. (Robert Scholes, *Semiotics and Interpretation* [1982])

Grace Notes makes intertextual reference to a long (though infrequently considered) tradition of what … I shall refer to as "the musical novel." At the same time, as a story about contemporary Northern Ireland, it engages with a (critically orthodox) tradition of colonial and postcolonial fiction foregrounding questions of representation, resistance, identity, and voice.

(Gerry Smyth, "The Same Sound but with a Different Meaning" [2002])

As it did in my opening chapter, the concept of intertextuality underpins this discussion in ways intimated by the difference between Robert Scholes' summary of intertextuality (derived from Roland Barthes, Julia Kristeva, and others) and Gerry Smyth's positioning of MacLaverty's *Grace Notes* within two specific intertexts. Indeed, even within Scholes' definition it is not immediately clear how to trace the circuitry of power inherent to intertextuality.[23] The notion, on the one hand, that a novel "engages" with prior traditions, as Smyth persuasively demonstrates in positioning MacLaverty's *Grace Notes* within the domains of both postcolonial fiction and the "musical novel" (Toni Morrison's *Jazz*, Jackie Kay's *Trumpet*, and so on) suggests an active consciousness, an authorial agency of some potency. While allowing for such an active and *conscious* "engagement," Robert Scholes, on the other hand, also regards an intertext as a text or texts "lurking" inside another, and like most things that lurk or skulk furtively, these hidden texts are poised to overwhelm and, perhaps, take over. Questions of scale, then, are lodged within conceptions of intertextuality, for an intertext can be something capacious like postcolonial fiction within which a novel like *Grace Notes* might be located, or something much smaller at work inside the novel itself. In this latter connotation, an implicit undercutting of the once all-powerful Author-God,[24] Scholes identifies something *within* a text, not a larger discursive space encompassing it, of which the author may not be fully aware. In the next chapter, I intend to argue that, at times, Beckett inhabits Paul Muldoon's writing in an almost parasitic fashion, for much like the country rat invited to supper (whom Michel Serres describes), or the guest seated next to a munificent host willing to satisfy his visitor's voracious appetite,[25] Beckett resides within Muldoon seeming, paradoxically, both to drain him of creative provender and enhance it. Mightn't much the same be said of the presence of Beckett within MacLaverty's writing: at times he is invoked strategically and thereby controlled; and at other times, he isn't? Authorial prerogative, the power of filiation, is thus implicated – or *seems* to be so – in a tug of war with *affiliation*. Stated in more benign terms, as Edward Said has done, "We must look more closely now at the cooperation between filiation and affiliation that is located at the heart of critical consciousness."[26]

Before turning to the Beckettian qualities of *Grace Notes*, many of which are subtle and affiliative – and unconscious – it might prove useful to recount some of the more overt or filial engagements in MacLaverty's fiction. Not surprisingly, as is also true of Friel's representation of the Troubles, many of these are not only Beckettian, but both Joycean and Shakespearean as well. The Joycean intertext in MacLaverty's *oeuvre*, for example, is announced by "Hugo" from *Secrets*, as the title character fancies himself an expert in all things Joycean and, at times, suffers from physical maladies that afflicted Joyce as well (like bad teeth that he grinds in his sleep). In MacLaverty's story Hugo, a pharmacy student, arrives at a small boarding house and acts as an informal tutor to the young boy who narrates the story, discussing *A Portrait of the Artist as a Young Man* with the boy when he is required to study it at school. Some months later, the boy volunteered to "do a seminar" on "A Painful Case" from *Dubliners* and again sought advice from Hugo, who by this time had moved to another house owned by his mother and completed a novel. Several years passed and the boy graduated, eventually becoming a scholar and lecturer himself, and near the end of the story he learns that Hugo has hanged himself in a barn and, further, that no one had ever read his novel. At his wake, Hugo's friends reveal a sense of guilt that they had not been assiduous enough in their efforts to stay in contact with him. They drink their beers as custom requires and laugh, "but not loudly enough to betray ourselves to each other" (*Secrets*, p. 92). Scholarship, loneliness, desperation, suicide – "Hugo" presents another painful case through its title character, a composite picture of Joyce's scholarly Mr. Duffy and suicidal Mrs. Sinico.

From *Secrets* to several stories in *Matters of Life & Death* some thirty years later, MacLaverty's short fiction invites comparison with *Dubliners*. Maiden sisters like the Misses Morkan in "The Dead," for example, resurface in their staid ways in "End of Season" from *The Great Profundo and Other Stories* (1987) and in the hauntingly beautiful "The Wedding Ring" from *Matters of Life & Death*, a story that seems to combine "The Dead" and "The Boarding House." In "The Wedding Ring," two maiden sisters Annie and Susan Walsh operate a small boarding house at which their niece, Ellen Tierney, worked. Like Mrs. Mooney's house in *Dubliners*, the Walshs' accommodates three to four men; like Mrs. Mooney's daughter Polly, Ellen or "Ellie" is nineteen and has fallen for one of the residents. Sadly, however, as MacLaverty's story begins, the Walsh sisters are preparing their niece's body for burial. While washing her niece, Annie, in her sixties and "the strongest person" Susan knew, spies a gold wedding ring dangling on a necklace around Ellie's neck and reads its tiny inscription: "For Ellie – my love and life" (*Matters of Life & Death*, p. 107). Amazed, she asks Susan about the ring, and then the truth slowly emerges: Frank Burns, the young man who had once lived at the house and who had appeared to Annie too familiar with Ellie, had given it to her. In a narrative flashback, Annie, echoing Lily in "The Dead," disparages men as "only out for what they can get" (p. 114) and, like Mrs. Mooney in "The Boarding House," she "dealt with moral problems as a cleaver deals with meat."[27] Once she foresaw the inevitable end of Ellie's familiarity with the young man, she summoned both her niece and Frank to announce her decision to send him packing: "Mr. Burns! I want to speak to you right this minute! Mr. Burns! And you too, Miss Ellie!" (p. 115). As "The Wedding Ring" concludes, each of the Walsh sisters feels the pressure of one further obligation: Susan, who supported her niece's relationship with Frank, braves the wind to walk to his new residence, relate the terrible news, and return his ring; moments earlier, Annie, in the roles of gynecologist and moral butcher, performed an anatomical inspection of her niece to ascertain that she had died a virgin.

Matters of Life & Death also features the often desperate, unfulfilled lives of older single women like Aunt Nora in "Matters of Life and Death 2," who in numerous respects resembles Maria in Joyce's "Clay"; of exiled writers like Andrew Younger in "Winter Storm"; and of lonely, abused young women like the talented young painter in "Up the Coast." And for some thirty years MacLaverty's fiction has featured more than its share of older priests on the verge of a spiritual breakdown, students trapped in oppressive institutions, and strong tensions between fathers and sons. In other words, MacLaverty's *oeuvre* shares both overt and more subtle intertextual relationships with Joyce's fiction, especially *Dubliners* and, in the case of his novel *The Anatomy School* (2001), with *A Portrait of the Artist as a Young Man.*[28] In *The Anatomy School* and, to a lesser extent, "Death of a Parish Priest" from *The Great Profundo*, these intertextual relationships expand to include Yeats, Eliot, and a host of other writers, not the least of whom is Shakespeare. "Death of a Parish Priest," like Joyce's "The Sisters," revisits a priest's final days. Like Joyce's Father Flynn, who breaks his chalice and is heard laughing in the confessional, Father Tom feels uncomfortable administering the sacrament, in part because of his dentures, which he has begun to remove before saying Mass. One cold day at Church, he feels sleepy and like poor Tom in *King Lear*, whom he quotes, shivers from the cold, not only from the freezing temperature outside, but because he doesn't "even have my Cordelia to weep over."[29] As he lies down to die on the Church floor, he is joined by a vision of Joy, a woman he loved long ago to "be close. Be warm. Be ... Joy" (*The Great Profundo*, p. 116). These examples constitute only a small portion of what is often a sumptuous intertextual relationship between MacLaverty, Joyce, and Shakespeare.

Shakespeare also appears prominently in *The Anatomy School*, first as a required writer for young Martin Brennan to study – at the beginning of the novel he has failed his final exams and is required to retake them – but later as an intertext for the Troubles. Lines from *Macbeth*, a text Martin reads intently, appear throughout the novel, with the play's author ultimately earning the grudging respect of the frustrated student: "Shakespeare was crap sometimes, but he was a hell of lot better than fucking Milton" (*Anatomy School*, p. 159). Shakespeare becomes even more popular with Martin after he and his friends steal a copy of the exam and discover that the first question concerns imagery in *Macbeth*. Not surprisingly, Martin's adolescent conversations – and thoughts – also feature a more predictable array of topics: "dirty pictures," wanking, and all manner of topics associated with the "pure codology" of attending an all-boys Catholic school. As he prepares his essay on *Macbeth*, he recalls some explicit pictures he had seen and becomes excited; his tumescence distracts him from his study, leading him to a doodle that looks either like a camel or weasel and to his confused memory of an exchange between Polonius and Hamlet. The Shakespearean intertext in *The Anatomy School*, then, adds comic dimension to the novel and later, after Martin graduates, it also provides an analogue to the Troubles. As his mother's tea companions gather in the parlor for refreshment and discuss a spate of recent killings, Martin wonders aloud how many more people will have to die before the conflict is over. Father Farquharson, immensely proud of his ability to recite from memory, recalls Malcolm's lines from Act Four of *Macbeth* as his contribution to the discussion: "I think our country sinks beneath the yoke:/ It weeps, it bleeds, and each new day a gash/ Is added to her wounds" (*Anatomy School*, p. 348). The priest's recitation allows Mrs. Brennan to change the subject momentarily by lauding the education he received compared to the "faffing about they go on with nowadays." Then, the conversation returns to Northern Ireland's wounds and a macabre intertext provided by nursery rhymes: "They say we're the world's experts here at putting the body back together again," Nurse Gilliland remarks. Mrs. Lawless promptly quips, "Humpty Dumpty land" (p. 348).

All of which leads us to Beckett. Allusions to Beckett in MacLaverty's fiction, in "The Drapery Man" from *The Great Profundo and Other Stories*, for example, and throughout *Walking the Dog* are largely comic, although I want to argue that nonetheless the effects of these citations are various and significant. "The Drapery Man" concerns Jordan Fitzgerald, an aging Irish painter living in Spain, his loyal younger friend, once his lover, and their now Platonic domestic arrangement. The arrangement might be regarded as a double-entendre invoking both Beckett's friendship with James Joyce, and Hamm and Clov's master-servant relationship in *Endgame*, which is echoed by MacLaverty in a number of ways: like Hamm, Jordan lives close to water and likes to be seated in the exact center of his studio; like Hamm, he is blind (and suffers from a bad heart; while Hamm hears a dripping in his head). As was the case with Joyce and Beckett, over twenty years separate MacLaverty's acclaimed artist from his younger "drapery man," the portrait painter's helpmate in the eighteenth century who did "all the time consuming bits – the lace and satin stuff" (*The Great Profundo*, p. 34). The narrator of the story, Fitzgerald's "drapery man" contributes not only by adding intricate details to paintings, but also by mixing pigments and preparing canvases, shopping, preparing lunch, and keeping "the place in order" (p. 35). Similarly, when Joyce was nearing completion of *Finnegans Wake*, Beckett was there, taking dictation and reading Book IV with a critical eye, particularly the last ten pages.[30] As both Deirdre Bair and Lois Gordon in their respective biographies of Beckett explain, the younger man "enjoyed doing 'little jobs for Jimmy' (adapting Nora's phrase) – reading to him ... doing anything at all."[31] And Joyce, like MacLaverty's painter, seemed almost always in need of help, even when the pair first met a decade earlier. Then, in the fall of 1928, both Joyce and his wife Nora were suffering from ill health: his eyesight had suffered a recent "collapse," and in November she was recovering from a hysterectomy. Joyce and Beckett's friendship endured until the time of the former's death in 1941. MacLaverty's drapery man makes a similar commitment to his mentor: "There is now a kind of unspoken acceptance that I am here until he dies" (*The Great Profundo*, p. 39), as Clov may well remain with Hamm in *Endgame*, although he has threatened to leave and is "dressed for the road" in the play's closing tableau.

More overt allusions to Beckett surface in "The Drapery Man." The aging painter, for example, loves to hear Flann O'Brien and Beckett read aloud, which his young associate does upon request. Fitzgerald "even laughs" at hearing Beckett's writing, entertained by it, while the narrator finds the prose "almost impossible ... and quite, quite meaningless" (*The Great Profundo*, p. 31). Impossibility later devolves into antipathy, as the narrator appraises his own fecklessness as an artist's apprentice: "I have become involved in painting but am useless at it – as useless as Beckett's secretary is at writing, if he has one – as useless as Beckett is, come to think of it" (*The Great Profundo*, p. 34). But Beckett and the Beckettian are hardly "useless" to MacLaverty (both in this story and in several from *Walking the Dog*); rather, he is often the source of a quite mischievous humor – and, ultimately, much more. One example of Beckettian humor, as I have discussed previously, emerges in Beckett's critical conflation of language with the body, words with bodily processes and fluids. Words "ooze" in Beckett or drip in their inadequate evacuation of thought, which is why – as in Joyce – neologisms have to be produced and etymologies stretched to encompass a "slumbrous collapsion" of sense. But bodily processes can also serve as the foundation of wit or the catalyst for seduction, as occurs in "The Drapery Man" when Fitzgerald first met his assistant. At the younger man's hotel and out of earshot of the boy's mother in the early moments of their now long relationship, Fitzgerald leaned over to the young man and asked if he would like to accompany him home: "And I'll show you my retchings" (*The Great Profundo*, p. 32).

In "At the Beach," the most substantial story in *Walking the Dog*, Beckett and the Beckettian perform similar comic functions as a middle-aged couple, Jimmy and Maureen, are on holiday in Spain. Married for twenty-five years and enjoying a rare time of intimacy without their children in tow, they initiate the vacation with episodes of love-making conducted at an unprecedented and exhausting pace. The afterglow of their first congress prompts Maureen's recollection of the flight they had just taken, one in which Jimmy had placed a sticker the airline had provided on his forehead: "Wake for Meals." Maureen laughed at the sight, which prompted Jimmy's witticism:

> "It's what life's all about," he said. He put on his salesman's voice. "Have you seen our other best-selling sticker, sir? *We give birth astride the grave.*"[32]

Paraphrasing Pozzo's line in *Waiting for Godot*, Jimmy also echoes the pun about Irish wakes in *Finnegans Wake*: it's not a funeral, but a "funferal." As the story progresses, Jimmy's sense of humor becomes one of the few redeeming qualities of his otherwise coarse and piggish character: he ogles younger women at every turn, he drinks too much, and interrogates his exasperated wife about her prior sexual experiences. His humor takes on a kind of Beckettian quality when recounting his own sexual past, as his linguistic invention originates in the body:

> In those days I was a vicious bastard – every time I went out with a woman I went straight for the conjugular. (*Walking the Dog*, p. 80)

In a story that draws clear lines between a woman's loneliness and a rare moment of contemplative solitude when Maureen visits an ancient Spanish cloister[33] – and includes the almost comic extermination of ants that invade the couple's holiday flat – Beckett provides moments of laughter in a marriage that has deteriorated into hollow rituals and perfunctory lovemaking.

If Beckettian language provides comic spaciousness to the otherwise stifling dimensions of this marriage, and if one origin of both linguistic invention and comic potential in Beckett is the body, then MacLaverty utilizes the Beckettian more generally in *Walking the Dog* as a comic counter-text to the otherwise bleak stories in the volume: three of the volume's nine stories emphasize sectarian tensions, even as they have infiltrated so presumably unifying a ritual as the wake of a dead neighbor; "At the Beach" and "The Grandmaster" offer extended pictures of dysfunctional relationships between husband and wife, and a mother and her teenaged daughter; and the concluding story occurs largely in a hospital where a man visits his dying and alcoholic friend. In a counterpuntal structure, MacLaverty adds ten prose fragments to the volume, most of which are shorter than two pages, featuring an anonymous wit named "your man." In one of these, "*O'Donnell* v. *Your Man*," Mrs. O'Donnell is outraged that "your man" has written a story broadcast on BBC radio that contained the word "fuck." Apparently, after sitting down to enjoy a ginger beer and a program on her radio, one of Mrs. O'Donnell's more sensitive friends suffered shock and severe gastroenteritis as a result of the "fearful word" she had heard. Once exposed to it, she could not "unthink" it, which led to the further distress caused by a consideration of such lexical variants as "fuckable, fuck-wit, fucker, fucking, fuck-bollock," and so on (*Walking the Dog*, p. 149). Her gastric calamity was also occasioned by her discovery of the remains of a small snail that had found its way into her bottle of ginger beer. She hadn't initially seen the snail given the opaque glass of the bottle and, of course, had no reason to expect that one would have taken residence there; but when she poured the liquid into a tumbler, there it was. But neither had she any reason to fear that the objectionable "fuck" would be employed in a story broadcast by the BBC. Like the manufacturer of the ginger beer, an author should devise systems which prevent the contamination of their products; thus, your man should take immediate steps to make certain that such monstrous expressions never again despoil his writing. Or so Mrs. O'Donnell insists.

In the fragment "St Mungo's Mansion" that precedes Mrs. O'Donnell's complaint, "your man" receives a letter detailing the financial plight of the mansion, which is scheduled to be bulldozed unless money can be raised. A committee has formed to save the mansion with proceeds from a celebrity cookbook; the implication being "that your man is a celebrity or, if not that, then at least someone prominent in public life ..." (*Walking the Dog*, p. 167). "Your man," solicited for a recipe and an anecdote to accompany it, complies by submitting instructions for boiling eggs: fill a saucepan with water, insert the eggs, boil for a few minutes, peel, apply seasoning, and so on. His "anecdote," in actuality the title of a story he has contemplated writing, is equally sparse: "A THREE-LEGGED HORSE CALLED CLIPPITY." And his sentiment?

> *Hope the above is helpful to saving Saint Mungo's Mansion. Yours sincerely, Samuel Beckett.*
>
> *Your man is not really Samuel Beckett but it amuses him to think that he is*. (*Walking the Dog*, p. 168)

Perhaps it amuses MacLaverty as well to include such references, but what I want to argue is that Beckettian irony in *Grace Notes* works similarly to that in *Walking the Dog*: it responds to the "Troubles" – and to memories of the Troubles – and the psychical damage it has caused, offering an alternative absent from *Cal*. This assertion is also meant to suggest another everyday casualty of the Troubles: language. As Helen Cuffe, reading of sectarian violence in the *Irish Times* admonishes her son in Johnston's *The Railway Station Man*, "Appalled, stunned, sickened, outraged – None of those words mean anything any more. Overworked. Demeaned."[34] Language has suffered a "collapsion" of meaning.

One last example of intertextuality in MacLaverty's writing recalls Porter Abbott's notion that later works in Beckett's oeuvre accrue "intertextual complexity" because of their relationship to earlier ones. As I have suggested, a similar dynamic obtains between early and more recent MacLaverty. The tragic narratives of *Cal* and *Lamb* give way in his more recent writing to a wicked sense of humor and a comic capacity not only to parry the darker implications of the "Troubles," but also to undercut the pathos of his earlier work. One instance of this in *Walking the Dog* is "A Visit to Norway," the entirety of which reads as follows:

> *In Heathrow the girl at Security, feeding bag after bag through the X-ray machine, says to your man,*
>
> *"May I ask what's in your cardboard tube, sir?"*
> *"A reproduction of a woodcut – "The Kiss" – by Edvard Munch."*
> *"I much prefer his mezzotints," says she, patting his chest, his thighs and buttocks.*
>
> (p. 123)

The tenor of this exchange contrasts sharply with the vulgar, routinized quality of the security girl's inspection. Like music in MacLaverty's writing – from Elvis Presley to Haydn and Schubert in "My Dear Palestrina"; from *A Time to Dance*; from blues in *Cal* to Catherine McKenna's *Vernicle* in *Grace Notes* – this interchange about modern art effects a rupture in the fabric of an everyday reality in which such security procedures have become commonplace. Here, in other words, a temporary space emerges to inhabit, and contemporary life – or super-modernity, as some describe it – supplies us with an abundance of such transitory locales.[35] Yet, because of the Troubles and the security measures they necessitate, the originating *place* of violence is not entirely supplanted by the *non-place* of art: "the first is never completely erased, the second never totally completed."[36] It is, rather, that an alternative, hybrid reality emerges, a grace note in space, not in the time elapsed between musical tones. Equally important, this scene also references the dust jacket of the first American edition of *Cal* (published by George Braziller in 1983), on which *The Kiss* is displayed in the center of a green background. As such, the allusion in *Walking the Dog* constitutes an invitation to recontextualize or "ironize" Munch's stark image in relation to *Cal*: to transport *The Kiss* from Cal's tragic world to the comic groping of security guards.

GRACE NOTES AND THE BECKETTIAN

The discovery of the square root of two is a capital event. The accumulation of plague-stricken corpses in the streets of Athens is not ... For a mathematical discovery is testimony to the affirmative capacity of thought and, as such, of interest to the philosophical mind ... The disasters which punctuate human history cannot serve as a point of departure for philosophy. Suffering cannot be its theme. For the Good is always its proper aim and end.

(Andrew Gibson, *Beckett and Badiou: The Pathos of Intermittency* [2006])

Auschwitz confirmed the philosopheme of pure identity as death. The most far out dictum from Beckett's *End Game* [sic], that there really is not so much to be feared any more, reacts to a practice whose first sample was given in the concentration camps ... Absolute negativity is in plain sight and has ceased to surprise anyone. (Theodor W. Adorno, *Negative Dialectics* [1966])

Thus Andrew Gibson begins his recent study of Beckett and Badiou.[37] In its own way, "The discovery of the square root of two is a capital event" resonates as strikingly as such opening sentences as "The sun shone, having no alternative, on the nothing new" from *Murphy*; or "I shall soon be quite dead at last in spite of all" from *Malone Dies*. Later, in his articulation of Badiou's reading of Beckett with those of contemporary "Beckettians," Gibson advances two theses that inform my consideration of *Grace Notes*. The first, as much of the above intimates, concerns Badiou's disputation with what Gibson terms a "whole critical tradition" that construed Beckett as an absurdist or "existentialist, a nihilist or tragic pessimist": "In its very admiration of Beckett, the tradition has declared its distance from him."[38] The second thesis emerges from what Gibson regards as Badiou's emphasis of the "logic of reversal" in Beckett's work. Such a logic, and here Gibson refers to the work of Leslie Hill,[39] privileges a kind of indifference manifested in Beckett's writing in which opposites are not joined in "dialectical union" but are hollowed out or emptied momentarily of meaning. Yet, following Hill's lead, Gibson adds that this indifference does not necessarily constitute an assault on meaning per se, but is rather an activation of "sense making"; that is, in Badiou's terms, such a process captures the "emergence of truths in their newness."[40] Catherine McKenna's musical composition *Vernicle* effects such an emergence by taking binaries, well-defined markers of sectarian tension and the Troubles, and transforming them into a separate truth without collapsing into dialectics. The result, in short, is an act of affirmation.

The larger contexts of Catherine's symphonic work are just as important. To recall earlier discussions of Tyrus Miller's late modernism and of Declan Kiberd's Irish "classics," one such context is essentially comic and sumptuous in its expansion of subjective space even though this space is marred by sectarian tension and, in Catherine's case, a history of depression. Another, represented by the passage above (taken from Adorno's negative dialectics), moves in an opposite direction. For the first, irony, riant sensibility – Samuel Beckett. A subjectivity formed in a crucible of violence, Chance, and at times a numbing sense of loss; an ill-perceiving, ill-speaking subject wandering in the dim void of *Worstward Ho*. Or Derry. Or Belfast. Or at various points in *Grace Notes* on what Catherine glumly regards as the "geography of the places of death" in Ireland: "Cornmarket, Claudy, Teebane Crossroads, Six Mile Water, the Bogside, Greysteel, the Shankill Road, Long Kesh, Dublin, Darkley, Enniskillen, Loughinisland, Armagh, Monaghan town."[41] A walker out for a stroll, like Catherine's great-grandfather, rendered deaf one day by a bullet cascading off a wall near his right ear, the otic brother of Beckett's Pozzo, fully sentient one day, diminished the next. Nonetheless, these victims of a capricious Chance persist, at times with an admirably wry sense of humor: "On. Say on. Be said on. Somehow on," *Worstward Ho* begins, and MacLaverty's protagonist finds a way to persist, to go on. For the second context, represented by allusions to the mass murder of Kiev Jews at Babi Yar, there is Adorno's thesis that "all post-Auschwitz culture … is garbage"; and with this degradation of culture follows the shattering of the individual, whose downfall "brings the entire construction of bourgeois existence down with it."[42] And then there's the aesthetic that such a reality seems to cultivate, part of which Catherine, a student of musical composition in *Grace Notes*, so much admires in her Russian mentor, Anatoli Ivanovich Melnichuck: "Melnichuck's music had a spareness and an austerity which she loved … [T]here was also something very spiritual about everything he wrote" (p. 62). Spareness, austerity, spirituality, Babi Yar – all of these topics are pertinent to another understanding of Beckett and my reading of *Grace Notes*. And, when combined with the riant spaciousness cultivated in the novel's later pages, we might then reconstrue MacLaverty's novel within the intertext of the Beckettian.

But that is not all or, rather, that is not my only interpretive claim about both *Grace Notes* and MacLaverty's *oeuvre* of Troubles literature. To invoke one last critical paradigm, this one from Fredric Jameson's adumbration of a "political unconscious," my interpretive "transcoding" of MacLaverty, as Jameson might phrase it, is intended to demonstrate that a Beckettian "master narrative" exists to be recuperated by readers *only* because it preexists in the unconscious of MacLaverty's oeuvre. "The idea is," Jameson explains, that if "interpretation" in terms of "master narratives" remains "a constant temptation, this is because such master narratives have inscribed themselves in the texts as well as in our thinking about them . . ."[43] They exist, in other words, in the political unconscious. MacLaverty *and* his protagonist in *Grace Notes*, both of whom endeavor to represent the Troubles, come to the enterprise with what might be termed shared or collective assumptions, some conscious and some not; my "mediation," Jameson might say, represents the devising of a code to understand their respective representations without any obligation to read them as identical or even as similar. Instead, Jameson underscores, "one cannot enumerate the differences between things except against the background of some more general identity. Mediation undertakes to establish this initial identity . . ."[44] Quite clearly, I have succumbed to the temptations Jameson identifies.

My emphasis of a comic, largely affirmative Beckettian quality to *Grace Notes*, much like a conventional reading of *Finnegans Wake*, begins with the relationship of the book's opening and closing sentences. To underscore their irony, I have conflated them below:

She went down the front steps and walked along the street on the main road. (*Grace Notes*, p. 3)

....

Bravo.
She rose. (*Grace Notes*, p. 277)

She, Catherine McKenna, descends the steps at the beginning of the novel on her way to the airport and her flight to County Derry to attend her father's funeral.[45] In a former church converted into a concert hall, its stained glass windows and religious iconography rendered indistinguishable by darkness, she rises at the novel's end to acknowledge the audience's enthusiastic reception of her symphony, complete with Lambeg drums played by four Orangemen from Portadown. Her father, as we learn earlier, despised Orangemen and their "nonsense" drumming, as Catherine recalls while traveling home to attend his funeral. Indeed, he denigrated Lambeg drumming and the Orange parades in which they are featured as displays of "Sheer bloody bigotry" (*Grace Notes*, p. 8) – "Nothing to do with the betterment of mankind or the raising of the human spirit" (p. 9). Her use of the drummers, then, is hardly coincidental. Neither is it accidental that

Catherine's father Brendan died of a "massive heart attack" not long after he lost his temper over the IRA's policy of "Blowing the hearts out of all the wee towns" – "It's our own kind doing this to us," he was heard to lament (p. 15). Caught between Orange bigotry and Catholic violence, between the arrogant domination of one tribe and the self-destructive agenda of his own, Brendan McKenna and his neighbors live in what Catherine regards as a "place of devastation" (*Grace Notes*, p. 10). Yet, in the refulgent moment captured by the novel's last sentence, Catherine's triumph – her rise above the violence, an unforgiving mother, an abusive lover, and her at times severe depression – is complete.

Well, not *perfectly* complete, as her best friend Liz jokes before she stands and someone yells "Bravo": "Linguists would insist on that man shouting *brava*" (*Grace Notes*, p. 277). But we, most likely, will excuse this lexical error, because in a novel like *Grace Notes*, one laden with moments of excruciating darkness, this moment of triumph – and comic irony – is to be savored. Catherine descends, she rises, even if her audience includes at least one person oblivious to the gendered implications of language. The novel prepares its readers for such myopia about gender, for when Catherine had earlier won the Moncrieff-Hewitt Award for her Piano Trio and asked a judge how a young composer might get work performed, he responded, "He should try the Society for the Promotion of New Music." Noting her bemusement, the judge asks, "What was wrong with that?" "'He's a she. He's me,'" Catherine answered (*Grace Notes*, pp. 63–64). And we can finally laugh, too, after languishing with Catherine in the voids of her loneliness and depression.

In so doing, the presence of Beckett in *Grace Notes* becomes discernible in ways more significant than quibbles over the gender of nouns (or interjections!) – these lexical preoccupations echo Hamm, Clov, a pesky flea, and the debate over "laying" or "lying doggo" in *Endgame*. One, for example, involves the subtle analogy in the novel between art after Auschwitz, to borrow Adorno's formulation in reading Beckett, and art during the Troubles. "After Auschwitz," Adorno maintains, "our feelings resist any claim of the positivity of existence as sanctimonious, as wronging the victims; they balk at squeezing any kind of sense, however bleached out, of the victims' fate."[46] Moreover, as he asserts in discussing *Endgame*, the very conception of the individual that underpins existentialism is obliterated by the Holocaust:

The catastrophes that inspire *Endgame* have shattered the individual whose substantiality and absoluteness [were] the common thread in Kierkegaard, Jaspers, and Sartre's version of existentialism. Sartre even affirmed the freedom of victims of the concentration camps to inwardly accept or reject the tortures inflicted upon them. *Endgame* destroys such illusions. The individual himself is revealed to be a historical category, both the outcome of the capitalist process of alienation and a defiant protest against it, something transient himself.[47]

The integrity of the individual, in this case Catherine McKenna, and catastrophes of the kind Adorno describes – if it is not too impertinent to suggest the analogy – must finally inform any reading of MacLaverty's novel and of *Vernicle*, Catherine's composition.

MacLaverty forges a historical parallel between the Holocaust and the Troubles – and implies the presence of World War II in the unconscious of the present – through Catherine's Russian mentor Melnichuck. And MacLaverty's suggestion of the presence of the past war in the contemporary Troubles is hardly unique. Most obviously, Johnston's "railway station man" carries with him the trauma of a particular moment – the bombing of an asylum for the insane – and other images from the war like the firebombing of Dresden surface in representations of the Troubles. In *Proxopera* (1980), for example, Benedict Kiely's feisty narrator connects contemporary violence to its antecedents both in a more remote Irish history and more recent atrocities of the war:

The Apprentice Boys of Protestant Derry, the maiden City, close the gates before Tyrconnel and the troops of James Stuart. The long memory lives on. With riots and ructions and bombs and bloody Sundays as much a maiden now as Dresden on the morning after.[48]

For that generation of critics who regarded Beckett as an existentialist or nihilist, the generation whom Gibson juxtaposes to more recent readers, the notion that World War II underlies MacLaverty's "Beckettian" political unconscious will hardly seem surprising. In this juxtaposition, memories of the Troubles, like those of the Holocaust, cannot ever be entirely vanquished. Relentless, they follow one back to Scotland or to the beaches of Spain when on a much-needed holiday. They echo in a news report on the radio while preparing a meal or changing a diaper; they linger disturbingly in the dialect of a passer-by.

But how does one accomplish more than a perfunctory "coming to terms" with the atrocity? How, as James Young asks in a probing essay on "Memory and Monument" written in response to the controversy occasioned by Ronald Reagan's planned visit in 1985 to the Bitburg cemetery in Germany, where the graves of both Waffen-SS and Wehrmacht soldiers lie, does one avoid the most egregious historical misstep: "The real danger lies in an *uncritical* approach to monuments, so that a constructed and reified memory is accepted as normative history – and then acted upon as if it were pure, unmediated meaning."[49] *Vernicle* is Catherine's musical monument of the Troubles, a metaphor established much earlier in *Grace Notes*. While walking through a cemetery and reading headstones, she spied the grave of Paddy Fleck, once a young IRA officer, and wondered about "writing something" for him: "What would it be like …? Was the nationalism Janáček represented different from the kind espoused by the Provisional IRA?" (*Grace Notes*, p. 85).

The connection between the Holocaust and *Vernicle* is equally clear. As I have mentioned, Catherine is initially attracted to the "spareness" and "austerity" of Melnichuck's music, its fragmentary quality, when she hears it for the first time on the radio; after that, she "bought anything of his" she could find (*Grace Notes*, p. 62). Later, she travels to Kiev to study with him, and her memories of the experience surface throughout the book: the coldness of rooms, the food lovingly prepared by Melnichuck's wife Olga, his black mongrel dog trying to mount her while she sat at the piano.[50] When the talk in Kiev turned to music, to Shostakovich in particular, Olga explained to Catherine the origin of his "Babi Yar Symphony":

> Babi Yar is a place of death. In 1941 the Nazis made all the Jews of Kiev come together and they took them to Babi Yar – thirty-five thousand – men, women, children – and they shot them and put them down in a ravine to be buried. Evtushenko wrote a poem and Shostakovich put it in a symphony. (*Grace Notes*, p. 126)

The atrocity at the gorge known as Babi Yar, as Young and others have noted, occurred between September 29 and October 1, 1941. There, Nazis forced Jews into the ravine, where they were slaughtered. Many victims were forced to work, to dig or bury others, before being murdered themselves, and some historians estimate the number killed to be 33,000 men, women, and children. Young, like Melnichuck in *Grace Notes*, insists that those killed should not be regarded as "prisoners of the war" or "citizens of Kiev": most were killed "for having been Jews," a fact elided in a recent monument built to commemorate the event.[51] On her visit to Kiev, Catherine's mentor becomes agitated after hearing his wife say "Babi Yar" and makes precisely the same point: "He says they were all Jews who were killed … The beginning of anti-Semitism is talk, is hatred – the end is Babi Yar" (*Grace Notes*, p. 127).

Recalling Babi Yar on her trip back home to Scotland from Northern Ireland and her father's funeral, Catherine, as I have mentioned, thought of the geography of the "places of death in her own country": Cornmarket, Claudy, and so on (*Grace Notes*, p. 127). Yet, ending this grim cartography, she reached a conclusion exactly the opposite of Adorno's in "Trying to Understand *Endgame*":

> Yet somehow she knew that her act of creation, whether it was making another person [i.e., her daughter, Anna] or a symphonic work, defined her as human, defined her as an individual. And defined all individuals as important.
> (*Grace Notes*, pp. 127–28)

For her, music turns Adorno's abject *subject* – who consists "of nothing but the wretched realities of their world, which has shriveled to bare necessity" ("Trying to Understand *Endgame*," p. 251) – into an *individual*, one who has the determinative power, however delimited, to transform "wretched realities" into non-spaces. One might also ascribe this to the power of irony and, at times, the value of ironic laughter.

Babi Yar, or MacLaverty's Northern Irish version of it, underlies both Catherine's liberal-humanist view of the world and *Vernicle*. For in *Vernicle* Catherine successfully transforms, thereby controls, the one thing she, like so many Northern Catholics, hates the most; the one thing that for many Catholics symbolizes sectarian violence: Orangemen drumming. Moreover, the brutal pounding of the Lambeg drums, in its unrelenting repetitiveness, also parallels the other constant in her life: depression. Like so many depressives, Catherine at one point in the novel seems doomed to repeat over and over the fragmented thoughts that torture her:

> Not only the days repeating but the everyday thoughts repeating. Endless loops. Like a refrain. Over and over again. Her mind flagellating itself . . . The same thing. A chorus. A refrain. Recapitulation. The same thing . . . Glum. Dumb. Down . . . Endless repetition. (*Grace Notes*, p. 199)

The Beckettian quality of this passage and condition scarcely requires unpacking. And then there are the tears, a seemingly endless cascade of them. The narrator of *Ill Seen Ill Said*, despite his plaintive question "What is the word? What the wrong word?" describes it well enough:

> Riveted to some detail of the desert the eye fills with tears. Imagination at wit's end spreads its sad wings . . . Tears . . . Tears. (*Nohow On*, p. 56)

So does Julia Kristeva in *Black Sun Depression and Melancholia*: "Faced with the impossibility of concatenating," depressives "utter sentences that are interrupted, exhausted, come to a standstill." The work of mourning "for an archaic and indispensable object" – "mourning for the Thing" – shatters the capacity for concatenation.[52]

But, oddly enough – or, in this instance, propitiously enough – Kristeva relies upon a familiar metaphor to characterize the depressive's non-concatenated speech: its "frugal musicality," its "monotonous melody," its "repetitive rhythm."[53] The Kristevan "black sun" of depression, that "eerie galaxy" with its "invisible, lethargic rays," produces a kind of sparse enunciation that competes with silence and repetition for the prize of tropic dominance in depressive discourse. Much the same might be said of Catherine's musical composition. In certain passages of *Vernicle*, during the first movement, for example, the four Orangemen pound the Lambeg drums ferociously and, in so doing, also pound the spirit of the audience into an utter darkness. Here, the darkness of depression rivals the devastation of Babi Yar:

Their aggression, their swagger put her in mind of Fascism. She was not trying to copy the vulgarity of Shostakovich Seven – the march of the Nazis on Leningrad – but that was the effect. A brutalising of the body, the spirit, humanity. Thundering and thundering and thundering and thundering. When the drums stopped … the only thing that remained was a feeling of depression and darkness. Utter despair.
(*Grace Notes*, pp. 272–73)

Mercifully, the second movement revives the audience, providing relief from the ruthless thunder. Babi Yar meets the Bogside, the Holocaust meets the Troubles, Beckettian repetition meets the discourse of the depressed. And, rather amazingly, the spirit still soars, as the word "vernicle" connotes. When asked about it earlier by Miss Bingham, her former piano teacher, Catherine, who had studied its etymology, defines "vernicle" as the badge a medieval pilgrim wore upon returning from a shrine or other sacred site.[54] It also connotes the imprint of Christ's face on Veronica's handkerchief after she offered to wipe his brow during the Agony, a definition that holds little appeal for Catherine. For her, "vernicle" means both surviving depression and returning from the Troubles: "Proof that you'd been there. In a land of devastation. At the bottom of the world. And come through it – just" (*Grace Notes*, p. 245). *Vernicle* takes you to such a place marked by thunderous and terrifying drumming, and then deposits you on the other side after enduring the visit. It marks a process of moving on – "Nohow on," perhaps – just barely.

And then some idiot who can't read the program, or who lacks sufficient linguistic competence to salute a female composer properly, shouts "*Bravo*." And we laugh with Liz and Catherine, purposefully ignoring any signification that would detract from the moment. These moments occur several times near the end of the novel, forming fecund grace notes, fleeting non-places to inhabit. "Grace notes – ," MacLaverty's narrator speculates, "notes which were neither one thing nor the other. A note between notes. Notes that occurred outside time." A few sentences later, he adds: "This is decoration becoming substance" (*Grace Notes*, p. 133). Or, perhaps, it is a kind emptiness or nothing becoming substance, the emptiness of Beckett's *Texts for Nothing*. As Anthony Cronin reminds us, for its French title *Textes pour rien*, Beckett, as MacLaverty does later for *Grace Notes*, borrows from a musical term, "mesure pour rien," signifying a bar's rest.[55] Such a caesura is not therefore a guarantee of Progress, a thoroughly discredited Victorian notion parodied by the title *Worstward Ho*. Rather, such ironic laughter accompanies Catherine's momentary victory, the rise after the descent, cautioning us about inferring more from the occasion than we should.[56]

For Tyrus Miller, and for Abbott too, albeit for slightly different reasons, such laughter is significant – and related complexly to modernism. Late modernist works like *Endgame* and *Murphy*, as Miller argues and I have underscored earlier, signal Beckett's "reflection on a peculiar type of laughter as the zero degree of subjectivity." This laughter, variously described as "mirthless" and "self-reflexive," comprises "an index of a minimal residue of humanness."[57] More important, in the late modernism Miller theorizes, such laughter creates what Kristeva before him in *Desire in Language* (1980) termed a "riant spaciousness" or "mode of spatiality," and is evident in texts the telos of which is to "shore up … a subjectivity at risk of dissolution."[58] One further refinement. In Miller's understanding of late modernism and mine of MacLaverty, "one type of grotesque representation occupies a special thematic place" in the late modernist text: an "obsessive depiction of pure corporeal automatism" (tics, fits, "involuntary eruptions") and "bizarre ailments."[59] There is no reading Beckett without noticing this preoccupation – from the stinking feet and breath of *Waiting for Godot*, to Mr Madden's "treponema pallidum" in *Mercier and Camier* – and its comic potential. Laughter is connected to both the frailty of the body and some of its less appealing products in *Grace Notes*, which at times seems a veritable catalogue of such matters: dirty nappies, toothless smiles, defective ears, and so on.

Before the performance of *Vernicle*, for example, Catherine experiences both nausea and the peristalses of diarrhoea, which send her to the lavatory where she is confined for a disconcerting length of time. Worried about her, Liz enters the ladies' room to see if Catherine is well enough to return to the hall. She is, and as she prepares to wash her hands, the soap dispenser "deposited a white splurge in her palm. She showed it to Liz and laughed":

> "Don't say a word."
> "You're awful," said Liz. (*Grace Notes*, p. 263)

This randy humor continues when, once back in their seats, Liz mentions a line about sex in the program. She then notices that Catherine is shaking badly from nerves, yet laughing too:

"You're shaking," said Liz, her eyes widening.
"You think I haven't noticed? It's all the orgasms I've missed."

(*Grace Notes*, p. 266)

These examples of humor and the bodily in Beckett and MacLaverty are in no way offered as confirmation of the latter's status as a late modernist, as a writer to be tethered somewhere between modernism and postmodernism. Nor is this the occasion to parse arguments about late modernism as either an explanatory or a periodizing concept. My point is, rather, that Samuel Beckett – albeit never mentioned in *Grace Notes* – plays a crucial role in the novel and in MacLaverty's later fiction more generally, and that this role is most evident in the laughter and subjectivity of his characters.

This thesis is intended to corroborate the affirmationist Beckett both Gibson and Badiou before him have wrested from a tradition that too often tends to regard the Beckettian in nihilistic ways. Such a thesis, however, *must* be able to accommodate the critical remembering upon which Adorno, Young, and others insist. Importantly, as Young stipulates and I noted earlier in regard to the letter to the editor in "On the Roundabout," critical remembering demands *communal* remembering: "The usual aim in any nation's monuments," Young observes, "is not solely to displace memory or to remake it in one's own image: it is also to invite the collaboration of the community in acts of remembrance."[60] Catherine's audience, sitting in an auditorium surrounded by traces of religious sensibility, collaborates in reexperiencing a march, and a terror, Catherine knows all too well. We might, at the risk of overreaching, include the audience's experience of viewing Beckett's later play *Catastrophe* (1982), written as part of "A Night for Václav Havel," organized as an expression of support for the playwright held prisoner for over four years in Czechoslovakia. For James Knowlson the protagonist of *Catastrophe*, displayed on a plinth while the Director autocratically prepares him for theatrical presentation, stands in for the imprisoned artist or for political prisoners more generally. This figure of abjection, dressed in old gray pajamas, shivering from the cold (while the all-powerful Director is attired in fur) and helpless to resist any manipulation by the Director or his assistant, also recalls Holocaust victims. In particular, for Knowlson the Director's demand that the victim's skin be whitened to resemble the flesh of a corpse "recalls images of the concentration camp or Holocaust victim."[61] It is almost impossible, then, to watch *Catastrophe* without experiencing feelings of complicity in exacerbating the Protagonist's helplessness and of admiration for his final raising of his head, an action explicitly rejected as a possibility by the Director.

Perhaps, in the final analysis, this is *too* much transcoding, and perhaps the genealogy of "riant spaciousness" – the subjective expansiveness created by lexical and bodily humor in *Grace Notes* – might serve to recommend more interpretive caution. Appropriating the term from psychoanalytic understandings of early infancy, Kristeva views adult and "belated dispositions of laughter" as commemorating an "archaic laughter-space" where child and mother once met. Such a space recalls the "riant wellsprings of the imaginary," a place prior to subject-object dichotomy and the mirror stage of ego development; here, "space and time coexist" in the infant's laughter and its resonance of prenatal oneness.[62] For Miller to transport this concept of laughter from Kristevan psychoanalysis and semiotics to the cultural register of fiction between the World Wars is no small feat. And for me to attenuate this theory even further is, admittedly, risky interpretive business. Yet, MacLaverty's later work – *Walking the Dog* and *Grace Notes* in particular – seems to invite a rereading of both subjectivity and laughter in his entire body of fiction. Beckett and the critical exegesis of late modernism provide the means for doing this. More important, such an inquiry might reposition the Beckettian as especially significant to representations of the Troubles, and not merely from that perspective that might construe the term as reducible to nihilism or existentialism. It might be possible to argue, finally, that if they are to be appropriately critical and communal, historical representation and cultural memory alike require both the horrific and the comic, the catastrophic and the affirmative. In this way, if in no other, Bernard MacLaverty's oeuvre, like Brian Friel's, accrues even greater importance as a new Northern Ireland struggles to be born. So does Beckett's.

NOTES

1. Eamon Quinn and Alan Cowelle, "Ulster Factions Agree to a Plan for Joint Rule," *The New York Times*, March 27, 2007, Foreign Desk, p. 1. On May 8, 2007, it was announced that Ian Paisley would serve as first minister of a new Northern Assembly and that Martin McGuinness would assume the post of deputy first minister.
2. Alain Badiou, *Theoretical Writings*, ed. and trans. Ray Brassier and Alberto Toscano (New York and London: Continuum, 2000), p. 148.
3. R. F. Foster, *Modern Ireland*, p. 586. For a summary of Unionist ideology, 1969–1975, see John Daniel Cash, *Identity, Ideology and Conflict: The Structuration of Politics in Northern Ireland* (Cambridge: Cambridge University Press, 1996), pp. 151–202. In this chapter, Cash reprints sections of Paisley's January, 1975 broadside, "A Call to the Protestants of Ulster," which refers to "traditional enemies" as "devotees of that godless monster which has drenched Ireland with blood for many generations – the godless monster of a United Ireland" (p. 192).

4. Theodor W. Adorno, "What Does Coming to Terms with the Past Mean?" in *Bitburg in Moral and Political Perspective*, ed. Geoffrey Hartman (Bloomington: Indiana University Press, 1986), p. 115. In a prefatory note, Hartman observes that *Aufarbeitung* in Adorno's title is "inadequately translated" as "Coming to terms with." "The German phrase," by contrast, "has psychoanalytic as well as political connotations," suggesting a "reprocessing" of old materials into "something new" (p. 114).
5. Ricoeur, *Memory, History, Forgetting*, p. 54.
6. Although *Lamb* (New York: George Braziller, 1980) does not represent the Troubles, it inflects the conversation between clerics at a home for wayward boys "miles from nowhere on a promontory jutting its forehead into the Atlantic wind" (p. 18). In the opening chapter, Brother Benedict tells his colleague that nationalist trouble is "something we should keep at the front of our minds," that "we'll be a united country again," and that "In the course of history we cannot mourn individuals" (p. 9). All quotations from this volume will be followed by page numbers in the text.
7. This fear of increased violence is justified by data reprinted by Cash in *Identity, Ideology and Conflict* that indicate the dramatic increase in shootings and bombings in Northern Ireland between 1970 and 1972. Shootings: 213 (1970), 1,756 (1971), 10,628 (1972); Explosions: 153 (1970), 1,022 (1971), 1,382 (1972). The deaths of army and police officers also soared from 2 in 1970 to 146 in 1972 (p. 152).
8. Bernard MacLaverty, "A Happy Birthday," in *Secrets and Other Stories* (1977, rpt. New York: Viking, 1984), pp. 29–30. All further quotations from this volume will be followed by page numbers in the text.
9. It is demonstrable that things changed, economically speaking, in both Northern Ireland and the Republic, as the millennium was coming to a close. In *Postcolonial Dublin: Imperial Legacies and the Built Environment* (Minneapolis: University of Minnesota Press, 2006), Andrew Kincaid asserts, "For promoters of the new economy, Ireland is a shining example of a deregulated, free-market economy finally crawling out from under the rock of statist interventions and social welfare" (p. 175).
10. Paul Bew, Peter Gibbon, and Henry Patterson, *Northern Ireland 1921–1996: Political Forces and Social Classes*, rev. edn. (London: Serif, 1996), pp. 173–74.
11. Foster, *Modern Ireland*, p. 587.
12. Bew, Gibbon, and Patterson, *Northern Ireland*, p. 167.
13. Bernard MacLaverty, "On the Roundabout," in *Matters of Life & Death and Other Stories* (London: Jonathan Cape, 2006), p. 2. All further quotations from this volume will be followed by page numbers in the text.
14. Adorno, "What Does Coming to Terms with the Past Mean?" p. 117.
15. MacLaverty, *Cal*, p. 7. All further quotations from the novel come from this edition and will be followed by page numbers in the text.
16. Kennedy-Andrews, *Fiction and the Northern Irish Troubles*, p. 91.
17. In O'Brien's *House of Splendid Isolation* (New York: Farrar, Straus & Giroux, 1994), Josie O'Meara writes in her diary that after a wanted terrorist enters her remote world, "Death is everywhere now. It rattles like jugs" (p. 93).

18. Kott, *Shakespeare Our Contemporary*, p. 132.
19. Stephen Watt, "The Politics of Bernard MacLaverty's *Cal*," *Éire-Ireland* 28 (Fall 1993), p. 138.
20. Watt, "The Politics of Bernard MacLaverty's *Cal*," p. 146.
21. H. Porter Abbott, "Late Modernism: Samuel Beckett and the Art of the Oeuvre," in Brater and Cohn (eds.), *Around the Absurd*, p. 77.
22. Atik, *How It Was*, p. 52.
23. Robert Scholes, *Structuralism in Literature* (New Haven: Yale University Press, 1982), p. 145; Gerry Smyth, "'The Same Sound but with a Different Meaning': Music, Repetition, and Identity in Bernard MacLaverty's *Grace Notes*," *Éire-Ireland* 37.3–4 (Fall/Winter 2002), 6.
24. The term "Author-God" comes from Roland Barthes' "The Death of the Author," in which a text is construed not as "a line of words releasing a single 'theological' meaning (the 'message' of the Author-God) but a multi-dimensional space in which a variety of writings, none of them original, blend and clash." See Barthes' *Image – Music – Text*, trans. Stephen Heath (New York: Hill & Wang, 1977), p. 146.
25. Michel Serres, *The Parasite*, pp. 7–8.
26. Edward W. Said, *The World, The Text, and the Critic* (Cambridge, MA: Harvard University Press, 1983), p. 16.
27. James Joyce, *Dubliners*, p. 63.
28. Bernard MacLaverty, *The Anatomy School* (New York: W.W. Norton, 2002). All quotations from this volume will be followed by page numbers in the text.
29. Bernard MacLaverty, *The Great Profundo and Other Stories* (New York: Grove Press, 1987). All quotations from this volume will be followed by page numbers in the text.
30. For a brief account of Beckett's relationship with Joyce at this stage of the composition of *Finnegans Wake*, see Deirdre Bair, *Samuel Beckett*, pp. 296–97. See also Lois Gordon, *The World of Samuel Beckett, 1906–1946* (New Haven: Yale University Press, 1996), especially pp. 58–60.
31. Gordon, *The World of Samuel Beckett*, p. 58.
32. Bernard MacLaverty, *Walking the Dog and Other Stories* (London: Penguin, 1994), p. 65. All further quotations from this volume will be followed by page numbers in the text.
33. These fleeting moments of peace have become almost conventional in contemporary Irish fiction. After meeting Roger and selling one of her paintings, Helen Cuffe in Jennifer Johnston's *The Railway Station Man* (London: Penguin Books, 1984) awakens with a sense that she suddenly knew what "ecstasy" meant, though later the feeling was gone (p. 79). Similarly, Katherine Proctor in Colm Toíbín's *The South* (London: Penguin Books, 1990), believes she has found "the sacred core of the world" in a deserted square in Barcelona, feeling as if she "was right to be here" (p. 12).
34. Johnston, *The Railway Station Man*, pp. 15–16.
35. This formulation is indebted to Marc Augé's distinction between "places" and "non-places" in *Non-Places: Introduction to an Anthropology of Super-Modernity*,

trans. John Howe (London: Verso, 1995), pp. 77–78. Contemporary or "super-"modernity, because of its accelerated speed, produces "transit points," temporary abodes such as this security checkpoint in *Walking the Dog*.

36. Augé, *Non-Places*, p. 79.
37. Andrew Gibson, *Beckett and Badiou: The Pathos of Intermittency* (Oxford: Oxford University Press, 2006), p. 1.
38. Gibson, *Beckett and Badiou*, p. 117.
39. See Leslie Hill, *Beckett's Fiction: In Different Words* (Cambridge: Cambridge University Press, 1990), pp. 6ff.
40. Gibson, *Beckett and Badiou*, p. 120.
41. Bernard MacLaverty, *Grace Notes* (New York: Norton, 1997), p. 127. All further quotations from this novel will be followed by page numbers in the text.
42. Adorno, *Negative Dialectics*, pp. 367; 370–371.
43. Fredric Jameson, *The Political Unconscious: Narrative as a Socially Symbolic Act* (Ithaca: Cornell University Press, 1981), p. 34.
44. See Jameson, *The Political Unconscious*, pp. 40–42.
45. It is worth noting, too, that Part One of the novel involving Catherine's return home occurs after Part Two, which culminates with the wildly successful inaugural performance of *Vernicle*, her symphonic work. (The end of Part One, literally the last word in Catherine's story, is similarly affirmative, "Credo," although it is clear her belief concerns her daughter and herself, not Catholicism or Christianity more generally [p. 138].)
46. Adorno, *Negative Dialectics*, p. 361.
47. Adorno, "Trying to Understand *Endgame*," p. 47.
48. Benedict Kiely, *Proxopera*, p. 35. Like the concentration camp, Dresden emerges as a motif in contemporary literature from Kurt Vonnegut's *Slaughterhouse Five* to several plays of Peter Shaffer. A line in Shaffer's *Lettice and Lovage* (London: Andre Deutsch, 1988) explains this motif, as Lotte describes her father's exodus from Germany: "He used to say [Dresden] was the most beautiful city on earth. Then in the war the Allies burnt it to the ground defending civilisation." (p. 49).
49. James E. Young, "Memory and Monument," in Hartman (ed.), *Bitburg in Moral and Political Perspective*, p. 104.
50. MacLaverty's inclusion of the mongrel with the "pink crayon" between its legs recalls both Joyce and Beckett's use of canine congress in, respectively, *Ulysses* and *Mercier and Camier*. Its juxtaposition to the meditation on death at Babi Yar constitutes a melding of the sacred and the profane, nature and culture, in the tradition of Joyce and Beckett. It may possess Adornian overtones as well, as the reified culture represented by classical music – the man-made world of music and Naziism alike – cannot control what little is left of nature.
51. Young, "Memory and Monument," p. 105.
52. Julia Kristeva, *Black Sun: Depression and Melancholia*, trans. Leon S. Roudiez (New York: Columbia University Press, 1989), pp. 33, 40.
53. Kristeva, *Black Sun*, p. 33.

54. It is not accidental that, while thumbing through an encyclopedia, Catherine recalls finding an entry for "Somme." One implication is that this site of a prominent World War I battle – something underscored by Frank McGuinness's *Observe the Sons of Ulster Marching Towards the Somme* (1986) – also resides in the political unconscious of the Troubles.
55. Cronin, *Samuel Beckett*, p. 402.
56. Abbott, "Late Modernism," pp. 77–83. Here he traces Beckett's repetitive parody of the "Victorian trope of onwardness" from *Watt* through *Worstward Ho*, the latter title of which evokes Charles Kingsley's Victorian saga.
57. Miller, *Late Modernism*, pp. 58, 60.
58. Miller, *Late Modernism*, p. 63.
59. Miller, *Late Modernism*, p. 64.
60. Young, "Memory and Monument," p. 112.
61. See Knowlson, *Damned to Fame*, pp. 596–98.
62. Julia Kristeva, *Desire in Language: A Semiotic Approach to Literature and Art*, trans. Leon S. Roudiez (New York: Columbia University Press, 1980), pp. 283, 286.

CHAPTER 4

"Getting round" Beckett: Derek Mahon and Paul Muldoon

The lamentable change is from the best,
The worst returns to laughter. Welcome then,
Thou unsubstantial air that I embrace:
The wretch that thou hast blown unto the worst
Owes nothing to thy blasts. (4.1.5–9)

–Edgar in *King Lear*

Harry, I find I have to read innumerable sentences you now write twice over to see what they could possibly mean ... In this crowded and hurried reading age you will remain unread and neglected as long as you continue to indulge in this style and these subjects.

–William James to his brother Henry in Colm Toíbín, *The Master* (2004)

I can call up old ghosts, and they will come, But my art limps, – I cannot send them home.

– Paul Muldoon, "Old Ghosts," in *The End of the Poem* (2006)

There are moments in *How It Was: A Memoir of Samuel Beckett* in which Anne Atik portrays the aging writer in the early 1980s as exhibiting the weighty effects not of drink or ill health, but of one or another text, one or another preoccupation. *King Lear* provides one compelling instance of the latter, and here more than the ghost of Shakespeare inhabiting contemporary Irish writing is at issue – a ghost whose largely genial visitations we have witnessed in Brian Friel's plays and Bernard MacLaverty's fiction. In April of 1981, for example, Atik recalls sharing her response to Paul Scofield's performance in Peter Brook's film version of *King Lear* with Beckett, to which he remarked that he had borrowed "vile jelly" from the scene in the play in which Gloucester's eyes are plucked out for his new text, *Ill Seen Ill Said.* He added, in reference to Shakespeare's play, not just this gruesome moment, "Impossible to stage."

Atik recounts another visit over two years later in August of 1983 in which Beckett again visited her home, now more "wobbly on his legs." He'd been reading *King Lear* again, he confided, and once more underscored both the play's complexities – "Unstageable; wild; scenes and words impossible to stage" – and the salience of Edgar's lines: "The worst is not / So long as we can say, 'This is the worst'" (4.1.27–28). "They're very important," Beckett emphasized.[1] In *Damned to Fame*, James Knowlson corroborates this account of the persistence of Shakespeare's play in Beckett's thoughts, describing how he copied quotations in his notebooks from Edgar's Act Four speech and referred to the new text he was writing as "Better worse," which later became *Worstward Ho*.[2] One provenance of these two late – and very great – works, *Ill Seen Ill Said* and *Worstward Ho*, then, is *King Lear*, which near the end of his life Beckett found irresistible. More significant than the play's impossible demands in staging, Edgar's resolve in the face of the worst was something Beckett could not "get round."

"Getting round" things – prior texts, striking images and events – was the subject of Paul Muldoon's F. W. Bateson Memorial Lecture at Oxford in 1998. Given the complexity of the topic, Muldoon, as his wont, invented a term – the "ungetroundable" – to limn a potent relationship that finally exceeds more commonplace notions of influence, even if at times he doesn't seem fully aware of the implications of this assertion. In his introductory remarks to "Getting Round: Notes Toward an *Ars Poetica*," Muldoon cautioned his listeners that influence constituted the subject of the lecture "in so far as it's possible for a writer to detect, and then dissect, the influences on his or her work without seeming impossibly self-regarding."[3] This intimation of a writer's solipsism, however, scarcely amounts to the only point of vulnerability in the argument that ensues; more problematic is the fact that "influence" fails to convey the full implication of Muldoon's neologism. Indeed, throughout the lecture he outlines the more powerful imposition of one text or author upon another – of one "ungetroundable" image or another – upon authorial consciousness, something akin to the effect of *King Lear* on the aging Beckett. For while early in his career in *Dream of Fair to Middling Women* Beckett almost casually alludes to the play when depicting Belacqua as being in love from the "girdle up" with Smeraldina-Rima,[4] the elder Beckett, as his confession to Atik some fifty years later reveals, was held in thrall by something far more potent. By the time Beckett had reached his seventies, *King Lear* was something he simply could not get round.

But there is more to the idea than this. Identifying Roland Barthes and Jacques Derrida in his lecture, Muldoon initiates a brief, somewhat vexed foray into literary theory, particularly the idea of intentionality. He begins by urging "theorists" to abandon the claim that there is no "father-author": "Let them try to get round the ungetroundable fact that the poet is the first person to read or, more importantly, to be read by the poem." (So, there *is* a "father-author" or Author-God, but he's a comparatively puny deity, a first reader or even an object to be read, with limited ability to discern what influences him.) Muldoon distinguishes this first reader from a New Critic, from a W. K. Wimsatt or a Monroe Beardsley, both of whom he also names, and, while seemingly attributing the intentional fallacy to New Criticism, counters that "what must be determined is the intent of the poem." The poem itself, Muldoon insists, "creates the role" of the first reader, "and all subsequent readings must take that into account" ("Getting Round," p. 120). This questionable treatment of New Criticism aside, an obvious question arises: if a writer's intentionality proves too marshy a ground upon which to pitch an interpretive tent – a position outlined in the opening paragraph of Wimsatt's formalist manifesto *The Verbal Icon*[5] – how does one recover a *poem's* "intention"? How does a poem "read" authors, and how do we as readers more removed from this originary site "take that into account"? More broadly, and recalling my summary of literary criticism under siege some chapters back, aren't these the kinds of questions that lead to the disparagement of literary criticism and the allegation of its massive irrelevance to our times?

Perhaps. Yet anyone who has ever seriously considered the project of critical exegesis must sympathize with Muldoon's thesis, however imperfect. All writers *are* readers first. They are also citizens, hence even the most hermetic writer is a "witness to history" ("Getting Round," p. 123), as Muldoon's *Quoof* (1983), for example, demonstrates by bearing uncommon witness to the Troubles in Northern Ireland that engulfed Ulster at the time.[6] Such witnessing, he adds in quoting Seamus Heaney, may also lead to a poem's "applicability beyond its own vivid occasion" as a means "of comprehending ironies and reversals more extensive than the personal crisis which it records" (p. 123). More germane for my purposes, however, is the possibility that history, much like a literary antecedent or striking image, can prove as "ungetroundable" as *King Lear* was for Beckett in the 1980s.

For many Northern writers, to take one instance from an almost endless litany of atrocities, the spectacle of young women being tarred and feathered has seemed impossible to avoid. This grotesque piece of street theatre, staged in novels as different as Eoin McNamee's *Resurrection Man* and Robert McLiam Wilson's *Ripley Bogle*, prises its way into the poetry of Heaney and Muldoon as well. Heaney's *North* (1975), for example, employs the image of a woman's shaven head (the ritual of tarring and feathering usually begins with a hair shearing) and other signs of brutality in several poems, most strikingly in "Punishment" when the poem's speaker indicts his own passivity while viewing such barbarism:

> I who have stood dumb
> when your betraying sisters,
> cauled in tar,
> wept by the railings ...[7]

The "little adulteress" with a "tar-black face" had been compelled to play the role, as Heaney's speaker ruefully acknowledges, of a "poor scapegoat" while he, the "artful voyeur," cast the "stones of silence." Muldoon's "The More a Man Has the More a Man Wants" from *Quoof* expands the registry of female victims in a transhistorical direction:

> Someone on their way to early Mass
> will find her hog-tied
> to the chapel gates – ...
> Her lovely head has been chopped
> and changed.
> For Beatrice, whose fathers
> knew Louis Quinze,
> to have come to this, her perruque
> of tar and feathers.[8]

The images of a once beautiful face twisted in pain, of the "lovely" head made hideous while the woman is helplessly chained to a railing or chapel gate, of a mob in a lather eager to confirm its ochlocracy in the name of religion or sectarian loyalty – for Heaney and Muldoon, these scenes proved ungetroundable.[9] And for Muldoon in particular, just as significant is the way in which the young victim of the Troubles stands for – or literally becomes – another woman from a totally different history. The two are communicated by the one, or actually *become* the one; a point about the "ungetroundable" to which I shall return in my conclusion.

The same spectacle arrests the attention of Robert McLiam Wilson's eponymous narrator in *Ripley Bogle* and, albeit to a lesser extent, that of a minor character in Eoin McNamee's *Resurrection Man*.[10] An incident of tarring and feathering receives extended treatment in the former, providing an occasion for Ripley's otherwise unremarkable father to intervene and, later, motivating two cowardly Provos to shoot the elder Bogle in retaliation for his action. Relating the scene in minute detail, the world-weary Ripley concedes that the tarring and feathering of Mary Sharkey, punishment for becoming pregnant with the "lamb" of a corporal from the Royal Engineers, was "a little strong even for [his] steel-plated stomach." Incensed by her putative betrayal of community, a band of "patriotic youngbloods" tied her to a lamppost, stripped her, shaved her head, and later boiled the tar in front of her. Bogle's neighbors stood by passively, much like Heaney's speaker in "Punishment," none possessive "of the bollocks" to act. After the pitch was "chucked" over the terrified girl, Mary's "deathly wails" caused Ripley to become "hysterical" and incited his father Bobby to spring into action. For Ripley, the incident was unforgettable.[11]

In *Resurrection Man,* a novel replete with kneecappings, bombings, torture, and murder, this particular ritual rises above the homogenizing effects of the media and crosses sectarian lines as a practice staged in Catholic and Protestant neighborhoods alike. While recovering in hospital, Artie Wilson, one of Victor Kelly's many victims in the novel, stops in front of a television set to watch the ghastly results of a now familiar spectacle:

> On television he watched pictures of girls who had been tarred and feathered for going out with British soldiers. They were left dangling from lampposts like crude fetishes ... He remembered having seen it happen in the Village to a girl who was engaged to a Catholic. The women had shaved the girl's head indoors while the men stood outside with the tar and feathers, smoking and chatting. It seemed a form of initiation prescribed by custom.[12]

More than just an instance of mob action, tarring and feathering constitutes a *point de capiton* or "quilting point" where strands of sectarian hatred, gender inequality, and voyeurism meet. As such, in the "necropolis" that Belfast and all of Ulster had become – a place where "the bombed dead were spilled on the street like cheap fruit," sentiments from Wilson's later novel *Eureka Street*[13] – this perverse "form of initiation," as it did for Heaney and Muldoon, proves "ungetroundable" for Ripley and his father.

The "ungetroundable," given these examples, might seem more akin to trauma than influence, but this is not necessarily so. To take a more literary example, the "better worse" oxymoron Beckett found so compelling in Edgar's lines in *King Lear* seems ungetroundable in Derek Mahon's account of meeting the "great man" in Paris in the autumn of 1981. Beckett, who appeared to Mahon more "erect and athletic" at seventy-five than Atik portrays him, was dressed nattily in a tweed coat and jeans for the meeting, and at one point in their conversation began "waxing lyrical about the benefits of age: loss of memory, of vocabulary." "It's great," Beckett is reported to have said, referring to his own "happy decrepitude."[14] Loss of sensory capability and the inevitable slide into decrepitude, like the encroaching stones of *Ill Seen Ill Said,* need not obliterate hope – or humor either, as Mahon observes:

> And indeed [Beckett's] apprehension of the "real world" is painfully, if often hilariously acute. "Born of a wet dream and dead before morning," he might have led a happy death, but the blackest humor, if not exactly cheerfulness, keeps breaking in, for an important thing to remember about Beckett is that he is one of the funniest modern writers ...[15]

Affirmation, as Badiou terms it, or, in the perhaps even more utopian thought of Ernst Bloch, a sense of hope in the "Not-Yet-Become," might be seen to drive Beckett's witticism to Mahon that he has been "looking forward" to aging "all my life." Life's inevitable encroachments, its process of pejoration as Pascale Casanova describes in her study of *Worstward Ho*, need not be a source of fear but rather, like thought itself for Bloch, signal a "venturing beyond."[16]

In even suggesting a utopian dimension to Beckett's work, I have clearly gone too far, or, at the very least, confirmed my membership in the league of misguided readers Terry Eagleton has recently identified: "[T]here are always critics on hand to scour [Beckett's] remorselessly negative texts for the occasional glimmer of humanistic hope, in a world where rank pessimism is felt to be somehow ideologically subversive."[17] Nevertheless, as I hope to show, an affirmative, riantic, and expansive Beckett informs Mahon and Muldoon's writing, surfacing at moments that are otherwise suffused with loss, loneliness, and death. As such, he makes for a welcome contemporary in a post-9/11 and post-Katrina world, though for both poets the Beckettian is far more nuanced than this. For Muldoon, as I have mentioned previously, Beckett and the Beckettian define Irish liminality in *To Ireland, I*. More significant, however, are the multiple appearances of Beckett and his characters in Muldoon's elegy "Incantata" from *The Annals of Chile* (1994), a complicated poem that, like "Yarrow" from the same volume and "Sillyhow Stride" from *Horse Latitudes* (2006), records a speaker's effort to move beyond grief over the loss of loved ones. "Black humor," as Mahon describes the source of laughter in Beckett, breaks into these elegies to do battle with cancer, with sorrow, and finally with death itself. More so than most commentators, Mahon understands this process well, and throughout some of his most influential poems, Beckett also surfaces, but in ways quite different from, albeit compatible with, his appearances in Muldoon. These latter visitations might more accurately be described as incidents or events, sudden and incisive, determinative and necessary to illuminate what might otherwise be regarded as a bleak impasse. As such, they are consonant with Badiou's discovery in Beckett of a "lesson in affirmation, a lesson made more powerful and poignant as one has multiplied all the reasons that show how impossible any affirmation is."[18]

Before exploring these dimensions of the Beckettian, I want to return briefly to Muldoon's "ungetroundable" and his sense of the "strategies a poet might develop" to negotiate some of the nearly "insurmountable difficulties facing him or her." These challenges include "poetic influence," "poetic technique," and a more prickly matter he terms "poetic utility or efficacy," which presses the obligation of Irish writers to regard the reading and writing of poetry as "social duties, essential acts of citizenship" ("Getting Round," p. 108). Inherent to the ungetroundable and to poetic utility, therefore, is the overriding presence of the historical moment. But not just any moment. Just as the notion of influence posits the imprint of prior writing and writers on later ones, poetic utility implies the determinative role of a specific history on the present scene of writing, a doubling or overlap of discrete entities from different domains not unlike the yoking together of a metaphysical conceit, which Muldoon references in his lecture. Not surprisingly, a plethora of analogies to world history and literature surface in, even organize, poetic responses to the Troubles. In Michael Longley's "Letters" to three Irish poets, for example, the trope emerges of a poet who plays "[his] guitar while Derry burns";[19] in several images in Ciaran Carson's *Belfast Confetti*, broken or malfunctioning clocks register both the precise moment of a specific explosion and the more general sense of time being, as in *Hamlet*, "out of joint"; and so on. Quite obviously, the Troubles, for Northern writers and artists, was "ungetroundable," but so too was the drive to understand this moment by way of other histories, other struggles, other writing. And for both Muldoon and Mahon, Beckett has proved an irresistible, "ungetroundable" figure, more potent than the majority of influences both writers reveal so freely – and deploy so variously – in their work.

So, too, not insignificantly, is *King Lear*. Marina Carr describes returning to Shakespeare and *King Lear*, often along with the work of the Greek tragedians, Eugene O'Neill, and Tennessee Williams, obvious influences on such plays as *On Raftery's Hill*, *Ariel*, and *The Mai*; and, as we have seen, Shakespeare's play exercised a significant influence on Friel. In fact, one of his earliest works for the radio, *This Hard House* (1958), takes its title and plot from *King Lear*, and Carr's children's play *Meat and Salt* (2003) adapts aspects its narrative for a younger audience.[20] Mahon, too, employs Lear in portraying acute isolation in "North Wind: Portrush":

> I shall never forget the wind
> On this benighted coast.
> It works itself into the mind
> Like the high keen of a lost

Lear-spirit in agony
Condemned for eternity

To wander cliff and cove
Without comfort, without love.[21]

For Mahon, *King Lear*, too, has worked itself into the mind. Moreover, the allusion reveals what Eamonn Wall finds so compelling in both Beckett and Eavan Boland – namely, the positioning of place "near or at the source" of these writers' "creative flow"[22] – as Mahon demonstrates how place, when its identity is not homogenized out of existence by an encroaching Americanization, can be suffused with imaginative potential. The insinuation of Shakespeare's play into the speaker's psyche in "North Wind: Portrush" thus mirrors Muldoon's "ungetroundable" – images have "made their way into [his] consciousness" ("Getting Round," p. 107) and have taken up residence there.

So it is with *King Lear* in Muldoon's "Yarrow," written to eulogize his mother, a victim of cancer, which also claimed the lives of his former lover Mary Farl Powers, for whom "Incantata" was written, and both his sister Maureen and musician Warren Zevon, who are memorialized in "Sillyhow Stride." In a flashback in "Yarrow," the speaker's "ma" reminds him of women's dangerous sexuality by quoting Lear's infamous disparagement "but to the girdle do the gods inherit" (4.6.124);[23] at another moment, the speaker flippantly decides to drink to "Goneril's bland-/ishments and Cordelia's smart-ass '*Nada*'" (*Annals of Chile*, p. 56). These are the kinds of allusions some critics find tedious in Muldoon's poetry, as I shall discuss later, and can be "gotten round" fairly readily. A more telling pattern emerges, however, from an image in Shakespeare's play around which Muldoon could not navigate so easily: Lear's last-act plea to Cordelia to join him in prison where "We two alone will sing like birds i' th' cage" (5.3.9). Carrying his dead daughter in his arms into the last scene, the grieving, pitiable father in Shakespeare's tragedy extends the image:

Cordelia, Cordelia, stay a little. Ha!
What is't thou say'st? Her voice was ever soft,
Gentle, and low, an excellent thing in a woman.
(*King Lear*, 5.3.272–74)

In one section of "Yarrow," Muldoon laments, "That silver-haired mother o'mine./With what conviction did she hold/that a single lapse … would have a body cast/into the outer dark." Then, he quickly adds: "Dost thou know Dover?/The foul fiend haunts poor Tom in the voice of a nightingale"

(*Annals of Chile*, p. 89). Earlier, referring to his zapping of his television's remote control, he riffles quickly through a hodgepodge of potential diversions which include a Spanish *Lear*, a boxing match, an interview with art critic Robert Hughes, and a video of Michael Jackson performing his famous "moonwalk."

Why even mention this pastiche while unpacking a nexus of images consisting of Shakespeare, death, grief, and the feminine voice? Because in the same stanza Muldoon also oddly recalls watching a nature show in which "that same poor elk or eland" is "dragged down by a bobolink" (*Annals of Chile*, p. 47). The bobolink, a North American bird known for its singing, resurfaces later in the poem in connection with an eighteenth-century performance of *King Lear*:

> For that bobolink was no more your common oriole
> than was Barton Booth
> your common bletherskite: his 'Blow,
>
> winds, and crack
> your cheeks! Spit, fire! Spout, rain!'
> would cut through the cackle like the mark of Zorro.
>
> (*Annals of Chile*, p. 171)

An image cluster thus evolves in "Yarrow" in which a singing bird – a nightingale or bobolink – possesses the uncanny power to "bring down" animals – an elk or an eland (the latter commonly regarded as the most powerful species of antelope). That uncommon voice, like that of eighteenth-century actor Barton Booth, celebrated for his impersonations of Lear, King Hamlet, and Brutus, resembles that of Cordelia – and of Muldoon's mother. Yet, unlike Cordelia's "soft, gentle, and low" voice, that of Muldoon's mother was also sufficiently forceful to slice through the idle "cackle" of bletherskites, and its resonances inhabit Muldoon just as surely as the foul fiend haunts poor Tom's psyche in the voice of a nightingale. Like characters in Beckett who exist in bodies reduced to little more than the "fixed localisation [sic] of the voice,"[24] Muldoon's mother is fixed and localized in death, yet her voice remains active and mobile.

This image cluster accrues meaning in "Yarrow" as Muldoon's sorrow overlaps with Lear's desperate belief that Cordelia's lips are moving, that she is still breathing, and that she retains a voice. In expressing his sense of loss for his mother, Brigid Regan, to whom *The Annals of Chile* is dedicated, Muldoon returns again and again to the image of Lear staggering onto the stage in the play's last scene with Cordelia in his arms; it was something he could simply not "get round," just as Beckett could not shake Edgar's "better worse" speech and all it suggests. More precisely, within Muldoon's quite varied deployment of *King Lear* in "Yarrow," a dead woman's voice – sweet as a songbird's, but strong and piercing – can "take down" even the most formidable of animals and therefore also leave a psychical mark or wound on a grieving son. One might add that implicit in this image is the reality that the voice, as Mladen Dolar describes, "appears as the link which ties the signifier to the body"; moreover, because the "first obvious quality of the voice is that it fades away the moment it is produced," every time it resurfaces it tends to vanish.[25] Yet each time it is heard it may also scar the grieving son's psyche like Zorro's slash of his mark in "Yarrow," or linger painfully in the mind, as Cordelia's does in Lear's.

This essay thus argues a position diametrically opposite that of William James in the epigraph above from Colm Toíbín's *The Master*: a writer like his brother Henry, contrary to William's view, does not simply "indulge" in a style or capriciously pursue a "subject."[26] Rather like the James Joyce and Samuel Beckett Casanova describes – our interpretive premises are, in the end, not so *entirely* different – both Mahon and Muldoon got round things in the securing of their own literary space. For Casanova, Beckett "first had to find a way around the literary alternatives – realism or Symbolism – imposed by the internal struggles of the Irish field" as far back as Yeats and the rise of the Irish Literary Theatre. Then, he was forced to "overcome" Joyce's "apotheosis of the word" before he could take his own place in the distinguished genealogy that is Irish literature.[27] Mahon and Muldoon have also staked their claims in this heritage by inserting Ireland into one arena neither Joyce nor Beckett visited: a postmodern culture in which America reigns supreme. There is, frankly, little new in my observation, as critics of both poets have discussed their postmodernity, with the typical view underscoring Muldoon's almost promiscuous embrace of this culture and Mahon's loathing or fear of an encroaching Americanization (as his volume *The Yellow Book*, to take one example, reiterates).[28] Still, neither poet is synonymous with the capricious, fully empowered agent William James misapprehends his brother to be. Neither poet merely "chooses" these positions or topics.

More to the point of this essay, then, neither Mahon nor Muldoon can simply elect to "get round" Beckett any more than, for Casanova, Henry Roth or Arno Schmidt could get round Joyce or the Spanish writer Juan Benet could get round William Faulkner:

The worn notion of "influence" is plainly too simple and too vague to be of any use in trying to account for the affinity Benet felt for Faulkner. For far from dissimulating, or remaining silent about what he owed to Faulkner – unlike the majority of "influenced" writers who insist above all upon the originality of their inspiration – Benet openly acknowledged his filiation and constantly emphasized, by way of explicit homage, the many parallels between their work.[29]

Such terms as "parallels," "filiation," or acknowledgment, however, are far too tame, too decorous to denote the at times pathological dimensions of the "ungetroundable." Beckett, in other words, cannot summarily be "sent home" like the ghost to whom Muldoon refers in *The End of the Poem* (2006), a catalogue of lectures about poetry and the poetic process suffused with terms that further tend to erode William James' critique of his brother's writing. In what follows, I hope to show why – and why this matters to our understanding of the Beckettian.

DEREK MAHON: "BURBLES" AND THE BECKETTIAN

The presence of Beckett is simply everywhere [in Mahon's poetry].[30]

(Gerald Dawe, "Heirs and Graces: The Influence and Example of Derek Mahon" [2002])

Gerald Dawe's observation appears in various formulations throughout Elmer Kennedy-Andrews' anthology, *The Poetry of Derek Mahon* (2002), its strongest articulation advanced by Bruce Stewart who regards Beckett as Mahon's "mentor" in contemplating an unshakeable "metaphysical unease."[31] Stan Smith agrees, adding that in Mahon "the apocalyptic dwindles, as in Beckett, into the endless repetitive attrition of things in which the world wears down, for ever. The Beckett comparison is one that Mahon not only invites but openly acknowledges ..."[32] Among its several virtues, Smith's essay charts the predominance of the words "light" and "dark" (and roughly equivalent terms) in Mahon's volume *Poems 1962–1978*, a "striking assemblage of frequencies" that would motivate any reader of Beckett to take note. Indeed, the play of light and dark, black and white, is fundamental to Beckettian theatre and to the mise-en-scènes of such later prose pieces as *Ill Seen Ill Said* and *Worstward Ho*, as in the description of the protagonist in the opening paragraph of the former:

> There then she sits as though turned to stone face to the night. Save for the white of her hair and faintly bluish white of face and hands all is black. (*Nohow On*, pp. 49–50)

White "splotches" of lambs in the grass and black drapes in the old woman's cabin; white snow and black veil; the encroachment of white stones in the black night so that "Everywhere every instant whiteness is gaining" – these repetitions command our attention.

Such oppositions and repetitions can be construed in various ways, and Mahon reads them, if the evidence of Beckett's presence in his poetry is any way indicative, in a manner compatible neither with Eagleton's "remorselessly negative" metaphysics nor with the philosophical dead end Andrew Gibson distills from Steven Connors' work on Beckett's repetition. Because this latter matter pertains to Badiou's insistence upon Beckettian affirmation – and because it also might help explain Beckett's appearances in some of Mahon's most accomplished poems – it merits quotation at some length:

> [A]ccording to Connor, Beckett tends to dissolve the difference between repetition and difference itself … Connor's concept of a Beckettian "self-constraint" actually bears a certain resemblance to what Badiou means by "restricted action." But Connor's Beckett can imagine nothing beyond the self-constraining movement of his art.
>
> As Connor describes it, the ineluctable ambivalence of repetition in Beckett thus traps him … There is no exterior to this purgatory. There cannot be, because the power of the relationships between repetition and difference transcends time and history. For Badiou, however, this is not the case, because there is always the possibility of an event.[33]

As I have mentioned, the temporal metaphors Badiou deploys in theorizing the event, a cornerstone of his philosophy (or anti-philosophy), are especially significant. One of the most revelatory of these emerges in his reading of lines from the penultimate paragraph of *Worstward Ho*: "Enough. Sudden enough. Sudden all far. No move and sudden all far"[34] (*Nohow On*, p. 116). "Something happens" in this passage, and it happens with inexplicable speed. The thrice repeated "sudden" indicates not a purgatory of stasis or fixity, not a liminality between opposing formations, but a transition. While for Badiou it remains "impossible to know" whether the "grey black that localises [sic] the thought of being" is "destined for movement or immobility" ("Writing of the Generic," p. 6), the perspective of the *cogito* has changed. Suddenly in *Worstward Ho*, although journey and fixity may be superimposed, one upon the other, "all" is now "far." It wasn't before.

I might pause here and admit that in my characterization of Badiou's notions of events and situations I have privileged a temporal dimension that suits my interpretive purposes. Morerover, a more accurate, philosophically more acceptable rendering of such concepts as "event" and situation would require a fuller discussion of *Being and Event*, particularly Parts IV and V (meditations 16–25), a more conscientious appraisal of his appropriations from Cantor's set theory, and much more. That I lack the time and the competence for this undertaking should, by now, be apparent. Still, Badiou's assertions about the event and the *evental site* are highly relevant to this explication of the Beckettian qualities of Mahon and Muldoon. The evental site, for example, is not "part of a situation" (*Being and Event*, p. 175) and an event itself does not "immediately concern a situation in its entirety" (p. 178). An event, Badiou explains, is "always in a point in a situation"; these are not "natural" or "neutral situations," which are "solely facts" (p. 178). Moreover, "either the event is in the situation, and it ruptures the site's being 'on-the-edge-of-the void' by interposing itself between itself and the void" or it isn't, and "its power of nomination is solely addressed, if it is addressed to 'something,' to the void itself" (p. 182). In my view, Beckett's appearances in Mahon and Muldoon's writing often convey the sense of a local, momentary rupture in a larger situation; often they occur at the edge of a void that exists in proximity to nonbeing, to death, and to desolation. While my summary of Badiou, therefore, has of necessity been reductive, my hope is that it will illuminate the sites where Beckett emerges in this poetry.

This connotation of the Beckettian exists in a complementary relationship with definitions of the term advanced in earlier chapters – with riantic spaciousness, for instance, and with the importance of imagination, however diminished in later Beckett. And this sense of the Beckettian appears throughout Mahon's poetry, illuminating, I think, a fundamentally different presence than the one Stan Smith and Bruce Stewart identify. In "An Image from Beckett," to take one obvious example, the question arises of what precise image the poem's title references, a question most readily answered by pointing to the fourth stanza and the famous image it redacts from *Waiting for Godot*: "the gravedigger/ putting aside his forceps." Michael Allen has done a masterful job of demonstrating how Mahon, by revising the rhyme scheme as the poem existed in *Lives* (1972) for later publications in 1979 and 1991, moves away from the "articulation of uncertainty and marginality" by altering numerous unstressed endings into stressed ones that communicate a sardonic and elegant (a Beckettian?) toughness.[35] One might add clarity to Allen's analysis and inquire further about this redrawn image: if the gravedigger puts aside the forceps he wields in *Waiting for Godot* – if birth and death are no longer coeval – then where exactly is the Beckettian image in the poem?

Answers to this question may reside in two other prominent image patterns: that of black and white – as Smith has catalogued so usefully – and that of stasis and sudden change. On several occasions in "An Image from Beckett," the two patterns coincide, as in the opening stanza:

> In that instant
> There was a sea, far off,
> As bright as lettuce.

And in the third stanza:

> Also, I think, a white
> Flicker of gulls
> And washing hung to dry –

And a few lines later:

> Then the hard boards
> And darkness once again.
> But in that instant
> I was struck by the
> Sweetness and light ... (*Collected Poems*, p. 40)

The process in which "knuckle bones" of the dead are transformed by the "rich earth" in the poem's tenth stanza, "second by second/ To civilizations," conflates both patterns, atomizing the long process of history into seconds. Within each, change occurs. The landscape continues to haunt Mahon's speaker, as we learn near the poem's end, but it is hardly a scene of stasis or total darkness, even if in the poem's concluding stanza Mahon's speaker expresses the hope that future generations will have both the time and light necessary to read his will. The image of the gravedigger's forceps is composed of both temporal and visual elements; and, if this is so, then the Beckettian image in the poem's title is comprised of flickers, instants, darkness *and* whiteness, sweetness and light.

Similar motifs inform "Beyond Howth Head," where echoes of Joyce and Beckett predominate within a textual pastiche of multinational references and literary allusions. In the poem's early stanzas, Mahon portrays the incursions of American and Western European mass culture into Ireland, a postmodern condition represented even more directly by the relentless tourism Mahon indexes throughout *The Yellow Book*. Near the middle of "Beyond Howth Head," Mahon summarizes the process about as bluntly as it can be put: Washington, "its grisly aim/to render the whole earth the same," bombs Ireland relentlessly from its B-52s. In this late capitalist economy, in this transnational world, traditional rock-built houses, "townlands," and "homespun cottage industries" are overwhelmed by night music from Long Island and Cape Cod, television from the BBC, and imported Volkswagens in a kind of "empiric joie de vivre." Yet, even in the midst of this cultural encroachment, a pair of young lovers kissing in a parked car "torches down the dark" dispelling "tired disbelief" and prompting this weightier question:

> The pros outweigh the cons that glow
> from Beckett's bleak reductio –

> and who would trade self-knowledge for
> a prelapsarian metaphor,
> love-play of the ironic conscience
> for a prescriptive innocence? (*Collected Poems*, p. 53)

The Beckettian glow is rivaled in the next stanza by another kind of "flash, an *aisling*, through the dawn/where Yeats's hill-men still break stone" (p. 53). And in this flash of light, another understanding is enabled that redeems speaker and reader alike from potential despair. This reading of "Beyond Howth Head," *pace* Milton's *Areopagitica*, conceives of good and evil as twins cleaving together in the rind of one Edenic apple tasted. So too are life and death. Mahon knows this and in this stanza his speaker implies that yet another pair inhabiting this prelapsarian metaphor are "prescriptive innocence" and "ironic conscience," the latter being preferable to the former even if its exorbitant price is mortality.

Mahon then invokes the tradition of vision poetry in "Beyond Howth Head" in which an analogous coupling of life and death emerges. In this poetry, the figure of the shape-changing aisling promises a weary poet that his country has revived sufficiently to defend itself from yet another invasion. From this perspective, "Beyond Howth Head" chronicles the most recent invasion of Ireland by a superior force, one bent on subjugation and conquest: namely, postmodern techno-culture. Discussing Brian Merriman's *Cúirt an Mheán-Oíche*, written about 1780, as conveying an "old sovereignty" myth, which began typically with a poet occupying a "liminal zone frequented by fairies," Kiberd notes that often "the shape-changing woman epitomized the psychic problems which would have to be overcome by any ambitious man if he were to attain his destined greatness."[36] Such a background illuminates a causal relationship developed in the opening stanzas of Mahon's poem in which traditional Ireland is destroyed by foreign cultural products, an invasion specified in the poem's middle stanzas by the B-52s blasting away local difference. Thus, the underside of today's Celtic Tiger is the society mocked in "'Shiver in your tenement'" from *The Yellow Book*: a "pastiche paradise of the postmodern."[37] This "paradise," defined by a "new harshness" and connected to a rampant "sado-monetarism" (*The Yellow Book*, p. 25), motivates the speaker of "An Bonnán Buí" to ponder an otherwise outrageous articulation of a soulless postmodernity with the Troubles in Ulster:

> Do we give up fighting so the tourists come
> or fight the harder so they stay at home? (*The Yellow Book*, p. 27)

As "Beyond Howth Head" comes to a close, Mahon's speaker identifies a further encroachment in the onset of darkness:

> And here I close; for look, across
> dark waves where bell-buoys dimly toss
> the Bailey winks beyond Howth Head
> and sleep calls from the silent bed; …
> And I put out the light
> on shadows of the encroaching night. (*Collected Poems*, p. 57)

Darkness, dark waves, dimly-lit buoys – in an inversion of the whiteness of stones gaining ground in *Ill Seen Ill Said*, blackness overwhelms light at the end of the poem.

The leitmotif of black and white, therefore, might be regarded more precisely as a Beckettian motif in Mahon's poetry, especially when it is articulated with the temporal oppositions of instantiation and gradual encroachment. Stated in another way, within the larger incursion of darkness in "Beyond Howth Head" life flashes, glows, and occasionally erupts with the suddenness of change in *Worstward Ho*. This is not to claim that this same motif informs all of Mahon's poetry, but merely to suggest that it is more likely to appear when Beckett is somewhere nearby. So, for instance, a far more prosaic instance of the black/white opposition appears in "The Yaddo Letter," written by Mahon to his children in 1990 from the Yaddo Writers Colony in Saratoga Springs, New York. At times, the poem reveals Mahon the father imparting his wisdom to the children he obviously loves and misses; at other moments, a melancholic, nostalgic Mahon recalls the wonderful times they enjoyed together in London, "before Mummy and I split up."[38] However maudlin its sentiment, however potentially "tedious and trite" Mahon's sententiousness might become, "The Yaddo Letter" offers thoughtful paternal advice that, in one instance, quite consciously invokes the motif under discussion:

> … no black
> without its white, like a hot sun on the ice of a Yaddo lake.
> Children of light, may your researches be
> reflections on this old anomaly. (*Hudson Letter*, p. 30)

This "old anomaly" presents the opposition black/white as a prosaic binarism, an uncomplicated version of the larger pattern Smith discerns in Mahon's poetry, and a far cry from the more nuanced Beckettian affirmation and sudden evental change I have tried to trace.

The Hudson Letter (1995) features more overt references to Beckett in "Burbles," short verses that translate and adapt eight of the several dozen very short poems or "mirlitonnades" Beckett wrote in French on envelopes, scraps of paper, and in one instance the label from a bottle of Johnny Walker Black Label whisky.[39] As James Knowlson explains, Beckett's "sadness" over the deaths and declining health of several friends "spilled over" into these "numerous little poems" written mostly in 1977 and 1978. Initially calling them "rimailles," "rhymeries," or "versicules," Beckett copied them in a commonplace book he carried and finally settled on the term "mirlitonnades" when referring to them.[40] And, while Knowlson praises some of these poems as "beautifully crafted," if occasionally gloomy, some critics have discovered little art in Mahon's "Burbles." Hugh Haughton, for instance, disparages them as eight "grotesque lyric fragments after Beckett," and seems pleased that Mahon "banished" them from *Collected Poems*, arguing that Beckett's presence, so overt and meaningful in earlier poems like "An Image from Beckett" and "Exit Molloy," is far more evident in such later poems "Antarctica" and "Ovid in Tomis" than in these "discarded translated bagatelles."[41] Implicit in this deprecation, especially insofar as the later poems are concerned, is the notion, taken from a comment Mahon himself made in the introduction to *The Sphere Book of Irish Verse* (1972), that "poetry of lasting value" finds its source in "metaphysical unease," a sentiment that critics commonly equate with Mahon's affinity for Beckett.[42]

Mahon's "burbles" and Beckett's mirlitonnades, however, provide meager support for this critical preoccupation with "unease" or the thesis that Mahon's poetry resembles what Beckett himself, speaking of Thomas MacGreevy's poetry, termed the "existential lyric,"[43] as both poets approach mortality with an impish, even inappropriate humor that creates riantic expansiveness as often as nihilistic rumination. Beckett's mirlitonnades also relate to another motif developed here, as they are commonly referred to as "bird calls" or squawks.[44] "Mirlitonnade" connects these verses to a mirliton, a musical instrument, according to the *OED*, resembling a kazoo which, "when placed in the mouth imparts a nasal or buzzing quality to the voice." Hamlet's response to Polonius' blather as "Buzz, buzz, buzz" and Molloy's comment that words resembled "the buzzing of an insect" seem apposite to this context. Consistent with Badiou's view of Beckett's characters as compartmentalized voices, voice becomes a foregrounded term, but one quite distinct from Cordelia's soft and low tones. Rather, his mechanical voice screeches raucously, a carnivalesque inversion of the solemnity associated with mourning the death of a loved one and, in two verses, the calm associated with a cemetery.

In one mirlitonnade, for example, the result of his attempt to escape the distractions of Paris, Beckett traveled to Tangiers, visiting the Saint-André cemetery there on two separate occasions. He was moved to compose two verses on persons interred there, Arthur Keyser and Caroline Hay Taylor, which become the third and fourth of Mahon's burbles. Here is Beckett's original concerning the Keyser memorial:

ne manquez pas à Tanger
le cimetière Saint-André
morts sous un foullis
de fleurs surensevelis
banc à la mémoire
d'Arthur Keyser
de couer avec lui
restes dessus assis (*Poems 1930–1989*, p. 89)

And here is Mahon's rendition in "Burbles":

do not forget when in Tangier
the graveyard of St.-André where
the dead lie in a field of stone
covered with flowers and overgroan
a bench raised to the memory
of Arthur Keyser rest your bum
And sit in spirit there with him. (*Hudson Letter*, p. 21)

How are we to understand the relationship between Mahon's "bagatelle" and the Beckettian?

To begin, beneath the title "Burbles," Mahon inserts the phrase "*after Beckett*," implying that his verse is more than a translation; rather, it takes after Beckett in filial fashion just as a son may "take after" his father, or Mahon takes "after Baudelaire" in *The Yellow Book*. In his eight-line version of a seven-line original, "where" is added to Beckett's second line to underscore, I think, the sense of place as a site of events, however miniscule: the cemetery is not just a point of interest on a map – or a site of moribundity – but a place where things, however tiny, happen. The grounds themselves, for instance, are an exorbitant mess ("*un foullis*"), which Mahon can punningly advert to as "overgroan," combining the lexical with the bodily in his joke. Words, as we have seen, ooze in Beckett like secretions or drip a drop at a time, and "Overgroan" thus continues a Beckettian trope in which the failings of words parallel the less appealing processes of bodily functioning. As a gaseous bubble or natural process, "Burble" complements this conceit. In a similar lexical vein, it would be difficult to find a visitor's "bum" in Beckett's original, though we encounter a podex in *Watt* and a flurry of such terms throughout Beckett's *oeuvre*. The largest irreverence in both mirlitonnade and burble, however – recall that Mahon commends Beckett in his "A Tribute to Beckett on his Eightieth Birthday" as "one of the funniest of modern writers" (*Journalism*, p. 62) – is the identification of the bench as dedicated to Arthur Keyser (1856–1924), a travel writer who published "Trifles and Travels" (1923) and *From Jungle to Java* (1928), the latter of which records his impressions of Indonesia. The irony of sitting respectfully – of resting one's tired posterior – on a bench memorializing a travel writer coincides too neatly with the collapse of fixity and movement in the Beckettian to be ignored. This possibility, added to the bodily associations of "overgroan" and "bum," intimates the existence of a familiar Beckettian quality in Mahon.

Then there is the burble concerning the memorial to Caroline Hay Taylor at St. André's cemetery. Mahon's burble follows Beckett's poem closely in most respects: each is six lines long, each relates exactly the same facts, little is added or subtracted. Each depicts Taylor as remaining "true to her belief" (fidèle à sa philosophie) that "there is hope while there is life" (qu'espoir il y a tant qu'il y a vie), and each mentions that she escaped Ireland with this view intact. But Beckett dates this flight as occurring "en août mil neuf cent trente-deux," which Mahon "translates" as "in August nineteen-twenty-two." Why make this revision? Did Mahon's considerable facility with French fail him at this moment? Probably not. The most obvious explanation is that, in this memorable place, an Irishwoman – an aisling transplanted from Irish mythology to this remote scene well beyond the Hill of Howth – retained her unflagging optimism at a historical moment least hospitable to the cultivation of hope. As is well-known, the Civil War in Dublin raged in 1922, a by-product of the Anglo-Irish War and a harbinger of violence looming ahead. The Troubles in the North of which Mahon seems so acutely aware, the Troubles he cannot escape even when walking the streets of New York or London, renders him little more than an Irish bohemian far from the "original 'Ballroom of Romance'" as he puts it in "Global Village" by way of an allusion to William Trevor (*Hudson Letter* 41). Altering the date of the memorial's inscription, then, allows Mahon to imply that Caroline Hay Taylor remained forward-looking in circumstances least likely to cultivate hope or affirmation; by contrast, 1932 in Beckett's original exercises a far more restricted connotation.

In these ways, Mahon's "burbles" recall the speech from *King Lear* that Beckett could scarcely get round. Not surprisingly, one of Beckett's mirlitonnades – the first published in *Poems 1930–1989* – recalls Edgar's optimism in the epigraph with which this essay began:

en face
le pire
jusqu'à ce
qu'il fasse rire (*Poems 1930–1989*, p. 74)

"In face of the worst, it *is necessary to laugh.*" And laughter can be induced as quickly as one can set one's rump down on a bench or coin the term "overgroan." To be sure, sorrow and the "fulgurating" pain of the "trilogy" – or of September 11 – can overtake with equal rapidity. But in this darkness there may always be a flash of white. This is the thesis of Mahon's third burble:

> each day a great desire
> one day to be alive
> though not without despair
> at being forced to live. (*Hudson Letter*, p. 21)

This burble, like Beckett's original, transcends the binaries of life/death and hope/despair (although one should not equate laughter with optimism, as some of the above comments may seem to do). Here, the speaker aspires to be alive "one day," suggesting that at present he is not alive, and recalling the tradition of the dead speaking in Irish literature. Mahon's verse expresses a prospective desire for life that overpowers murmurs of despair and, in doing so, summarizes one trace of the Beckettian in his work.

Similarly, the "overgroan" lawns of St. André and the idea of a "bum" resting on Arthur Keyser's bench reiterate the necessity of Beckettian laughter in the face of death, which *can* often be equated with the "worst" – a laughter so beautifully related in Tom Murphy's *Bailegangaire* where, as Mommo recalls, "Great gales of laughter [followed] each name of the departed" as it was read; families "skitherin' and laughin' – Ih-hih-ih – at their nearest an' dearest."[45] In making this assertion, I of course run the risk of reading into the later Beckett a lightness or optimism that not only Eagleton has refuted, but Beckett's biographers caution against as well. James Knowlson puts the matter succinctly in his characterization of the mirlitonnades:

> The apparent slightness and playfulness of form of these late 1970s "poèmes courts" (or miniature poems) should not disguise the seriousness and, to use Beckett's own word, "gloom" of their themes.[46]

"Gloom," though, however inimical to the cultivation of humor, does not diminish its importance. Beckett's mirlitonnade posits that it is "necessary," and as we shall see, a similar imperative informs Muldoon's work, one of several Beckettian elements of his poetry.

PAUL MULDOON'S BECKETTIAN WORM

> Beckett appears "again and again" in ["Incantata"] ... Here too are Beckett's creations: Krapp, Belaqua, Hamm and Clov, Vladimir and Estragon. All are in one sense tragic figures, confronting a world bereft of any hope of betterment, let alone redemption. Their resilience, their ability to "go on," is based on a kind of existential stubbornness ...[47] (Clair Wills, *Reading Paul Muldoon* [1998])

Part of what cultures do is select from among the works that were valued in the past, assign contemporary significance to those works, and pass them on to the next generation.[48] (Gregory Machacek, "Allusion" [2007])

Again and again Lear enters with a rare
and radiant maiden in his arms
who might at any moment fret and fream. (Paul Muldoon, "Yarrow" [1994])

In her memoir, Anne Atik mentions another matter that seems as relevant to this discussion as her intimation of the "ungetroundable" power *King Lear* exerted on the aging Beckett: his growing distaste for the allusive quality of his earlier writing. She recalls that

In later life Beckett grew impatient with the "juvenile" literary allusions very densely embedded in his early work. Although a great reader, he disliked flaunting a too-visible wardrobe of learning; yet how could his intensive, extensive reading not enter his writing? Reading is passed down to others the way parents pass down their traits. (*How It Was*, p. 52)

Reviewing Beckett's *Collected Poems in English and French* for the *New Statesman* in 1977, Mahon reveals a similar impatience, complaining of a "displeasing undergraduate cleverness" too much on display in Beckett's early poetry, although in another essay Mahon advises his readers not "to make too much" of literary influence on Beckett's work because it is, finally, "sui generis" (*Journalism*, pp. 56, 60). The former assessment begs a number of questions: What distinguishes exhibitions of a preening undergraduate cleverness from more resonant quotation, say those in such later works as *Ill Seen Ill Said* and *Worstward Ho*? Does such an aesthetic standard merely record the frequency of allusions in a text? Or are some specific kinds of reference preferable to others? More particularly, what if one were to consider seriously Atik's very good question that, however unintended, recalls the sovereignty of the Beckettian pensum: How could reading or learning, particularly as Atik metaphorizes it as a determinative force analogous to the genetic code, *not* enter a writer's production?

These inquiries seem especially apropos to a consideration of Paul Muldoon, precisely because his most vocal detractors often object to the allusiveness and eclectic intertextuality of his poetry. Such censure contrasts with the critical reception of Mahon's work, which Rory Brennan judges to be the result of a "wide erudition [that] is never shown for its own sake." For Brennan, Mahon resembles "some Third World artisan who can fabricate musical instruments from scraps and oddments ... cobbled from bits of history and intellectual hubbub."[49] This kind of esteem – though much in evidence in reviews of Muldoon's *The Annals of Chile*, the focus here – was not universally proclaimed by its readers. Helen Vendler, for example, predicted that the volume would induce in American readers both "admiration" and "exasperation," the latter catalyzed by the "many private references " in Muldoon's poetry which could create a "feeling of loss before his Joycean game of baffle-the reader."[50] Nearly a decade later, she begins her review of Muldoon's *Horse Latitudes* (2006) with precisely the same question: "How allusive should a poem be? Should readers be helped by notes?"[51] Invoking the example of T. S. Eliot's addition of explanatory notes to later printings of *The Waste Land*, Vendler answers the question in the affirmative. More critical of *The Annals of Chile*, William Pratt railed at Muldoon both for being "outrageously and unabashedly allusive" and for indulging in an "elaborate word game with little meaning ..."[52] While conceding that a "network of allusions" in Muldoon's earlier volume *Madoc* may have been "too recherché to be useful" but "too insistent to be dismissed," Lawrence Norfolk hailed Muldoon as "one of the most inventive and ambitious poets working today."[53] Richard Tillinghast regarded *Annals* as evidence that Muldoon is "one of the two or three most accomplished rhymers now writing in English."[54] And Seamus Heaney endorsed its "opulence and maturity which still leave room for huge playfulness," adding that in spite of the book's Joycean "combination of the everyday and the erudite," it is also "entirely sui generis, a volume that vindicates Muldoon's reputation as one of the era's true originals."[55]

Heaney's commendation of Muldoon's originality underscores a paradox Gregory Machacek examines in both authorial deployments and critical studies of allusion. Synonyms for allusion – *borrowing* and *echo*, to name two – typically "imply that the allusive text is of lesser stature than the text evoked through allusion." Not so. One can bask in allusion by employing innumerable echoes or verbal adaptations and still be proclaimed an "original," as both Beckett and Muldoon have been. That is to say, although Muldoon's style has at times been damned for its artificiality, as we have seen it has also been applauded as uniquely ingenious in attempting to resolve tensions between the natural and the plastic.[56] More broadly, as Machacek observes, such terms as "allusion" and "intertextuality" – touchstones in critical responses to Muldoon's poetry and concepts emphasized throughout this book – are so "beset by limiting assumptions, conceptual murkiness, and terminological imprecision" that they often underlie the kind of apparent paradoxes mentioned above. Authorial borrowing or appropriation, therefore, ought not be understood merely in a diachronic fashion – a writer referring to or adapting the phraseology of an earlier writer – but also in a synchronic way in which a text is shown to participate intertextually "in the discursive space of a culture."[57] From this latter point of view, a text *must* engage with literary, historical, and other nonliterary phenomena. How could it do otherwise? For this reason, Heaney in one breath can laud Muldoon as one of the era's "true originals" and, in another, endorse his work's erudition and "huge playfulness," qualities associated with allusion. Playfulness, of course, can devolve into "game-playing," or be something more akin to a surf of the Internet than a decoding of the consideration of the author – and clearly some readers enjoy paddling in waves more than others.

This topic, though, concerns more than playfulness, however much this quality is evident in Beckett, Mahon, and Muldoon; and Machacek scrutinizes allusion in ways that might prove useful in discerning the Beckettian in Muldoon. These include the distinction between "learned references" and "phraseological adaptations." The former variety, so prominent in Muldoon's poetry, requires a writer and reader to share a cultural literacy and even to value the same texts in roughly approximate or at least compatible ways. Helen Vendler's complaint confirms this requirement, as she felt ill-equipped to decode Muldoon's many "private" references.[58] Phraseological adaptations operate differently. First, they have to be recognized as originating elsewhere, as there is a difference between referring to *King Lear* or to characters from the play and borrowing the phrase "vile jelly," as Beckett does for *Ill Seen Ill Said*. The latter is an instance of "covert borrowing" and its source may go unnoticed by some readers, while an overt reference to *Lear* – or Lear will not: readers either know the play or they don't, in which case they know they are likely missing something. Second, while a reference to *King Lear* might trigger a wide, almost limitless, array of speculations, the concrete specificity of "vile jelly" propels us specifically to the scene of Gloucester's abuse. In Machacek's improved literary critical lexicon, this moment constitutes a reprise of the original, which it may "echo" precisely or not.[59] In recognizing the reprise, a reader instantly joins a kind of cognoscenti, so that when Larry Doyle in Bernard Shaw's *John Bull's Other Island* compares a beefy Englishwoman who "eats not wisely but too well" with a sylph-like Irish colleen who "eats not wisely but too little," the informed reader is invited to juxtapose this quip to Othello's last-minute confession to Lodovico (and to admire Doyle's wit as well). An uninformed reader will simply allow the sentence to pass by.

Such observations still fail to answer the question prompted by the aging Beckett's antipathy to allusion in his earlier writing, though this distaste should not imply the absence of allusion in his later texts. As the example of "vile jelly" confirms – and one could cite Beckett's playful revision "worstward ho" for the title of his prose piece, or "Better hope deferred than none" from *Company* – all allusions are not equal; thus, all were not banished from his later writing. There *is*, it seems, a difference between reference and phraseological reprise, though Muldoon in the lectures that comprise *The End of the Poem* does not parse the issue with such exactitude. On the contrary, he seems to insist that all writing marks an intertextual gathering point of prior literary and non-literary phenomena. So, for example, Emily Dickinson's "I tried to think a lonelier Thing" is "ghosted" by Sir John Franklin's ill-fated 1845 voyage to find a northwest passage between England and North America; Stevie Smith's "I remember" is "faintly ghosted" by William Wordsworth's definition of poetry from the preface to the *Lyrical Ballads* as "the spontaneous overflow of powerful feelings … recollected in tranquility"; Seamus Heaney's "Keeping Going" contains the "ghostly presence" both of John Hume and Lord Chief Justice Widgery who presided over the "Bloody Sunday" inquiry; and so on.[60] For Muldoon, "ghosting" is another way of metaphorizing intertextuality, a kind of synecdoche for his larger observation about Yeats' "All Souls' Night":

> As I've tried to suggest, the text or texts to which "All Souls' Night" might stand as an epilogue is not so much *A Vision* but a selection of poems by Keats, a writer whom Yeats categorised in a 1913 letter to his father as the "type of *vision*," and from whom he *conglomewrites* [my emphasis] key words and images.
>
> (*The End of the Poem*, p. 27)

Writing is, for Muldoon, a conglomerate production; a properly critical reading, in turn, operates on this premise and works at unraveling texts – and words within them – that, given the Latinate origins of this neologism, are conceived as gatherings together of linguistic and discursive balls.

For a writer like Muldoon who claims to loathe critical prescription and programmatic systems of interpretation, as John Redmond has pointed out, this view of writing as always already an aggregation of texts may be *the* only aesthetic imperative:

> Muldoon remarks that "difficulty for its own sake is anathema to me. My aim [in 'Madoc'] was to write something that you could zoom through, rapidly turning the pages" … Writing and reading are forms of work for Muldoon but they are not privileged forms of work … At the same time we should not see them as *less* privileged forms of work. It is work which is the privilege.[61]

Unpacking allusions, however, is hardly the only labor in reading Muldoon. For, as Redmond acknowledges, Muldoon "complicates the reading process" in a manner reminiscent of Robert Frost by refusing to embark upon a "quest for certainty" or ground his poetry in any specific philosophy, citing a passage from "Yarrow" quoted earlier as an example:

For that bobolink was no more your common oriole
than was Barton Booth
your common bletherskite ... (*Annals of Chile*, p. 171)

Earlier, I stressed the notion of voice both in this passage and throughout "Yarrow" and continue to urge its significance. Redmond, by contrast, emphasizes the importance of "no more" in the stanza's first line as a device that "helps Muldoon create an air of conversational evasiveness." Instead of a "precise, definite answer, we are given some, but only some, idea of whatever is in question" through such constructions as "no more ... than," constructions which intentionally blur boundaries and create ambiguity:

As in Frost the idiomatic, conversational style creates an impression of transparency, an impression which proves false as soon as the reader *slows down* and thinks carefully.[62]

This impression of transparency may also prove an invitation to misread. After one slows down to consider constructions like "no more than," the conglomerate nature of Beckettian and Muldoonian textuality becomes more apparent, though their conglomewritings also differ considerably in terms of the cultural realms from which they borrow.

Like "Yarrow," "Incantata" from *The Annals of Chile* bears this out, confirming the fact that for Muldoon writing is always already "conglomewriting"; ideas and the sentences expressing them are inevitably bound up with other phenomena in the discursive ball that "conglomerate" denotes. And like allusions in Laurence Sterne's *Tristram Shandy*, at least as it is characterized in *To Ireland, I*, Muldoon's adversions are not always "high-flown,"excessively "literific" or "literose," as a poem like "Sillyhow Stride" demonstrates with its various references to John Donne's poetry, the Everly Brothers and Warren Zevon's repertoires, the merits of various electric guitars and amplifiers (Crate, Fender, Marshall), and much more. Equally important, in his reading of Sterne, Muldoon also underscores Irish writing's "disregard for the line between sense and nonsense" and its obsession with the "slip and slop of language" (*The End of the Poem*, p. 107). Like the body, however, words often prove inadequate to a task, necessitating a "conglomewrite" here or a Joycean "funferal" there. Thus, a phraseological adaptation or reprise like "worstward ho," on the one hand, might be denigrated as an unfortunate display of undergraduate cleverness; on the other hand, this meld of "westward" and "worstword" might be regarded as a synopsis of the book's ironic narrative, all of which returns us to Anne Atik's question: How *could* Beckett's "intensive" and "extensive" reading *not* enter his writing? How *could* Muldoon's similarly extensive reading – and his intensive engagement with contemporary mass culture, particularly rock music – *not* enter his poetry? If the answer posits allusion's necessity or "ungetroundability," then we have reached a thesis quite opposite that implied by Muldoon's detractors: he doesn't allude to baffle the uninitiated or to show off; he does so because for him no other choice exists. Allusion, as today's techno-geeks might put it, is as "hard-wired" in his writing as strands of DNA are in the genetic code.

But all allusions are not equal. More precisely, my contention is that Beckett's presence in "Incantata" functions more like a parasite in an elegy replete with motifs of bodily invasion, worms, cancerous mutations, and so on. In Muldoon's conglomewriting – of which this poem is a conspicuous illustration – lines between text and allusion, host and parasite, grow increasingly blurred; much as cancer, etymologically related to the crab Joyce depicts in the "Circe" episode of *Ulysses*, consumes the dead or dying flesh of its victim, so too host and parasite become a single entity.[63] The major difference, the point at which this analogy breaks down, is that Beckett's presence in Muldoon's work is an enabling, not debilitating, invasion. In this regard, the Beckett of "Incantata" complements the Beckett of *To Ireland, I*, in which Muldoon proclaims him the "Lord of Liminality himself" (p. 12), for this liminality is, paradoxically, central to Muldoon's conception of Irishness, just as Beckett becomes central to Muldoon's elegy. Recall that in *To Ireland, I* Muldoon illuminates various strategies "devised by a range of Irish writers for dealing with the ideas of liminality and narthecality that are central … to the Irish experience" (p. 5). In this logic, Beckett is the "lord" or epitome of an irreducibly Irish displacement; peripherality defines Irishness, as does Beckett. Similarly, in the trope of parasitic contamination the borders between center and periphery, host and guest collapse, just as those between poetic text and prior text, text and cultural intertexts, gradually disappear.

This metaphor informs "Incantata" in part through the poem's references to Mary Farl Powers' lithograph *Emblements* (See Figure 1), with its legion of ravenous worms moving inexorably toward their goal. Both the metaphor and lithograph, perhaps surprisingly, create a playfulness in the poem, an odd quality in some respects given its elegaic purpose in responding to Powers' death. Even more surprising, her decline in health marks a production, much like that of a worm's path through a cankered potato, an infestation productive of both an occulted language to be deciphered and *Emblements*. Such an invader most resembles Michel Serres' parasite and Beckett himself in Muldoon's poem: a "guest" who effects a "break in a message," yet one who also "gives rise to a new system, [a new] order that is more complex than the simple chain. This parasite interrupts at first glance, consolidates when you look again."[64] The new order that results marks a

Figure 1. Mary Farl Powers, Emblements (1981). Reprinted by permission of the Estate of Mary Farl Powers

more complicated affirmation of humanity than existed before, and in so doing enhances the prospect of Beckett remaining our contemporary in an increasingly dangerous world. This hybrid entity of interruption, loss, and affirmation grows inside of the text into a deeper consolidation, a new logic in which boundaries between host and guest topple. Beckett is thus the worm, as it were, in the blighted potato of Muldoon's text.

"Incantata" begins with an echo of the opening stanza of his earlier poem "Mary Farl Powers: *Pink Spotted Torso*" from *Quoof*. Here is the latter:

> She turns from the sink
> potato in hand. A Kerr's Pink,
> its water-dark
> port-wine birthmark
> that will answer her knife
> with a hieroglyph. (*Poems 1968–1998*, p. 113)

In Powers' art, the potato's "birthmark," another product of the genetic, is transformed into an ideogram, a ramification enabled by her creative knife.

By contrast, in the opening of "Incantata," the hieroglyph is a "print of what looked like a cankered potato," a potato being eaten into a giant sore like those during the Great Famine affected with a blight often described as a "vampire fungus." Refining this trope, and following the lead of Powers' *Emblements*, the second stanza focuses directly on parasitical eating and specifies the diners: "army-worms" enjoying a "nightmarish *déjeuner sur l'herbe*." This parasitic infestation, juxtaposed to Edouard Manet's painting of a leisurely picnic on the grass, evolves into the image of the "grass widow" in the third stanza – the inebriated young Muldoon would often abandon Powers as a "grass widow" so he could pursue further intoxications – and by association widowhood leads Muldoon to the word "viduity" in *Krapp's Last Tape*: "There is of course the house on the canal where mother lay a-dying," Krapp's younger voice intones on the tape, "in the late autumn, after her long viduity" (*Shorter Plays*, p. 59). The utterance of this odd word brings the action of Beckett's drama to a standstill, interrupting the playing of the tape and sending Krapp offstage to retrieve a dictionary, find the word, and muse over its possibilities. Yet perhaps this isn't precisely an interruption; perhaps "viduity" itself in Beckett's text resembles a parasite not merely eating into Krapp's listening time, but also producing a new action that affects the entirety of the play. Similarly, Beckett first appears in "Incantata" as an interruption; in fact, he is a parenthesis – "(remember how Krapp looks up 'viduity')" – lodged between the cause of Powers' abandonment and its effect. Already, then, we are in a Krapp-like world of loss, narrative interruption, and a parasitism productive of conceptual noise – hence, subtle change – in the system of the poem.

Both the title "Incantata" and this reference to the viduity of Krapp's mother alert readers that, as is so often the case in Muldoon (and Beckett), language will at times undergo modification or mutation. This elegy is both a cantata and an incantation, a musical composition and a magical spell, just as viduity denotes widowhood, but also recalls the vidua bird (widowbird or indigobird), a small African passerine bird resembling a finch known for both its black and bright indigo plumage. Muldoon, much like Beckett, betrays a fascination with these paradoxical dimensions of words and names, as the former reveals through a lengthy etymological meditation on the name "Beckett" in *To Ireland, I*.[65] Yet another example of Muldoon's absorption in etymology emerges in the lines from "Yarrow" in the epigraph above that offers the possibility that "at any moment" a dead Cordelia might "fret and fream." As a verb, "fream" seems vastly inappropriate to this image, as it denotes the capacity to "roar, rage, [or] growl, spec. of a boar" (*OED*). This amplification of a voice lovingly described as gentle, sweet, and low into a porcine roar, if it announces the return of Cordelia's life, may nonetheless be allowable, however tortured the association. But "fream" also possessed a unique definition in the late seventeenth century when used as a noun: an "arable land worn out of heart and laid fallow till it recover" (*OED*). This obscure usage creates the uncanny juxtaposition of a fretting howl of life and a land lying moribund until it can be restored to fecundity; hence, the trope promotes Cordelia as a figure of the nation itself, a kind of aisling promising revival. The word "viduity" possesses a similar kind of incongruity in evoking both the blackness of mourning clothes and the brightness of a bird's plumage (perhaps coincidentally, vidua birds are also brood parasites that lay their eggs in other birds' nests and imitate their hosts' songs).

At this early point in the poem, however, this flash of brightness in the lexical dark is too faint to mollify Muldoon. He chastises himself for his former idea of "R & R" – "getting drunk" – and in the third stanza laments the results of his inebriety: he would land "back home in Landseer Street deaf and blind" and find himself "all at sea but in the doldrums" in his relationship with Powers. Then, things change abruptly, as they do again later in the poem at stanza 24, as Tim Kendall points out, when Muldoon initiates a long catalogue of diminished realities with the refrain "That's all that's left."[66] In the fourth stanza, however, it's the tone that changes with the mock-heroic entrance of "His Nibs Sam Bethicket" who, along with Sartre, is said to "temper" Powers' *Summa Theologiae* that the "things of the world sing out in a great oratorio" and bespeak a kind of natural order (*Annals of Chile*, p. 14). But what more does Muldoon mean by linking an allusion to Thomism with Sam Bethicket? Perhaps two things: that God is, in fact, no longer the center of or primary cause in Powers' worldview, as He was in Aquinas' theology; and that the seriousness of philosophy is always susceptible to comic undercutting, as in the jangle of words in *Finnegans Wake* where the joking reference "Bethicket" originates:

> You is feeling like you was lost in the bush, boy? You says:/It is a puling sample jungle of woods. You most shouts out:/ Bethicket me for a stump of a beech if I have the poultriest no-/tions what the farest he all means.[67]

As one student of *Finnegans Wake* has noted, "Bethicket" presents "a picture of Beckett lost in a bush, or thicket, and the whole passage is a good-humored parody of Beckett's prose style."[68] A "jangle" of philosophies, much like "a jungle of woods," is potentially disarming, and while Muldoon was no "stump of a beech," he at times was just as befuddled by Powers' reaction to her incipient cancer as the young Beckett was by the

Wake. In other words, the parasitical worm is also a "thick" reader, one who, in his struggle to understand complexities that may exceed his comprehension, injects humor into a "farest" of interpretive possibility.

In the next several stanzas, allusions to Vladimir and Estragon, Nagg and Nell, similarly emerge not so much as indicators of a "relentlessly negative" Beckett, but as intimations of a comic affirmation. In the sixth stanza, to take perhaps the most striking examples in the poem, Muldoon reports sharing "a couple of jars" and ideas with Vladimir and Estragon; and in the seventh he reports Powers' commentary on *Endgame*:

> and you weighed in with "To live in a dustbin, eating scrap,
> seemed to Nagg and Nell a most eminent domain." (*Annals of Chile*, p. 15)

It is difficult *not* to regard these lines as providing evidence for Kiberd's thesis in *Irish Classics* of the sumptuous destitution of Irish literature in general and Beckett in particular, even if in "Incantata" and later poems Muldoon reveals the difficulty, as he phrases it in "Sillyhow Stride,"of "throwing up a last ditch/against the mounted sorrows."[69] At *this* moment, though, in *this* reading of Hamm's aging parents and their deplorable living conditions, Powers – who, like a dying Warren Zevon in "Sillyhow Stride" knew his "mesotheliomata/on both lungs meant the situation was lose-lose" (*Horse Latitudes*, p. 106) – refuses to succumb to despair. Moreover, while she cajoles Muldoon in the next stanza to "have no more truck" with "tiresome" literary "intrigues," this allusion to *Endgame* scarcely qualifies as such. The allusion's explicit affirmation mitigates the damage of tedious intrigue.

To be sure, Beckett on occasion appears in Muldoon's poems not only as one reference among others, no more or less privileged than any other, but also as a figure of decline. Such an accession, I hope, does not thoroughly discredit my project, though it *does* suggest the need for clarification. In a poem in *The Prince of the Quotidian* (1994), for example, Beckett shares time in a seminar Muldoon taught with Swift, Yeats, Sterne, and Joyce; and, as in *To Ireland, I*, in this course Muldoon seems more preoccupied with "the long sonata of *The Dead*."[70] Beckett is no more, perhaps even less, ungetroundable than Swift and Joyce. An even more significant challenge to my argument – to definitions of an affirmative *and* an "ungetroundable" Beckett – emerges in an allusion to Beckett in "As" from *Moy Sand and Gravel* (2002). "As" lists a series of analogies to a speaker's gradual capitulation to a significant other; hence, all save one of the poem's eleven nine-line stanzas end with the refrain, "I give way to you." Analogies in the poem originate in a roster of disparate phenomena, many of which seem inconsequential. In the second stanza, for example, as "hammock gives way to hummock/ and Hoboken gives way to Hackensack ... I give way to you." And in the third, "As vent gives way to Ventry/and the King of the World gives way to Finn MacCool/and phone gives way to fax ... I give way to you."[71] All convey the sense of the inevitability of change, yet some analogues seem entirely random, as Hoboken and Hackensack are not even connected by an interstate highway, only an alliteration. Other pairings are historical or bluntly factual: phones have in some ways been superseded by fax machines, butcher's string by vacuum packs (stanza 4), the Roman IX by the Arabic 9 (stanza 11). Still other analogies loom as mysteries or instances of convenient assonance. In what ways have "transhumance" given way to "trance," or "DeLorean, John" given way to "Deloria, Vine"? How is one to regard Spanish fly being superseded by Viagra (stanza 8), or *Howards End* giving way to *A Room with a View* (stanza 8)? The poem's penultimate stanza provides the strongest intimation of an answer, one seemingly incompatible with the Beckettian in "Incantata": namely, that these analogies are "symptomatic of a more general decline/ whereby a cloud succumbs to a clod/and I give way to you" (*Moy Sand and Gravel*, p. 40). Still, such a thesis hardly accounts for the eclectic comparisons proffered by the speaker.

A direct reference to Beckett appears in the fifth stanza of "As," located precisely in the middle of a random, at times vulgar, set of accessions:

> As Hopi gives way to Navaho
> and rug gives way to rag
> and *Pax Vobiscum* gives way to Tampax
> and Tampa gives way to the water bed
> and *The Water Babies* gives way to *Worstward Ho*
> and crapper gives way to loo
> and spruce gives way to pine
> and the carpet of pine needles to the carpetbag
> I give way to you. (*Moy Sand and Gravel*, pp. 37–38)

Here, the end of a line is connected to the beginning of the next either phonetically or lexically (Tampax becomes Tampa, water bed becomes *Water Babies*, the long "u" of loo becomes spruce); or phraseologically, as Navajo in line one connects to "rug" in line two, pine in line seven to "carpet of pine needles" in line eight. Are these symptoms of the "general decline" in stanza 10?

More particularly, what are we to infer from the reference to *The Water Babies* (1863), a fairy tale Charles Kingsley wrote for his son about an enchanted kingdom at the bottom of a river, and its giving way to

Worstward Ho? As many scholars have observed, Beckett's title is a parodic redaction of Kingsley's *Westward Ho* (1874), a popular Victorian adventure tale. In Kingsley's title, "west" is synonymous with progress, not with a journey toward death as in the conclusion of "The Dead." Amid various linguistic evolutions or devolutions – *pax vobiscum* paired with Tampax, crapper giving way to loo – a children's fantasy narrative gives way to a text that Badiou and Casanova regard as one of Beckett's most seminal achievements. Is this adversion to Beckett another example of a cloud yielding to a clod, or is it representative of another encroachment – the supplanting of literary fantasy by a more mature narrative? My thesis about *The Annals of Chile* and the Beckettian contends that "giving way" to Beckett is an affirmative capitulation, not a symptom of decline. Yet, pressing this thesis seems unnecessary. Better to say, perhaps, that in writing "Yarrow" in memory of his mother, Muldoon found *King Lear* to be ungetroundable; in writing "Incantata" and contemplating Mary Powers' death, Muldoon discovered that Beckett was similarly impossible to get round. Not so in "As" or *The Prince of the Quotidian*.

In "Incantata," Beckett and his characters return tout court in stanza 12 when Hamm and Clov, Nagg and Nell, Watt and Knott serve as emblems – *not* "emblements," a point to which I shall return – of a relationship floundering in the doldrums. Muldoon terms it a "standstill worthy of Hamm and Clov," but the poem does not bear this out as both lovers quickly wound each other with secrets; Powers metaphorically becoming a scorpion and delivering a sting to Muldoon. Within the listlessness of these doldrums, in other words, something *does* occur. Then, in the next stanza, she appears as "thin as a rake," bending over the copperplate of *Emblements* into which she "all but disappeared." The stricken gladiator or *retiarus* armed with net and trident in stanza 8 has in succession become a scorpion, a rake, and a worm, all of which, albeit armed with teeth or a sting, are slight and on the verge of disappearing. Here, as the next few stanzas clarify, one of the poem's chief paradoxes emerges: the parasite becomes the host, the worm becomes the potato, the devourer becomes the devoured. The poet with the tendency "to put/on too much artificiality" – so much so that Powers christened him "Polyester" or "Polyurethane" – is infected, too. As the cancer ate through her like a fungal blight through a potato, as cancer grew to cause "such a breach" in her that she "would almost surely perish," a new sense of mortality interrupts Muldoon's artificiality and tiresome literary intrigues. And with this change, Beckett's status as worm is refined yet again: the parenthesis that metamorphosed into a boy lost in the forest of Joyce's words now becomes emblematic of something else.

Emblematic of what? One possibility entails a reversal of Kiberd's thesis in which Beckett seeks not only to "express the impossibility of all expression," but also to draft a paradigm for Irish writing: namely, the discovery of "how sumptuous destitution can be" (*Irish Classics*, p. 17). Powers' assertion that Nagg and Nell imagined the starkly confined world of *Endgame* to be a "most eminent domain" certainly qualifies as the strongest expression of the sumptuary quality of destitution in Muldoon's poem. Yet, in another respect, just the opposite may also be the case as Muldoon expresses his grief in "Incantata" and wrestles with the image of his lover in decline, her body wasting away before his eyes. As a result, as I have mentioned, stanza twenty-four initiates a nineteen stanza sequence that delineates "all that is left" of his dramatically diminished world without Powers in it. Hardly feeding himself "on abstinence," then, Muldoon for much of the poem appears to document just how destitute a sumptuous cultural life can be.

This procession, however, is preceded by a crucial moment in the poem's twenty-third stanza in which allusions to Beckett resonate as Muldoon attempts to reconcile the relationships between imminent death, Powers' worldview, and her art:

> The fact that you were determined to cut yourself off in your
> prime
> because it was *pre*-determined has my eyes abrim:
> I crouch with Belacqua
> and Lucky and Pozzo in the Acacacac-
> ademy of Anthropopopometry, trying to make sense of the
> *"quaquaqua"*
> of that potato-mouth. (*Annals of Chile*, p. 20)

In the first two lines, Muldoon overstates Powers' agency, suggesting that her conviction that "nothing's random, nothing arbitrary" led her to "cut [her]self off" in her prime. Muldoon then quickly moves to an equally unlikely source of consolation: reading. The image of the "potato mouth" he "tries to make sense of" recalls the opening lines of "Incantata," when Muldoon contemplates Powers "lying there in your long barrow/ colder and dumber than a fish by Francisco de Herrera,/ as I X-Actoed from a spud the Inca/ glyph for a mouth" (*Annals of Chile*, p. 13). The "potato-mouth" evolves as a motif in the poem and eventually becomes a conceit for both Powers and her art. At the beginning of stanza 13, he imagines her bending over the copper plate of "Emblements" and all but disappearing into "its tidal wave of army-worms"; at the end of the stanza, he explains that he wanted the "cumbersome device" of the potato mouth to enunciate "something" both of Powers' spirit and that of *Emblements* (p. 17). The

"X-Actoed" glyph carved in the poem's opening lines is thus an overdetermined image representing Powers, her art, and in stanza 23 Muldoon's own self-reproach. But like most pictographs, the glyph and the occulted language from which it originates also convey broader meanings.

Through his allusions to Beckett in this stanza, Muldoon reveals his confusion *as a reader*. Like Sam Bethicket's project of navigating Joyce's jungle of words in *Finnegans Wake* and perhaps even more like Belacqua Shuah's difficulty with *The Divine Comedy* in "Dante and the Lobster" from *More Pricks than Kicks*, Muldoon is "so bogged that he could move neither backward nor forward" in understanding Powers' disease, her response to it, and the potato-mouth that symbolizes these.[72] Fortunately for the overtaxed Belacqua, Dante's Beatrice emerges in the opening paragraph of "Dante and the Lobster" to show him "where he was at fault" because "she had it from God, therefore he could rely on its being accurate in every particular" (*More Pricks than Kicks*, p. 9). Muldoon is not so fortunate, and by referring to Lucky's monologue in *Waiting for Godot*, he clarifies that one possible reading resides in "the *quaquaqua*" of the carved mouth, an echo of the "personal God" to whom Lucky refers. In Lucky's speech, however, "qua" functions as a modifier, suggesting an entity that serves as a deity or acts in that capacity: "a personal God quaquaquaqua with a white beard quaquaquaqua outside time without extension" (*Waiting for Godot*, p. 45); in Muldoon's stanza, by contrast, "qua' becomes an object of study in its own right, and one of its connotations is the cancer which has hollowed out the fatal "breach" in Powers.

The breach in the potato, like the breach of cancer, represents an incursion, yet it is also a mouth capable of speech, and as such it may serve as the provenience of a language or signifying system much as the images on the cover of *The Annals of Chile* suggest worms on the move through a Famine-era potato (See Figure 2). Through this trope Muldoon shifts the focus from the "public works of Puncher and Wattman" and the Judeo-Christian God in Lucky's monologue, to the process or functionality of cancerous mutation. What or who, as the "quaquaqua" evolves later into a "quoiquoiquoi," is represented by the potato-mouth? Meditating upon this question, one he can never really answer, Muldoon resembles Beckett's characters stranded in the "caca" of an academy and the "popo" of a science, institutions with limited abilities to explain such immensely complex phenomena. Again, certainty in Muldoon is replaced by the necessity of reading carefully, and even then the results may prove inadequate, something like Lear's reading of Cordelia's lips while awaiting her life-confirming

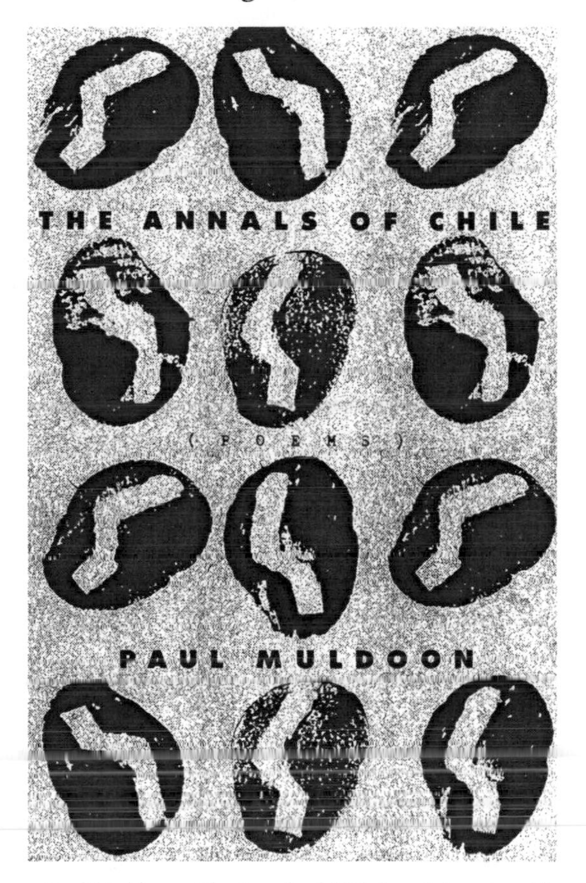

Figure 2. Cover, Paul Muldoon, *The Annals of Chile* (1994). Reprinted by permission of Farrar, Straus and Giroux

fream. At the end of the devolutions that follow this stanza, at the end of a long series of diminished realities prefaced by "That's all that's left," the act of reading remains.

And so does the act of writing or artistic production, as in the final lines of the poem when Powers, fresh from her work on *Emblements*, greets Muldoon fresh from his writing: "that you might reach out, arrah,/ and take in your ink-stained hands my own hands stained with ink" (*Annals of Chile*, p. 28). A final interpretive possibility fuses Muldoon's explanation of Beckett in *To Ireland, I* with the history of emblems and emblem books that *Emblements* seems to evoke. What exactly is an "emblement"? In some ways, it's like an "Incantata" – it's not a word the *OED* recognizes, and yet it is richly evocative nonetheless. Neither is an "emblement" an emblem in the historical sense, one common in the Italian and English Renaissances when emblems designed by Andrea Alciati, Geoffrey Whitney, Henry Peacham, and others possessed a clear tripartite structure: a motto, a picture representing it, and an epigraph unpacking the engraved image. In so doing – unlike Muldoon's reaction to Powers' art, her cancer, and her response to it – emblems deal in what might be termed interpretive certainties or redundancies by firmly delimiting meaning between the iconic and the linguistic, and then reiterating this meaning. In "Veritas Temporis Filia," for example – from Whitney's *A Choice of Emblemes* (Leyden, 1586) – an emblem so popular in sixteenth-century England that it was enacted as a living performance at Queen Elizabeth's coronation, old father Time leads his young daughter Truth from the cave where she was imprisoned by Envy, Slander, and Strife. This highly detailed iconography, supported by the epigraph – or is it the other way around? – invites us to read the scene and derive meaning from it consistent with the motto. In this emblem, Truth will eventually emerge, at which time she will be free of the distortions of Slander and Envy, and the moral at the conclusion of the epigraph reassures us of this inevitability: "Dispaire not then, though truthe be hidden ofte,/ Bycause at lengthe, shee shall bee sett alofte."[73]

By contrast, Powers' *Emblements* lacks both an explanatory epigraph and the closure of a motto. As the suffix "ment" implies, what we get instead in the lithograph is either always already a result (like establishment) or it is an act or process under way (impressment); thus, it is paradoxically both a finished product and a condition still in flux and underway. In short, it is both a material "thing" and a temporal moment; and in "Incantata" it is both a breach that has already been opened and a process of continual encroachment and genetic mistranslation. The cancer, like the blight in a famine potato, is already there – and is already always getting there. An emblement captures "something," as Clov might say, "taking its course" (*Endgame*, p. 13), as in Powers' lithograph and in her body too, as the cancerous parasite mutates into the afflicted host.

This is the most dramatic implication of the "ungetroundable": it is an epistemological claim of the inseparability of otherwise unrelated entities, often from two distinct historical moments or cultural registers, which like a host and its parasitic guest evolve into an irreducible singularity. A relative of the metaphysical conceit Muldoon so much admires, this "yoking together" lacks the violence of Dr. Johnson's poetic device. Rather, the ungetroundable, as Muldoon's poetry evinces, is a readerly fact. In "At the Sign of the Black Horse, September 1999" from *Moy Sand and Gravel*, for example, Muldoon's speaker, an obvious stand-in for Muldoon himself, surveys the damage caused by the flooding of a canal near his home in New Jersey. At the same time, he contemplates the Irish navvies who died well over a century earlier digging canals like this one in their new country; all the while, he gazes at his infant son Asher, wrapped snuggly in his pram in a shawl made in Ireland and a bonnet stitched by the boy's great-grandmother, Sophie. In Muldoon's imagination, the workers become Irish-Jews like Asher, who at one point becomes an image of a Holocaust victim. The navvies, "thousands of Irish schlemiels/who dug the canal," both keen and kvetch during their labors. Like Asher, they are Irish Jews; like Holocaust victims, they die, and the canal spills its banks with the detritus of their existence. History, in the form of muddy water laden with clay, hay, hair, shoes, and spectacles, races by on the opposite side of the street, overflowing the canal's banks and flooding the speaker's imagination, where two entities become one.

Similarly, in "The Loaf" from the same volume, Muldoon contemplates a hole in the wall of his old house excavated to accommodate a new dimmer switch. Looking inside the wall, he spies the residue of the two-hundred-year old home's original mortar, interlaced with the dried strands of horse hair once used to bind the material. It is hardly an accident that, in his essay on the "ungetroundable," the images Muldoon cites as impinging on his consciousness include a horse standing on a hill in New England, a hole in an eighteenth-century plaster wall, and an old Irishman who died digging the Delaware and Raritan Canal, which lies across the street from the old house. These images predominate his lecture and article; they reside also in the book of poetry he produced some time after the article was published. Like parasites, the horse's hair and gash in the plaster wall have become part of his imagination; like the parasite-host relationship, two images collapse into one: the horse and its hair into the wall, the navvy into the son. Muldoon could not get round these – and neither could he get round Beckett who, like the worm within the potato, resides within him.

NOTES

1. Atik, *How It Was*, p. 117. Perceptions about Beckett's physical well-being in the early 1980s differ from Atik's account, Derek Mahon's, for example, which is cited later. All quotations from this volume will be followed by page numbers in the text.
2. Knowlson, *Damned to Fame*, p. 593.
3. Paul Muldoon, "Getting Round: Notes Toward an *Ars Poetica*," *Essays in Criticism* 48 (April 1998) p. 108. All further quotations from this lecture will be followed by page citations in the text.

4. Samuel Beckett, *Dream of Fair to Middling Women*, p. 3.
5. In the opening chapter of *The Verbal Icon* (1954, rpt. New York: Noonday Press, 1958), Wimsatt and Beardsley discuss the "Intentional Fallacy": "We argued that the design or intention of the author is neither available nor desirable as a standard for judging the success of a work of literary art ..." (p. 3).
6. For a discussion of *Quoof* and the Troubles, see Clair Wills, *Reading Paul Muldoon* (Newcastle: Bloodaxe Books, 1998), particularly pp. 86–110.
7. Seamus Heaney, *North* (London: Faber and Faber, 1975), p. 38.
8. Paul Muldoon, *Poems 1968–1998* (New York: Farrar, Straus and Giroux, 2001), p. 130.
9. See Wills, *Reading Paul Muldoon*, pp. 94–97. For Wills, the religious setting of this atrocity is "not coincidental," as Muldoon aspires to a "critique of the link between authoritarian religion and civic intolerance" (p. 94). This "lesson for today" is transferred from inside the chapel to outside/public space as a warning to all who might contemplate a similar transgression against the Republican cause.
10. For a discussion of violence and meta-fiction in McNamee's novel, see Dermot McCarthy, "Belfast Babel: Postmodern Lingo in Eoin McNamee's *Resurrection Man*," *Irish University Review* 30 (Spring/Summer 2000), pp. 132–48. Taking his cue from the novel, McCarthy regards Victor Kelly as part media figure, a kind of "simulacrum of a past that has yet to be" (p. 148).
11. Wilson, *Ripley Bogle*, pp. 111–15.
12. McNamee, *Resurrection Man*, p. 51.
13. Wilson, *Eureka Street*, pp. 61, 15.
14. Derek Mahon, "A Tribute to Beckett on his Eightieth Birthday," rpt. in *Journalism: Selected Prose, 1970–1995*, ed. Terence Brown (Oldcastle: Gallery Books, 1996), p. 61. All quotations from this volume will be followed by page numbers in the text. See also *Samuel Beckett: The Last Modernist*, in which Anthony Cronin describes Mahon's meeting with Beckett in similar terms, underscoring Beckett's "general athleticism" at the time (pp. 573–74).
15. Mahon, "A Tribute to Beckett," p. 62.
16. For Casanova's reading of "generalized pejoration" in *Worstward Ho*, see *Samuel Beckett: Anatomy of a Literary Revolution*, pp. 18–26. "Venturing beyond" serves as a motif in Ernst Bloch's "Introduction" to *The Principle of Hope*, 3 vols, trans. Neville Plaice, Stephen Plaice, and Paul Knight (Cambridge, MA: MIT Press, 1995), vol. 1, pp. 1–18.
17. Terry Eagleton, "Introduction" to Pascale Casanova's *Samuel Beckett: Anatomy of a Literary Revolution*, p. 1.
18. Rabaté, "Unbreakable B's," p. 89.
19. Michael Longley, "Letters," in *Collected Poems* (London: Jonathan Cape, 2006), p. 56.
20. For a brief discussion of *King Lear* and Friel's unpublished radio play *This Hard House*, see Murray's introduction to *Brian Friel: Essays, Diaries, Interviews: 1964–1999*, pp. x–xi.

21. Derek Mahon, "North Wind: Portrush," in *Collected Poems* (Oldcastle: Gallery Books, 1999). All further quotations from this volume will be followed by page numbers in the text.
22. Eamonn Wall, *From the Sin-é Café to the Black Hills: Notes on the New Irish* (Madison: University of Wisconsin Press, 1999), pp. 120–21.
23. Paul Muldoon, *The Annals of Chile* (New York: The Noonday Press, 1994), p. 103. All further quotations from "Yarrow" and "Incantata" come from this volume and will be followed by page numbers in the text.
24. Badiou, "The Writing of the Generic," p. 10.
25. Dolar, *A Voice*, p. 59.
26. Colm Toíbín, *The Master* (New York: Scribner, 2004), p. 316.
27. Casanova, *The World Republic of Letters*, p. 319.
28. See, for example, John Kerrigan, "Paul Muldoon's Transits: Muddling Through after *Madoc*," in *Paul Muldoon: Critical Essays*, eds. Tim Kendall and Peter McDonald (Liverpool: Liverpool University Press, 2004), pp. 127–28. Kerrigan observes, "From the outset Mahon was sensitive to the Americanization of the planet ..." (p. 127).
29. Casanova, *The World Republic of Letters*, p. 339.
30. Gerald Dawe, "Heirs and Graces: The Influence and Example of Derek Mahon," in *The Poetry of Derek Mahon*, ed. Elmer Kennedy-Andrews (Gerrards Cross: Colin Smythe, 2002), p. 51.
31. Bruce Stewart, "'Solving Ambiguity': The Secular Mysticism of Derek Mahon," in Kennedy-Andrews (ed.), *The Poetry of Derek Mahon*, pp. 63, 62.
32. Stan Smith, "The Twilight of the Cities: Derek Mahon's Dark Cinema," in Kennedy-Andrews (ed.), *The Poetry of Derek Mahon*, p. 251.
33. Gibson, *Beckett and Badiou*, p. 125.
34. Badiou, "Being, Existence, Thought," p. 110.
35. Michael Allen, "Rhythm and Revision in Mahon's Poetic Development," in Kennedy-Andrews (ed.), *The Poetry of Derek Mahon*, p. 122.
36. Kiberd, *Irish Classics*, p. 182.
37. Derek Mahon, *The Yellow Book* (Winston-Salem, NC: Wake Forest University Press, 1998), p. 19. All further quotations from poems in *The Yellow Book* will be followed by page numbers in the text.
38. Derek Mahon, "The Yaddo Letter," in *The Hudson Letter* (Oldcastle: Gallery Books, 1995), p. 29. All further quotations from poems in *The Hudson Letter* will be followed by page numbers in the text.
39. Beckett's volume *Poems, 1930–1989* includes forty-three of these untitled verses, listed by their first lines. All quotations from this volume will be followed by page numbers in the text.
40. Knowlson, *Damned to Fame*, p. 568.
41. Hugh Haughton, "'The Importance of Elsewhere': Mahon and Translation," in Kennedy-Andrews (ed.), *The Poetry of Derek Mahon*, pp. 162, 154.
42. See, for example, Stewart "'Solving Ambiguity,'" who, in addition to making this point, argues that "Mahon seems to suggest that the very condition of

rootlessness that informs his poetry constitutes a *via negativa* by means of which the only valid metaphysics can be framed" (p. 62).

43. Mahon refers to this phrase with approbation in his review of Beckett's *Poems, 1930–1989*, and uses it as a title for the essay (see Mahon, *Journalism*, p. 56). In so doing, he slightly redacts Beckett's phrasing in his 1934 essay "Recent Irish Poetry," where he characterizes MacGreevy as an "existentialist in verse" (Beckett, *Disjecta*, p. 74).
44. The publishers refer to them as such twice in the volume *Poems, 1930–1989*, in both their Foreword (p. x) and in the Notes section at the end (p. 218).
45. Tom Murphy, *Plays: 2* (London: Faber and Faber, 1997), p. 157.
46. Knowlson, *Damned to Fame*, p. 569. Knowlson's comment about the critical neglect of these later poems might be extended to include the neglect of these poems by Beckett's biographers as well, as Knowlson is the only one who has much to say about them.
47. Wills, *Reading Paul Muldoon*, p. 182.
48. Gregory Machacek, "Allusion," *PMLA* 122 (March 2007) p. 534.
49. Rory Brennan, "Contemporary Irish Poetry: An Overview," in *Poetry in Contemporary Irish Literature*, ed. Michael Kenneally (Gerrards Cross: Colin Smythe, 1995), pp. 12–13.
50. Helen Vendler, "Anglo-Celtic Attitudes," *The New York Review of Books*, November 6, 1997, pp. 58, 59.
51. Helen Vendler, "Fanciness and Fatality," *The New Republic*, November 9, 2006, p. 26.
52. William Pratt, "World Literature in Review: English – Review of *The Annals of Chile*," *World Literature Today* 69 (Spring 1995), p. 365.
53. Lawrence Norfolk, "The Abundant Braes of Yarrow," *TLS*, October 7, 1994: p. 32.
54. Richard Tillinghast, "Poets are Born, Then Made," *New York Times Book Review* 144 (December 11, 1994), p. 25.
55. Seamus Heaney, "Paul Muldoon's *The Annals of Chile*," 1994, rpt. in *Finders Keepers: Selected Prose, 1971–2001* (London: Faber and Faber, 2002), p. 397.
56. John Redmond makes this point in "Indicting the Exquisite: Paul Muldoon's *The Annals of Chile*," *Thumbscrew* 1 (Winter 1994–95) p. 81.
57. Here Machacek is quoting from Jonathan Culler and invoking a notion of Kristevan intertextuality. See Machacek, "Allusion," pp. 523–25.
58. Vendler, "Anglo-Celtic Attitudes," p. 58.
59. See Machacek, "Allusion," pp. 526–30.
60. Paul Muldoon, *The End of the Poem* (New York, Farrar, Straus and Giroux, 2006), pp. 114, 144, 392. All further quotations from this volume will be followed in the text by page numbers.
61. Redmond, "Muldoon and Pragmatism," in Kendall and McDonald (eds.), *Paul Muldoon*, p. 98.
62. Redmond, "Muldoon and Pragmatism," pp. 100–01.
63. For a discussion of Joyce's fascination with etymology that bears on Muldoon's similar interest, see Stephen Whittaker, "Joyce and Skeat," *James Joyce Quarterly* 24 (Winter 1987): 177–92.

64. Michel Serres, *The Parasite*, pp. 8, 14.
65. See Muldoon, *To Ireland, I*, pp. 12–18. Here, as in *The End of the Poem*, Muldoon's use of the *Oxford English Dictionary* and other sources of etymology is much in evidence.
66. See Tim Kendall, *Paul Muldoon* (Bridgend, Wales: Seren, 1996), pp. 217–19.
67. James Joyce, *Finnegans Wake* (New York: Viking Press, 1939), p. 112, lines 3–6.
68. Atherton, *The Books at the Wake*, p. 16.
69. Paul Muldoon, *Horse Latitudes* (New York: Farrar, Straus and Giroux, 2006), p. 104. Further quotations from this poem will be followed by page numbers in the text.
70. Paul Muldoon, *The Prince of the Quotidian* (Oldcastle: Gallery Books, 1994), p. 24.
71. Paul Muldoon, *Moy Sand and Gravel* (New York: Farrar, Straus and Giroux, 2002), p. 36. Quotations from this collection will be followed by page numbers in the text.
72. Samuel Beckett, *More Pricks Than Kicks* (New York: Grove Press, 1972), p. 9.
73. Geoffrey Whitney, *A Choice of Emblemes* (Leyden, 1586), p. 4.

CHAPTER 5

Specters of Beckett: Marina Carr and the "other" Sam

> That's a good story. That's something-esque. What kind of "-esque" is it? I can't remember. I don't really go in for that "-esque" sort of stuff anyway, but there's nothing wrong with that story. Is there?
>
> –Katurian in Martin McDonagh, *The Pillowman* (2003)

> Indeed, from Friel's *Faith Healer*, through the long opening section of *Observe the Sons of Ulster*, to the retrospective narrators in *Dancing at Lughnasa* and *The Mai*, the Irish theatre in the closing decades of the twentieth century has been increasingly filled with monologues delivered to spectres of the past.
>
> –Christopher Morash, *A History of Irish Theatre, 1601–2000* (2002)

> ["First suggestion: haunting is historical, to be sure, but it is not *dated*, it is never docilely given a date in the chain of presents, day after day, according to the instituted order of a calendar. Untimely, it does not come to, it does not happen to, it does not befall, one day, Europe, as if the latter, at a certain moment of its history, had begun to suffer from a certain evil, to let itself be *inhabited* in its inside, that is, haunted by a foreign guest."]
>
> –Jacques Derrida, *Specters of Marx* (1994)

The "-esque" that Martin McDonagh's Katurian struggles to identify while being interrogated in *The Pillowman* is doubtless the "Kafkaesque," as one of his captors has just related a story in which a man, much like Joseph K in *The Trial*, is murdered for committing a crime of which he is profoundly ignorant.[1] The trajectory of this macabre tale – a prisoner's alleged guilt for committing a crime, his frustrated attempts to uncover its specificity, his execution – is too similar to that of *The Trial* to be ignored. The narrative of Katurian's story, "The Three Gibbet Crossroads," mirrors the progress of his own imprisonment, as he travels a similar path from accusation and confusion to death. Without too great a stretch of the critical imagination, then, one could assert that this brief recitation intimates the *influence* of

Kafka on McDonagh's play, one of several intertextual leads we might investigate and whose import we might consider.

In another metaphorical register, one to which Paul Muldoon gestures throughout *The End of the Poem*, *The Pillowman* might be described as "ghosted" by Kafka. For Muldoon, as I have mentioned, Emily Dickinson's "I tried to think a lonelier Thing" is "ghosted" by Sir John Franklin's ill-fated search for a northwest passage from England to North America; Stevie Smith's "I Remember" is "ghosted" by William Wordsworth's sense of recollection in the *Lyrical Ballads*; and so on.[2] These ghosts, like the ones of former club members who assemble in Ian Fleming's *Moonraker* (1955) to enjoy James Bond's fleecing of Hugo Drax at the bridge table, stay for a moment and then disappear into the night. As promiscuous as a one-night stand, ghosts seldom loiter or just "hang around"; rather, like the ghost of Joseph Swane in Marina Carr's *By the Bog of Cats* … (1998), they drop by to "say hello" before gently "stravagin' in the shadows."[3] By contrast, his sister Hester Swane's threat to return with her dead daughter Josie and begin a "ghostin'" of her former lover Carthage Kilbride, or the determinative voice of the dead Gabriel Scully in *Portia Coughlan* (1996), like Jacques Derrida's depiction of specters in *Specters of Marx*, scarcely connote a casual or occasional visitation. It is this latter variety of spirit, it seems to me, absent the sense of vindictiveness, that Tony Roche imagined when asserting that Beckett is the "presiding genius of contemporary Irish drama," its "ghostly founding father."[4]

Derrida's specters, however, bear more resemblance to the parasites Michel Serres theorizes than to Muldoon's ghosts, for like parasites, they are "foreign guests" who *inhabit*, not merely drop in for a chat, and – equally important – they are "untimely."[5] On this point, Derrida notes that "one can never distinguish between the future-to-come and the coming back of a specter," emphasizing that, like, say, the inevitable outbreaks of a herpes virus, "[a]t bottom, the specter is the future, it is *always* to come [my emphasis]."[6] This specter, of course, possesses other attributes less pertinent to our discussion. Borrowing from *Hamlet*, Derrida formulates the "visor effect," the specter's ability to lock us in its gaze and legislate action without being seen itself. In another context, I have likened this ability to that of the twenty-first century terrorist who lurks nearby, analyzing our vulnerabilities and poised to exploit them without warning.[7] In our present structure of feeling, one formed in part by 9/11 and Katrina, this specter, like a parasite, inhabits us, working to efface once secure boundaries of selfhood and identity. More to the point, Derrida asserts that spectral haunting "belongs to the structure of every hegemony."[8] It dominates in ways that a mere ghost never could (although occasionally Derrida's own terminology is itself too promiscuous, eliding meaningful distinctions between ghosts and specters).[9] This essay traces such a hegemony on the contemporary stage.

A "traditional scholar," Derrida remarks, "does not believe in ghosts" in large part because of his or her commitment to a "sharp distinction between the real and the unreal."[10] But what is unreal about "ghosting" or influence, about the pressure of the past on the present and, as the latter parts of this chapter and the following one underscore, the potentially distorting inverse pressure of the present on the past? Moreover, insofar as the incredulity of traditional scholars might be assessed, it is almost axiomatic that most don't trust the veracity of authors any more than they believe in ghosts. In *The Art of Literary Research* (1963), a primer widely assigned throughout the 1960s and 70s in postgraduate courses, Richard D. Altick promoted skepticism as a cardinal virtue of the literary critical enterprise, particularly when weighing authors' own commentary about their work: "Valuable though authors' autobiographical narratives may be, we can never accept them at their face value." Why? Because they invariably contain "just about every conceivable kind of memorial lapse and embellishment"; for this reason, although the best scholars may in other settings be generous and trusting to a fault, in the practice of their craft they must "cultivate a low opinion of the human capacity for truth."[11]

In truth, I am less interested in exposing purposeful lying or memorial embellishment than with troubling claims about a *ghostly* Beckett's effect on Marina Carr that have calcified into a critical consensus about the arc of her *oeuvre*. For, as I hope to show, one might easily dodge a ghost, entertain one at the Club with the deft play of a card, or even feel sorry for one, as John Banville's narrator does in *Ghosts* (1993):

> I seemed hardly to be here at all. This is how I imagine ghosts existing, poor, pale, wraiths pegged out to shiver in the wind of the world like so much insubstantial laundry, yearning towards us, the heedless ones, as we walk blithely through them.[12]

But there is no "getting round" or walking "blithely through" a specter. A critical mapping of Carr's evolution as a playwright might therefore be redrawn by a revised understanding of the Beckettian qualities of her writing. In this way, the first section of this chapter extends the premise of my readings of Paul Muldoon's *Annals of Chile* and Derek Mahon's poetry: namely, that for Carr, claims to the contrary notwithstanding, Beckett was – and *is* – "ungetroundable." One difference, however, is that while Beckett insinuated himself almost parasitically into Muldoon's response to Mary Farl Powers' cancer, much as *King Lear* did in Beckett's later prose, such contaminations scarcely affect all of his writing. My claim about Carr, conversely, contrary both to what she has said about the matter and how critics chart the trajectory of her canon, is that certain Beckettian elements prise their ways into virtually all of her work, from *Low in the Dark* (1989) to the more recent *Woman and Scarecrow* (2006). In an impressive corpus of plays in which haunting is a recurring motif, Beckett and the Beckettian are perhaps the most formidable specters of all. A similar thesis might be developed about Banville, who will be pressed into service on occasion in the discussion that follows. Not to make too fine a point of this, my contention is that to claim Beckett as a specter is not only to identify a past haunting, but also to anticipate his untimely eruption in Carr's most recent and future work.

Carr's plays, however, are not alone on the twenty-first century stage in revealing the effects of this spectrality – hence, Beckett's contemporaneity – and to demonstrate this, I want also to consider Sam Shepard's *Kicking a Dead Horse*, which was commissioned by and had its premiere at the Abbey Theatre in the spring of 2007. Clearly, this "other Sam" does not qualify as an Irish writer; thus, any treatment of his work might seem misplaced in a book whose title specifically delimits recent Irish writing as its object of study. Yet theatre historians would be hard pressed to find another non-Irish writer about whom the following sentiment, which appears on the cover of the Faber edition of the play, could apply: "*Kicking a Dead Horse* continues the Abbey's exploration of Shepard's work and the theatre's commitment to Shepard as one of the most important playwrights of a generation." In addition to conferring a sort of honorary Irishness upon Shepard, the Abbey thus imputes an urgency to his work for an Irish theatregoer and, in addition to producing this play, has revived *True West* in 2006 and *Fool For Love* in 2008. What terrain in Shepard's works is the Abbey keen to explore, and why in the twenty-first century would this geography be of particular interest to its audience? More to the point, how does any of this pertain to Beckett? The present chapter, then, attempts to do "double duty" as it were, outlining on the one hand the continued habitation of Carr by a Beckettian specter and, on the other, using *Kicking a Dead Horse* to assess ways in which the present reshapes the Beckettian into a rubric helpful in navigating the perilous straits of a post-9/11 world. The interpretive stakes of these readings, I believe, surpass corrections of critical studies of Carr and Shepard by evincing the determinative power of both a literary hauntology and a present-day traumatic moment, both of which have the capacity to shape our understanding of the Beckettian.

AT THE ABATTOIR: MARINA CARR'S TRAVELING GHOSTS, BECKETT'S TWO GODS

The ghosts I think of travel. I wouldn't think of the bog and wonder about ghosts.[13] (Marina Carr, "Interview" in *Reading the Future* [2000])

She was lovely … lovely indeed, made with a delicacy of which I would not have thought that bungler in the sky was capable.[14]

(John Banville, *Nightspawn* [1971])

Marina Carr admits her predilections for, even obsessions with, both ghosts and death, although she confides that, while her best friend in school had once been frightened by a banshee, she has never actually seen one herself. "On stage," Carr comments in regard to the latter, "there is nothing more beautiful than looking at the arc of a life and the completion of that life. … The tragedy of man is perhaps the only significant thing about him."[15] As Brian Friel's *Volunteers*, *The Freedom of the City*, and *Faith Healer*, among others, demonstrate, the dead seem to ramble on endlessly in contemporary Irish drama, often in a manner that replicates the "strange" act of Malone in *Malone Dies* of narrating an "account" of his own passing.[16] In bardic poetry such texts constituted a "cult of last words" and those critics who detect in *Woman and Scarecrow* telltale signs of the Beckettian are, in effect, claiming it as a present-day member of this cult. Indeed, ghosts and death are linked not only in Irish mythology, but also throughout Carr's *oeuvre*, for not only do the ghosts I have already mentioned appear in her plays but, given the narrative structures of *The Mai* and *Portia Coughlan*, after their respective deaths Carr's protagonists return to the stage, thereby adding an additional element of haunting to these plays.

Contrary to the implication of this contextualization – and to the fact, as Roche notes in the conclusion of *Contemporary Irish Drama*, that Carr enrolled at University College Dublin in 1988 intending to write an M. A. thesis on Beckett[17] – she insists that the principal influences on her writing are *not* Irish, and in a recent interview reiterated this position: "I certainly don't see myself in a direct line from all the great Irish playwrights of the past. I have read O'Casey, Beckett, and Synge, and would admire certain aspects of their work, but I'm not hugely influenced by them" (*Reading the Future*, p. 44). In this conversation, and in another with Melissa Sihra in 2001, she professes her admiration of the American theatre, of Eugene O'Neill's reverence for the "Greek feeling of tragedy" and of Tennessee Williams' poetic drama (*Theatre Talk*, p. 56), describing *The Glass Menagerie* and *A Streetcar Named Desire* as "hard to beat" as she acknowledges Williams' "huge" effect on her (*Reading the Future*, p. 56). On the levels of dramatic form and thematic preoccupation, and regardless of Altick's admonitions concerning authorial honesty, Carr ought to be trusted on this point; indeed, *The Mai*'s "gauzy realism" constitutes a veritable homage to Williams' *Glass Menagerie* and the fragile beauty of the memory play.[18] Similarly, the Greek inspirations of her "midlands plays," especially in their treatments of intrafamilial violence and sexuality reminiscent of the tragedies of Medea, Iphigenia, and Oedipus, recall O'Neill's monumental experiments *Strange Interlude* (1928) and *Mourning Becomes Electra* (1931). Carr's creation of the twins Portia Coughlan and her brother Gabriel, to draw the analogy even closer, parallels O'Neill's similar deployment of uncanny doubles in such plays as *Days Without End* (1932) and, most strikingly, *Mourning Becomes Electra.* Not so interested as O'Neill in weaving references to Freud into the fabric of the dramatic action, or in relating psychical splitting to specific historical traumas like the American Civil War (*Mourning Becomes Electra*) or World War I (*Strange Interlude*), Carr nonetheless reveals the influence of the Greek and American precursors she so readily acknowledges.[19]

Most critics accept these premises with barely a second thought, which in turn has led to a historicizing of Carr's career that, albeit useful, has also produced a restricted purchase of the Beckettian. A cheekier, more Beckettian formulation might argue that understanding of Carr's *oeuvre* has been "obnubilated" by the cloudy thesis that her earliest plays, particularly *Low in the Dark*, reveal a profound debt to Beckett; her middle plays from *The Mai* through *Ariel* form a distinctly different "phase"; and *Woman and Scarecrow* marks a return to Beckett. Paula Murphy, for example, regards Carr's early plays (*Ullaloo, Low in the Dark*) as exhibiting a "distinctly Beckettian style of writing"; *The Mai* marks "the beginning of a new phase" of "midlands plays"; and *Woman and Scarecrow* embodies a "move away from the thematic direction of the midlands plays and a further distancing from their realist dimensions."[20] Summarizing critical responses to the Royal Court's production of the play, Lyn Gardner offered a predictable reading of this "move" away from realism: *Woman and Scarecrow* is a "Beckett-like deathbed drama." While one reviewer found it depressing and another complained of its "stagnant" dramatic action, Gardner admired Carr's "robust humor" that "ensures the evening never becomes mawkish."[21] Writing for the *Times*, Sam Marlowe agreed, applauding Carr's "bittersweet" black comedy and happily imbibing the intoxicating brew of ingredients in her dramatic "cauldron": Greek mythology, Gothic romance, Shakespeare, and a pronounced "existential" leaning.[22] This "leaning," needless to say, was regarded as essentially Beckettian. A woman speaking in her last hours (as she prepares to die), a static narrative relieved only by momentary incidents, the operation of a bleak humor that works against sentimentality, allusions to Shakespeare (in this case, to *Hamlet*) – these elements of *Woman and Scarecrow* coincide with common understandings of the Beckettian. But, then again, such conventions obtain in most of Carr's plays and, from one perspective, rather oddly, the *least* Beckettian of these might very well be *Low in the Dark*.

This claim is offered both seriously and perversely, as a summary of the textual evidence might demonstrate, beginning with the echoes of Beckettian naming in *Low in the Dark*. The repetition of "M" in Beckett's work is superseded by "B" in Carr's play, as Murphy, Molloy, and Malone are supplanted by Bender and Binder, Baxter and Bone. The rhythm of the latter pair's names recalls that of Friel's Keeney and Pyne, and of comic pairs from the music hall and vaudeville stages. Sarahjane Scaife, who played Binder in the play's October, 1989 premiere, makes this very point when recalling the production: "Baxter and Bone work in tandem as characters, their theatrical power comes from their 'Laurel and Hardy meets [sic] Beckett' exchanges."[23] More relevant to the play's feminist politics, the names "Bend-Her" and "Bind-Her" connote the warping of women's lives under patriarchy, conditions exacerbated by women's constant pregnancy under the hegemony of the Catholic Church and its inflexible stance on reproduction (in this sense, the feminist critique of *Low in the Dark* resembles that of Italian comedian Dario Fo in such farces as *Can't Pay? Won't Pay!* (1974) particularly in an exchange between Bender and Binder about an imaginary child named "the Pope").[24] It is difficult not to discern echoes of such Beckettian tandems as Hamm and Clov, Winnie and Willie – "When-He" extricates her from the mound of earth, or "Will-He" ever do so in *Happy Days* – in the names of Carr's characters. And, to return to the prominence of "B" in Beckett's work, Tyrus Miller discusses the appearances of "Bim" and "Bom" in *Murphy*, noting that these names surface not only in *What Where*, but also in early drafts of *Waiting for Godot*, where Didi and Gogo were named Bim and Bom after two Russian clowns who "captured [Beckett's] imagination."[25] The names also surface in Belacqua's thoughts in "Yellow" from *More Pricks than Kicks* when he resolves to "arm his mind with laughter" in the face of a potentially frightening surgery (p. 164). Beckettian clowning is thus central to *Low in the Dark*, as Carr's naming implies.

Several comic devices in *Low in the Dark* also recall the verbal and physical antics of *Waiting for Godot* and *Endgame*. The play begins, for example, on a note of ironic understatement which, adapting Stanley Cavell's exegesis of comic strategies in *Endgame*,[26] involves the hidden literality or reality of some Beckettian exchanges:

BINDER: You look old today!
BENDER (*nonplussed*): I'll be older tomorrow. (*Plays 1*, p. 7)

Part of the humor of this dialogue originates in our recognition of the process of "leastening" underlying it: life follows a trajectory of diminution, of loss associated with aging. We all know this, but seldom in everyday conversations are we moved to ponder this reality; instead, in response to the deprecation that one appears older than usual, we expect and generally receive explanation or rationalization – "I didn't sleep well last night" or "I've been feeling ill recently." Carr, much like Beckett, denies us these familiar excuses in ways that are not so much unsettling as they are humorous. So, in one of Bender and Binder's many routines based on a narrative of romantic love, the reality of "leastening" intrudes:

BENDER: You live in a beautiful place.
BINDER: That's true … it's beautiful … yes, it is.
BENDER: Will we talk about us?
BINDER: What about us? We're alive, we're together, we're rotting.
(*Plays 1*, p. 37)

Again, our shared experiences of lovers' discourse – the conventions of which Bender demands Binder follow whenever she "breaks the rules" or veers from the expected narrative – seldom include this inevitability. Yet when Binder introduces the topic of mortality, they go on as if it were as inherent to the conventions of romantic narratives as "I love you," which Binder mouths with passion a few moments later. In other words – following Cavell – Carr, like Beckett, undoes clichés, and the result is often comic, if also sharply ironic.

A similar kind of "defeat of the implications of ordinary" language occurs later in this exchange between Baxter and Bone:

BONE: You're very aggressive.
BAXTER: I am not.
BONE: You are.
BAXTER: (*moves toward him, shouts*) I am not! (*Plays 1*, p. 43)

This comic undercutting echoes a similar exchange in *Endgame* between Hamm and Clov:

HAMM (*shocked*): I haven't made you suffer too much?
CLOV: Yes!
HAMM (*relieved*): Ah you gave me a fright!
(*Pause. Coldly.*) Forgive me
(*Pause. Louder.*) I said, forgive me. (*Endgame*, p. 7)

One can no more command another's forgiveness than the other can successfully refute the allegation of aggressiveness with shouting and menacing movement. But this exchange, too, produces a wry humor, as the stage picture undercuts the dialogue by working against it to invert its presumed meaning. In such a setting, dialogue itself grows circular or nonprogressive: while something indeed may be "taking its course," it has little to do with language and meaningful exchange. Rather, as in *Low in the Dark*, language provides the material for well-rehearsed stories and routines, old jokes and monologues; indeed, Curtains' story of a man and woman, with which the play begins and ends, encompasses all the stories and routines of the play in a larger meta-narrative that goes nowhere.

Carr thus appropriates a series of familiar comic devices from the Beckettian theatre, the most conspicuous of which include the knocking off of hats and the strategy of "capping the gag" in a series of one-line comedic thrusts and parries. The most famous of these, of course, leads to a meta-textual punchline in *Waiting for Godot* after Didi and Gogo decide that verbally abusing each other might prove entertaining:

VLADIMIR: Moron!
ESTRAGON: Vermin!
VLADIMIR: Abortion!
ESTRAGON: Morpion
VLADIMIR: Sewer-rat!
ESTRAGON: Curate!
VLADIMIR: Cretin!
ESTRAGON: (*with finality*) Crritic! (*Waiting for Godot*, p. 85)

Knowing that he has just been defeated, linguistically trumped – after all, Gogo has referenced the *lowest* rung of living creatures, critics, who reside far below the levels of rats and cretins – all Didi can mutter is "Oh." Similarly, after Curtains announces that she has purchased a new slip, Bender and Binder race through a series of questions:

BENDER: What colour?
BINDER: What size?
BENDER: Silk?
BINDER: Cotton?
BENDER: How much?
BINDER: Where?
BENDER: When?
BINDER: How?
BENDER: Why? (*Plays 1*, p. 31)

Exhausted, Curtains yells "Stop!" to conclude what evolves into a familiar pattern of banter in the play, though the conclusion of this rapid-fire series fails to rival the intellectual cut – the comically brilliant irony – of "Crritic" in *Waiting for Godot*.

This is not to say that all comic moments in *Low in the Dark* originate in the Beckettian. As Scaife recalls, for Baxter's cross-dressing the 1989 production exploited the audience's familiarity with Madonna – the "Material Girl" Madonna, that is, not the Mother of God – by costuming him in the grotesque cone-shaped brassière she made fashionable (or notorious). The largely comic whacking of Curtains with a carpet beater, the bevy of dolls to be breast-fed, the cross-dressing – such instances create humor in novel, often silly, ways. Scaife seems well justified in connecting this comic "energy" *not* so much with the Beckettian stage, but with the New York scene and the Off-Off-Broadway theatre both she and Carr experienced in the 1980s. Scaife mentions La Mama E.T.C. (Experimental Theatre Company) where several of Shepard's plays opened in the later 1960s and early 70s, along with those of Megan Terry, Lanford Wilson, Lee Breuer, Jean-Claude van Itallie and, in 1971, Beckett, when *Play* and *Come and Go* were produced with Breuer's *The Red Horse Animation*. Indeed, *Low in the Dark* would have fit neatly in a La Mama repertory with Shepard's *The Unseen Hand* (1969) or *Shaved Splits* (1970), with Charles Ludlam's early efforts from his "Theatre of the Ridiculous," and many others in this high-octane revolution in the American theatre.

At the same time, several lines in *Low in the Dark* confirm that, much like the arid landscapes of *Endgame* and *Happy Days*, the character's antic dispositions and repetitions of skits occur *within* the starkly mortal realities Beckett delineates. Curtains' story, that closes Act One, provides one of the more striking examples of this and echoes, an admittedly imprecise term, the conclusion of *The Unnamable*, quoted below:

> ... it will be the silence where I am, I don't know, I'll never know, in the silence, you don't know, you must go on, I can't go on, I'll go on.
>
> (*Three Novels*, p. 414)

Curtains' version foregrounds the couple's similar predicament:

> They agreed to be silent. They were ashamed, for the man and woman had become like two people anywhere, walking low in the dark through a dead universe. There seemed no reason to go on. There seemed no reason to stop. (p. 59)

In Act Two, Bender and Binder impersonate Italian lovers, at one moment dancing to a "romantic love song." As she holds Bender, Binder, playing the "greatest lover in the world," rhapsodizes about their lives together but vows "not to stop to think, never, because, *mi amore*, when you stop to think, then is *triste, molto triste*, because the universe, she is an incurable wound, blistering on the belly of the void, she is one vast unbearable grief" (p. 67). In these formulations, Beckett's and Carr's, movement and silence serve as antidotes to painful reflection: if one stops, one thinks; if one thinks or talks, she is led to the wound. Better to keep going in silence or, perhaps, to insist "Nohow on" when one arrives at a final pinhole in the "dimmost dim."

A familiar Beckettian metaphor surfaces later in *Low in the Dark* to communicate the inevitabilities of Being. Battling over the loss of an imaginary suitor, Binder deploys the term "menopause" as a weapon against Bender: "Menopause, hot flush, empty womb." Bender asks her mother to stop, and even begins to hit her, but Binder is unrelenting. Her retort that "The womb will be empty and the tomb will be full!" is a purposeful conflation of birth and death that recalls, among others, the opening line and motif of *A Piece of Monologue* – "Birth was the death of him" (*Shorter Plays*, p. 265) – and the metaphor of the gravedigger with forceps in *Waiting for Godot*:

> Astride of a grave and a difficult birth. Down in the hole, lingeringly, the grave-digger puts on the forceps. (*Waiting for Godot*, p. 104)

Curtains finally intervenes, yelling "Stop it!" and forcing the disputants off the stage. Both exit, only to be supplanted on stage by Baxter and Bone, the latter of whom appears "hugely pregnant" (*Plays 1*, p. 78) and is told that s/he needs to keep up on her exercises. The pair's arrival for calisthenics provides a low comic counterpoise to the Beckettian conflation of birth with the inevitability of death and recalls the exercising schtick of O'Casey's knockabouts in *The End of the Beginning* and Beckett's enjoyment of the comic disintegration it effected. This high-energy blend of ontology and knockabout humor characterizes Carr's Beckettian lean in *Low in the Dark*.

Yet, paradoxically, this early play – its broad humor notwithstanding – seems almost more despairing than the Beckett canon from which Carr appropriates so much. For regardless of its amusing skits and cross-dressing antics, *Low in the Dark* provides little sense of resistance or evental potentiality. Here, Badiou's understanding of the last lines of *Worstward Ho*, in which Beckett's narrator *suddenly* recognizes change and with it possibility, once again seems significant: "Enough. Sudden enough. Sudden all far. No move and sudden all far. At least" (*Nohow On*, p. 116). For Badiou, the subject's "dis-closure, whereby it incurs the risk of the Other … does so under the sign of the hope opened up by ontological alterity" ("Writing of the Generic," p. 22). The event, a complex and highly scrutinized foundation of Badiou's politics, is "of the order of an encounter that is amorous (love at first sight), political (revolution), or scientific (the eureka)." It "suspends the situational routine" and amounts to a "propitious ripeness of the opportune moment."[27] As important, as Daniel Bensaïd emphasizes, the event is highly aleatory and "characterized by the unpredictability of what might just as well not have occurred."[28] The sudden, unanticipated perceptual shift at the end of *Worstward Ho* and the surprising appearance of the boy outside Hamm's shelter in *Endgame* might qualify as events; similarly, the "slow fade up of a faint form. Out of the dark," the "empty dark," in *A Piece of Monologue* intimates possibility, for after this appearance the dark is no longer empty. Of course, if Godot were ever to arrive, as Badiou mused recently, this would surely qualify as the most significant event of all.[29] By contrast, Carr's characters – including the man and woman in Curtains' story – are afforded no such potentiality; the play's action produces no moments rife with possibility or amelioration. Instead, the dramatic world of *Low in the Dark*, as Clov remarks in *Endgame*, is "corpsed." Nothing to celebrate, the continual births of Bender's and Binder's infants add only more hungry mouths to the daily routine, just as the recurring story of the man and woman, while seeming to promise subjective dis-closure and the potential of movement, leads nowhere.

"Corpsed," however, is not necessarily a past participle of "corpsing," a term that gathers ontological traction in Banville's *Ghosts*. In fact, the participle injects two distinctly different meanings into Banville's narrative. Pondering his sense of estrangement from other people, his incompetence in forming meaningful relationships, Banville's protagonist proffers the analogy of an actor ruining a scene on stage: "I stumble among my fellow players, stammering out my implausible lines and corpsing at all the big moments" (*Ghosts*, p. 198). Earlier in the novel, however, an exhausted young woman employs this unusual term very differently:

> Corpsing: that was the word. She imagined being in bed here, in an anonymous little room up at the very top of the house, just lying in peace ... To be there, to be inconsequential; to forget herself, even for a little while; to stop, to be still; to be at peace. (*Ghosts*, p. 57)

Stopping and silence for Banville's young woman portend subjective inconsequentiality, a kind of momentary non-Being, whereas for Carr's characters such a respite can bring only further wounding. Thus, the juxtaposition of life and procreation to the inevitabilities of death and the decline of the body – in addition to Carr's widely comic strategies in *Low in the Dark* – might be regarded as Beckettian. But absent an event, a rupture or cut in the fabric of daily life leading to new possibility, *Low in the Dark* achieves a riantic spaciousness of limited proportion.

Insofar as Carr parodies and comically undercuts this ontology in *Low in the Dark* in ways that her later plays, for the most part, do not, her "midlands phase" *does* mark a significant change in her work. At the same time, however, the specter of Beckett never quite disappears from these plays, which manifest this hauntology in several distinct ways. If Beckett, for example, is accurately characterized by Muldoon as the "Lord of Liminality," then perhaps Carr might be similarly described. After all, Portia Coughlan is drawn to a third space near the Belmont River between her husband Raphael – in all his concreteness and gross materialism – and her dead brother, Gabriel, who died in the river; Scarecrow in *Woman and Scarecrow* quite literally inhabits a middle ground betwixt and between life and death, at one point entering a wardrobe to negotiate on Woman's behalf with the monster of death who resides there. An equally compelling instance of this – as described by Bernadette Bourke – was the Abbey's 1998 production of *By the Bog of Cats* .... The play "is set in a Beckettian no-man's-land" between the Kilbride house and Hester's caravan, between the stasis of community and mobility of the tinker.[30] This might also be defined as a "no-woman's-land" as well. As Anna McMullan aptly observes, Carr's women are "out of place in the traditional domestic positions of wife and mother, in the interior spaces of the kitchen or living room." As a result, characters like the Mai and Portia are "linked to rivers, lakes or bogs, which figure a more fluid, untamed space."[31]

There is little denying the gendered inscription of space in Carr, and McMullan is right to argue that space in *On Raftery's Hill* operates differently than it does in other plays, precisely because in it "the confines of the house reassert themselves with a vengeance. All resistance is crushed, all escape blocked."[32] Most obviously, Dinah Raftery has succumbed to the domestic-incestuous roles of daughter and wife to her father; and Sorrel, likened metaphorically to a rabbit being gutted for dinner, is raped by her father on the dinner table in a shocking assault which closes the play's opening act. McMullan's feminist decoding of domestic space, therefore, and her underscoring of the house's imprisonment of Red Raftery's daughters are persuasive. At the same time, a more Beckettian reading of space in *On Raftery's Hill* also presents itself, one that identifies the dramatic space in Carr's middle plays as not only liminal and inflected by gender, but also as always already corpsed and ontologized in familiar ways, particularly insofar as both Beckett and Carr frequently illuminate the boundaries between the human and the animal, and the human and the divine.

Such a reading returns us to the abattoirs that serve both as a site of containment and a motif in Beckett's "trilogy," and as places of employment for Shamie in Bernard MacLaverty's *Cal* and, not surprisingly, for Katurian in McDonagh's *The Pillowman*.[33] The most overt references to this discourse in Beckett's "trilogy" concern the toothless Big Lambert in *Malone Dies*, "highly thought of as a bleeder and disjointer" of pigs (*Three Novels*, p. 199), but Lambert's professional reputation amounts only to the most sensational adversion to human-animal relationships in these novels, as animals and their corpses literally cover their landscapes. Reflecting on his "state of decay," for example, Worm in *The Unnamable* considers that he might have left his gangrenous leg "somewhere off the coast of Java and its jungles red with rafflesia stinking of carrion" (*Three Novels*, p. 317); and he remarks later that few people ever visit his neighborhood "for fear of being overcome at the sight of the cattle, fat and fresh from their pastures, trooping towards the humane killer" (p. 327). In fact the slaughterhouse looms so near to the everyday, that Moran in *Molloy* remarks, "Coming from church [Jacques] would appear on my right, on my left if he came from the slaughter-house" (*Three Novels*, p. 97), connecting the abattoir with God. (In this capacity, Knott in *Watt* walks by a stream in Watt's garden and feeds young rats to their eager mothers and fathers, conflating the divine and the grotesque by remarking, "It was on these occasions … that we came nearest to God" [p. 156]). Most strikingly, even in *Lycidas*-like "new" pastures, in *Molloy* "slaughter-houses are not confined to towns, no, they are everywhere, the country is full of them, every butcher has his slaughter-house and the right to slaughter, according to his lights" (*Three Novels*, p. 29).

At least two issues inhere in this motif: one, the obvious imbrication of death with life; and, two, the "right" of a *man* to slaughter animals, non-humans, "according to his lights," a phrase which confers upon a butcher a warrant to kill unfettered by any ethical consideration. In *On Raftery's Hill*, Red Raftery exceeds this warrant and, in so doing, calls into question its validity. That the hill constitutes an especially perverse abattoir is well established by other characters' disgust with the reeking presence of dead animals on Red's property, creating the sense that the hill is encircled by carcasses in much the same way as Molloy is surrounded by slaughterhouses and the narrator of *Ill Seen Ill Said* is surrounded by – and suffering the encroachment of – stones. Visiting the Raftery house in Act One, Dara Mood announces that a person could "keel over wud the stink a rotten sheep and cows"[34]; Isaac Dunn, employing a Beckettian neologism to express a process of bodily decline, complains to Red of a "stink" emanating from "them dead sheep and cattle ya just lave maggotin the fields" (*On Raftery's Hill*, p. 19); and decrying his slovenly management of the family farm compared with that of her deceased husband, Shalome observes, "He kept this farm clean. ... Now it's just a river of slurry and rotten animals" (p. 31). Moments later, Dara complicates the motif by reporting that he saw Red cut the udders off of cows, then drag them to the river and hurl them in: "Cows is the most beauhiful creatures, gentle and trustin and curious and they've these greah long eyelashes ... This wan walked up to him and starts nuzzlin him and he goes ah her wud a knife" (p. 33). Dara's humanizing – and feminizing – of the cows, much like Sorrel's name and Red's association of his rape of her with the cleaning of a rabbit, purposefully thicken Carr's discourse of species in which women and cows both fall victim to Red's savagery. Both are sexually assaulted, as the mutilating knife wielded in the field becomes the phallic weapon so brutally deployed in the home. Bodies of water are similarly overdetermined in this image cluster, serving as more than a metaphor for a fluid feminine space. For throughout Carr's work, bodies of water – Owl Lake in *The Mai*, Belmont River in *Portia Coughlan*, Cuura Lake in *Ariel* – also function as graves for humans and animals; the slaughterhouse and dead mammals, both human and animal, circumscribe the action of these plays.[35] In the opening scene of *By the Bog of Cats* ... a dead black swan plays a similar role, as the action of the play begins and ends with blood staining the whiteness of the bog: first the swan's, then Josie and Hester's.

How might we read this framing motif? To begin, as thinkers including Derrida, Cavell, and Emmanuel Levinas have theorized, philosophical distinctions between humans and animals often rely upon the issue of language and, as Cary Wolfe argues, tenuously so. Lacking the capacity to phrase, Wolfe observes in summarizing Jean-François Lyotard's articulation of the "differend" and its relationship to the animal, "The 'silence' and 'feeling' of the mute are not available to the animal"; as a result, animals are prevented from "occupying any of the discursive positions for the ethical force of the differend to apply." Similarly, the animal, "because it does not have the means to bear witness, is a 'paradigm of the victim' who suffers wrongs but cannot claim damages." In the end, then, insofar as such ruminations trouble premises crucial to the category of human, "we may not be us, but at least we retain the certainty that the animal remains the animal."[36] In a more religious register, one all-too-evident in *Ariel*, "'humanity' sustains *itself* ... by means of a 'carnivorous' sacrificial structure that orders the relationship between the world 'of spirit' and the animal."[37] Turning his daughter Ariel into a sacrificial lamb, in other words, Fermoy

Fitzgerald feels assured of political victory; in this way, Ariel stands in not only for Iphigenia but for the animal as well. (In her ritualistic slaughter at the end of *By the Bog of Cats ...*, Young Josie Swane, attired in red pajamas, is contained in the same sacrificial structure.) When Ariel's voice is heard late in the play, Carr's stage description notes that she surrounds her guilty father much as dead sheep and cattle encompass Red Raftery's house. This particular hauntology begins with a spectral phone call: "*Note on ARIEL'S voice: once convention of the phone has been established, let ARIEL'S voice come from everywhere.*"[38]

One final connotation of the Beckettian might be inferred from this discourse of sacrifice: namely, that Fitzgerald's killing of Ariel is directed toward the "world of spirit" or, rather, to gods or God, thereby linking men *and* animals with a deity. This sacrificial structure is presaged in Watt's feeling of closeness to God when he feeds baby rats to their voracious relatives. And while this precise structure is not nearly so evident in the "trilogy" as in *Watt*, the tripartite "chain of being" of men, animals, and God informs all three novels. Questions abound, for example, about requirements associated with the taking of communion in the Catholic Church, a matter of great significance to this discourse as it marks the sole occasion when men consume God in the form of the transubstantiated host. On a train Watt meets Mr. Spiro, editor of a Catholic periodical, who responds to a reader's inquiry about appropriate procedures in the unlikely event of a rat or other animal consuming a consecrated host. In *Molloy*, Moran seeks advice from Father Ambrose about taking communion soon after drinking a pint of lager. A lively conversation ensues in which the priest observes that "Animals never laugh," adding a moment later: "Christ never laughed either ... so far as we know" (*Three Novels*, p. 101). (Perhaps there is one exception to the former case – the dove in *Watt* who shat in a priest's eye while he was exiting the church may have found the assault amusing!) Lacking the capacity for laughter, however, is only *one* index of God's difference from the human. Recall that in a moment of pique in *Waiting for Godot*, Didi snips at Gogo, "You're not going to compare yourself to Christ!" (p. 57), but Lucky's earlier monologue implicitly proffers this very comparison by allusion to divine apathia, athambia, and aphasia. God, in this construction, possesses a distinctly different – and diminished – relationship to language; moreover, God lacks the capacity for amazement or emotion in ways that parallel theorizations of the animal. Reiterating the significance of responsiveness in philosophical delimitations of animality, Wolfe reiterates that animals are "unable to respond with a response that could be precisely and rigorously distinguished from a reaction."[39]

My point is that Beckett's comic diminution of the divine also informs Carr's *oeuvre* and, not surprisingly, *Ariel* contains the most compelling examples of this representation and of the muddling of distinctions between the human and the animal. In the opening act, Frances Fitzgerald refuses Boniface's offer to hear more about her husband's traumatic childhood, insisting that she doesn't want to open a "buuk a butchery" that includes Fermoy's complicity in the murder of his mother, who had "eyelashes on her and the big beautiful mane … like a horse, like a beauhiful Egyptian horse" (*Ariel*, pp. 26, 27). The sordid story of her being thrown in a bag and "pegged to the bohhom of a lake" contrasts with her religious ardor and belief in the sainthood of her confessor. In an earlier conversation, Fermoy expresses a similar conflation of the animal and the divine by claiming that all he needs to get by is "horse sinse and God" (p. 17), but which or whose God? When his brother Boniface lampoons God as an "auld fella in a tent, addicted to broccoli," a low-comic and feckless figure, Fermoy objects:

No, God is young. He's so young. He's on fire for us, heaven reelin wud hees rage at not bein among us … Time manes natin to him. He rises from an afternoon nap and twinty centuries has passed. (*Ariel*, p. 16)

Boniface argues that this representation is impossible, as Christianity is predicated on the notion that God never sleeps, a premise Fermoy is quick to rebut: "My God slapes" (p. 16). Not surprisingly, this comic business accrues more sinister resonance as the play progresses, culminating in a redaction of Gloucester's lament in *King Lear*: "As flies to wanton boys are we to th' gods/They kill us for their sport" (4.1.36–37). Moments before Frances exacts her revenge for his sacrifice of Ariel, Fermoy attempts to rationalize his actions by echoing Gloucester's trope:

This is no playground and never was. This is where [God] hunts us down like deer and flays us alive for sport. (*Ariel*, p. 59)

These two Gods, the codger eating broccoli who lacks the capacity to sleep – Banville's "old bungler" in *Nightspawn* – and the angry young man who flays mankind for his amusement, surface throughout Beckett and Carr, culminating in *Woman and Scarecrow*, which in this reading identifies not so much a break or aesthetic "turn" in Carr's canon, but a logical continuation of a Beckettian haunting.

In addition, as this last example confirms, a Beckettian haunting might intimate a Shakespearean one as well – in the case of *Woman and Scarecrow* one identifiable not so much by traces of *King Lear* but of *Hamlet*. Most reviewers commented on the presence of Ophelia in Carr's dying Woman, however older and more jaded she appears, and for good reason, as Woman and Scarecrow debate this matter, eventually reaching the conclusion that Woman, unlike Ophelia, is dying of spite, not love. But later in the play, in a phraseological adaptation from *Hamlet*, Woman remarks that she is being "cut off in the blossom of [her] sins,"[40] all of which returns us to specters like King Hamlet. In this trope, Woman, like so many of Carr's protagonists, is already a ghost; and like a specter, like King Hamlet in Shakespeare's Denmark, Beckett and the Beckettian inhabit Carr, however much evidence of the habitation has changed throughout her career. There is little reason to suspect that this haunting will change, for specters are hardly friendly ghosts who just go away when they're bored or have been sufficiently entertained. They remain, as Beckett has in Carr's writing.

USING BECKETT TO KICK DEAD HORSES

This surge was intended to provide "breathing space" for the Iraqis. ... But while our troops are holding back the opposing team to let them make a touchdown, the Iraqis haven't even picked up the ball. ... The witnesses must tell us why we should continue sending our young men and women to fight and die. ... What is the likelihood that things will change dramatically and there will be political progress in the near term? *Are we merely beating a dead horse* [my emphasis]?

(Ike Skelton, Chairman, US House Armed Services Committee, September 12, 2007)

Kicking a Dead Horse is a small play ... with a very big subject ... The Bushes, father and son, have, like Moses, led Americans into the deserts of Iraq, creating an exodus from which there is no exit to a promised land. Like [Shepard's protagonist], they have ridden off into a dusty wilderness in a desperate attempt to keep alive their cowboy mythology, only for their horse to die under them and leave them stranded.

(Fintan O'Toole, "Metaphors for Modern Times," March 24, 2007)

Preparing to chair hearings in the US Congress in September, 2007 concerning the American troop surge in Iraq, Representative Ike Skelton (D-Missouri) had most likely not seen Sam Shepard's *Kicking a Dead Horse* earlier that spring, or studied Fintan O'Toole's response to its production by the Abbey Theatre. Somehow, however, in the muddle of figures of speech in a politician's brain – breathing space, touchdowns in football games, and so on – an inventory almost depleted by America's misadventures in the Middle East, Chairman Skelton arrived at beating dead horses. Some six months earlier, so did O'Toole, who recognized in Shepard's sixty-something cowpoke Hobart Struther those aging wranglers, George Herbert Walker Bush and his son, and thus linked the American southwest of *Kicking a Dead Horse* with the deserts of Iraq. Missing, however, from the congeries of metaphors in

Mr. Skelton's opening statement to his Committee is Samuel Beckett, who figured prominently in Irish responses to the play. Olwen Fouere, who played the Mai in the inaugural production of Carr's play at the Peacock Theatre in 1994, immediately seized upon the connection: "[Shepard]'s the Beckett of the prairies," she proclaimed after the play's premiere.[41] O'Toole drew an even finer comparison, asserting that Shepard's "metaphorical approach" to politics in *Kicking a Dead Horse* brings it into a generic kinship with Harold Pinter's *Mountain Language* and Beckett's *Catastrophe*. "Even when there is the option to be direct," O'Toole writes, "a metaphorical approach [to political critique] often makes aesthetic sense," as Bertolt Brecht's fables set in China attest.[42]

As O'Toole also concedes, *Kicking a Dead Horse* is about many things – "middle age and mortality, romance and realism, illusion and disillusion" – topics Shepard has developed throughout his career in ways that anticipate both the mise-en-scène and dialogue of his newest play. Almost from its beginnings Off-Off-Broadway over forty years ago, Shepard's writing has privileged the American west, particularly the desert, as a repository of value and the "authenticity" his hapless protagonist seeks. These concerns inform what is arguably Shepard's most significant work, that of the later 1970s and 80s, such as *True West* (1980), *Fool for Love* (1983), his film collaboration with Wim Wenders *Paris, Texas* (1984), and his collection of poetry and short prose, *Motel Chronicle* (1982). Especially at this moment, Shepard scoured the American landscape, seeking authenticity and juxtaposing it to the artificiality of the city: Los Angeles (and, by extension, Hollywood) in *True West* and Houston in *Paris, Texas*. This is not to suggest that America's rural communities – the southwest in *Curse of the Starving Class* (1978) and the midwest in *Buried Child* (1979) – are immune from the kinds of dysfunction, even incest and intrafamilial violence, that traumatize Carr's characters. But time and time again, Shepard's characters posit the hope that authenticity and *manhood* still exist in a postmodern world of simulations and hyperreality. Often, these exist in the desert, albeit in alienated forms.

Dismayed by early-1980s Los Angeles, Shepard puts the matter with vulgar directness in a short verse from *Motel Chronicles*:

> I've about seen
> all the nose jobs
> capped teeth
> and silly-cone tits
> I can handle
>
> I'm heading back
> to my natural woman.[43]

Throughout *Motel Chronicles* Shepard relates his affection for Westerns, for Burt Lancaster and Gary Cooper in *Vera Cruz* (1954), for instance, and for a rugged West that no longer exists. If a "natural woman" cannot be fabricated through the silicone implants and surgical "nips and tucks" of Hollywood, neither can a real "man," a construction of gender May hurls at Eddie in *Fool for Love*: "Anybody who doesn't half kill themselves falling off horses or jumping on steers is a twerp in your book." Eddie's response is unequivocal: "That's right."[44] Like the degeneration of men and women into advertisements of gender, even the state of Texas has suffered the prostheses of motels with their useless swimming pools scarring the land: "Poor Texas," one of Shepard's poems laments, "Carved into/Like all the rest" (*Motel Chronicles*, p. 26). Meanwhile, back in LA, "people here/have become/the people/they're pretending to be" (p. 42). Only his reclusive father seems ruthlessly authentic. Writing from New Mexico in *Motel Chronicles*, Shepard notes, "My father lives alone in the desert. He says he doesn't fit in with people" (p. 56).

All of these issues emerge in one of Shepard's signal dramatic achievements, *True West*, revived by the Abbey in 2006, a play that informs my brief reading of *Kicking a Dead Horse*. For the ersatz urban existence Hobart attempts to escape – artificiality wrought, in part, by his selling of Western artifacts to eastern museums and art galleries – is problematized in *True West*. At one moment, Austin, a struggling screenwriter in LA, sarcastically asks his alienated brother Lee, "You got anything of value? You got any tidbits from the desert?", and in another, Lee shouts in a rage, "This would never happen out on the desert. I would never be in this kinda' situation out on the desert."[45] The desert, then, in a binarism that is later deconstructed in the play, functions as the real when juxtaposed to the artificiality of Hollywood. Yet this "cowboy culture" or authenticity is itself susceptible to the contamination of Baudrillardian simulation. At one point, Lee relates to Austin his idea of a "true story" involving men chasing one another into the "endless black prairie," first in trucks and later on horses, and when offering Austin a credit as cowriter of such a script Austin scoffs, "I don't want my name on that piece of shit!" (*Seven Plays*, p. 38).

However improbable this screenplay, Shepard's representation of the relationship of men and horses – men and objects, more broadly – strikes an emotionally resonant chord. In *True West* Lee, who has just returned from the desert in search of his father, complains that he hasn't seen a good Western since *Lonely Are the Brave* (1962) starring Kirk Douglas. In particular, Douglas' mourning for his dead horse at the close of the film captures Lee's imagination:

> Ya' hear the horse screamin' at the end of it. ... Then there's a shot. BLAM! Just a single shot ... And [Douglas'] eyes close. And you know that he's died too. You know that Kirk Douglas has died from the death of his horse. (*Seven Plays*, pp. 18–19)

For Lee, this is a "real" Western, the kind of "true to life" story that doesn't get made anymore, the kind of film he convinces a producer needs to be revived. As Marc Robinson describes, plays like *True West* also feature the surprising centrality of objects, of things that acquire an "almost totemic status, or at least they contain so much ambiguous power that when a character uses them, or reacts to them, he is somehow expressing in the deepest way the essence of his condition." Such *things* – biscuits, books, Ping-Pong balls, and in *True West* the dozens of toasters Lee steals – both possess the qualities of everydayness *and* accrue "preposterous new importance" by catalyzing the possibility of "new departures" and "fresh responses."[46] Robinson's analysis recalls those connotations of the Beckettian relating to "thing theory" and Badiou's "event," the sudden encounter with value that sparks new possibility, even revolution, all of which leads us to the desert of *Kicking a Dead Horse* and Hobart Struther's predicament.

To begin, Shepard's stage-picture is both unique and oddly familiar: on the one hand, a dazzling, limitless vista; on the other, a freshly dug, though inadequate, grave and the overwhelming presence of death. The play's opening minutes, however, bear most resemblance not only to *Volunteers* or *Happy Days*, in which excavation and entombment are so prominent, but also to *Krapp's Last Tape*. Both plays feature protagonists in their sixties at moments of profound stasis; both Krapp and Hobart review their former lives in differently voiced meta-commentaries saturated with disdain and self-derision; and, most obviously, both characters appear as low-comic figures, even buffoons. Like Krapp, Hobart frequently stares vacuously at the audience; like Krapp, with his purple nose, the banana in his mouth, and the precarious peel on the floor designed for a pratfall, Hobart is depicted in the stage directions in overtly clownish ways (*"Each of these 'looks'* [at the audience] *should be very distinct and deliberate in the mode of the classic circus clown"*).[47] Both are plagued by amusing excesses, Krapp with his bananas and Hobart with his repetitive physical and verbal assaults on the dead horse. His first lines are "Fucking horse. Goddamn," sentiments he repeats several times, and he kicks the horse repeatedly until he experiences an emotional breakdown late in the play:

> *Hobart collapses in a heap on the horse's belly ... Slowly, he begins to weep softly, head tucked into his elbow. Long pause as he grieves. His arm slowly embraces the horse's belly. He keeps his head down, sobbing softly.* (*Kicking a Dead Horse*, p. 39)

Here, the Western hero, Kirk Douglas in *Lonely Are the Brave* or Gary Cooper in *Vera Cruz*, has been reduced to a clown, one who considers nonetheless the possibility of joining his horse in the grave so as to relieve his loneliness. As O'Toole emphasizes, Shepard's text is enlivened by humor, yet finally it "becomes, in the playing, more melancholy than madcap." While "melancholy" may not necessarily capture the tone of *Krapp's Last Tape*, neither does "madcap"; for by its conclusion, Krapp, like Hobart, has reasserted his stasis: "Perhaps my best years are gone. When there was a chance of happiness. But I wouldn't want them back" (*Shorter Plays*, p. 63). Krapp, in the play's closing tableau, stares straight ahead as he had at the play's beginning, frozen at his table; in the last moments of *Kicking a Dead Horse*, Hobart returns to the pit he was digging.

Still other parallels with Beckett resound in *Kicking a Dead Horse*. Scanning the expanse that surrounds him with a pair of binoculars, Hobart spies "Nothing – Nowhere ... Nada" (p. 11), a replica of Clov's actions and report in *Endgame*. Mounting a ladder, telescope in hand, and after making playful meta-theatrical gestures to the audience, Clov trains the glass on the outside world and announces, "Zero ... zero ... and zero" (*Endgame*, p. 29). Somewhat like Hobart, who uses God's name in various, usually profane, ways throughout Shepard's play, Clov responds to Hamm's interrogation about what he might have seen outside with, "What in God's name could there be on the horizon?" (p. 31). Both Beckett and Shepard enliven – and ironize – their plays with such phrases and clichés involving God, and frequently these are connected to either death or isolation. Hamm, for example, instructs Clov to catch and exterminate a flea "for the love of God!" (p. 33); and later expresses his hope that Clov will kill a rat in the kitchen with "Let us pray to God" (p. 54). At the same time, God, a bungling deity whose imperfect creation of the world cannot rival the mastery exhibited by the tailor in Nagg's story, becomes the butt of an old joke in *Endgame*.

The action of *Kicking a Dead Horse* is neatly framed by lines featuring the former God: Shepard's character mumbles to himself "Fucking horse. Goddamn" in the play's opening line (p. 10), and admits "I don't think I can think of God" in the play's final moments (p. 46). In between, he relies upon a familiar set of expletives and interjections: "Then stop blathering on to yourself, for Christ's sake" (p. 13); "Not that I require an audience, God knows" (p. 19); "Fucking goddamn horse" (p. 21); and so on. Equally important, "back in the days of AUTHENTICITY," as Hobart relates, Crazy Horse was bayoneted, "Not unlike Christ when you come right down to it ... Spears to the ribs. Sacrificed like some wild beast" (pp. 29–30). The relationship of animal, man, and God – of a sacrificial discourse in which all three, like Carr's Ariel, are implicated – obtains in *Kicking a Dead Horse* as well.

Traces of the Beckettian in Shepard's play also surface in the relationships between place and selfhood, between things and imaginings, and in the suddenness of events suggestive of new possibility. *Krapp's Last Tape* clarifies the connection between place and self, fixity and movement, when Krapp announces, "I love to get up and move about … then back here to … me. [*Pause*] Krapp." Objects and even the dust stirred up by movement function, in the end, as metonyms of him, as literally *his* dust: "I suppose I mean those things worth having when all the dust has – when all *my* dust has settled" (*Shorter Plays*, p. 57). Similarly, Hobart's project to recover authenticity is in reality a search for a more genuine self: "… and now there was a constant hankering for actuality. Hankering – How else can you put it? The sense of being inside my own skin" (*Kicking a Dead Horse*, p. 14). Not surprisingly, this genuine selfhood is bolstered by relationships with objects, the "things" that "thing theory" endeavors to describe. Hobart's expensive cowboy hat stands as the most meaningful of these, for after he begins to divest himself of his possessions – saddle, bridle, spurs, chaps – and heave them into the grave, a startling occurrence takes place: "… *a naked young woman emerges from deep in the pit, wearing Hobart's western hat and nothing else … The young woman approaches him slowly and silently from behind, takes off the hat and places it on Hobart's head*" (pp. 30–31). Totally unaware of her presence, he eventually discovers the hat on his head, and throws it once again into the hole, telling the audience: "I can't believe I did that again. This is getting dire. This is getting dark and dire" (p. 32).

And, perhaps it is. Yet telling himself in the play's closing moments to "dream something up" – a "bright – shining – sunny – day" (p. 46) – darkness recedes. The world brightens considerably and Hobart, eyeing his hat in the pit, descends into it. Then two things occur. First, the dead horse suddenly "slams forward, downstage, again with a mighty boom"; and, second, Hobart's voice is heard, as he sings from "deep in the pit" (pp. 46–47) the same song about "rambling" he had sung earlier when the girl mysteriously arose from the ground. Much like the earlier voices he hears from the "imagined faceless souls" who provide him with "some sense of company" (p. 19), Hobart in the final moments of *Kicking a Dead Horse* seems to have imagined a new possibility, encountered a new value. The sudden, unexpected movement of the dead horse accompanies this new possibility, though it doesn't seem to produce it.

In these ways, traces of *Company*, *Endgame*, and especially *Krapp's Last Tape* are evident in *Kicking a Dead Horse*. What seems less evident, in fact, is the twenty-first century political allegory O'Toole discerns in the play, as the terms "Iraq" and "Bush" never appear in Shepard's text. But in the play's most pointed piece of monologue, as a storm reaches its violent crescendo on stage, Hobart initiates a thumbnail sketch of an iniquitous American history: from the development of the Iron Horse to the chasing of the "heathen Redman down to Florida"; from the murder of Chinese workers and intransigent Mexicans, to the sucking of hills "barren of gold." Turning to more recent events, he recounts the damming up of rivers for "recreational purposes" and decries the fact that we have "Demolished art." Then, the climax: America has "Invaded sovereign nations. What else can we possibly do?" (*Kicking a Dead Horse*, p. 42). One answer is that we can represent such inglorious episodes in Beckettian ways, which means that however dark and dire – however absurd and low-comic – we can also endure and find new possibilities of moving on. If in only this way, Beckett remains our contemporary.

NOTES

1. Martin McDonagh, *The Pillowman* (London: Faber and Faber, 2003), p. 18.
2. Paul Muldoon, *The End of the Poem*, pp. 116, 144, 392, and *passim*.
3. Marina Carr, *By the Bog of Cats* … in *Plays 1*, p. 321. All further quotations from this play, *Low in the Dark*, *The Mai*, and *Portia Coughlan* come from this edition and will be followed by page numbers in the text.
4. Anthony Roche, *Contemporary Irish Drama*, p. 5.
5. Jacques Derrida, *Specters of Marx: The State of the Debt, the Work of Mourning, and the New International*, trans. Peggy Kamuf (New York and London: Routledge, 1994), p. 4.
6. Derrida, *Specters of Marx*, pp. 38, 39.
7. See Stephen Watt, "007 and 9/11, Specters and Structures of Feeling," in *Ian Fleming and James Bond: The Cultural Politics of 007*, eds. Edward P. Comentale, Stephen Watt, and Skip Willman (Bloomington: Indiana University Press, 2005), pp. 238–59.
8. Derrida, *Specters of Marx*, p. 37.
9. Helen Sword should be credited for making this observation in *Ghostwriting Modernism* (Ithaca: Cornell University Press, 2002), p. 163.
10. Derrida, *Specters of Marx*, p. 11.
11. Richard D. Altick, *The Art of Literary Research* (1963, rev. ed. New York: Norton, 1975), pp. 32, 20.
12. John Banville, *Ghosts* (New York: Vintage, 1994), p. 37. All further quotations from *Ghosts* will be followed by page numbers in the text.
13. "Interview" in Ni Anluain (ed.), *Reading the Future*, p. 49. All quotations from this volume will be followed by page numbers in the text.

14. John Banville, *Nightspawn* (1971, rpt. Oldcastle: Gallery Books, 1993), pp. 38–39.
15. "Marina Carr in Conversation with Melissa Sihra," in *Theatre Talk: Voices of Irish Theatre Practitioners*, eds. Lilian Chambers, Ger FitzGerald, and Eamonn Jordan (Dublin: Carysfort Press, 2001), p. 56. All further quotations from this interview will be followed by page numbers in the text.
16. Kiberd, *Irish Classics*, p. 40.
17. Roche, *Contemporary Irish Drama*, p. 287.
18. The term "gauzy realism" originates in Williams' production notes for and stage directions in *The Glass Menagerie*. Williams' audience, for example, sees the opening scene first through "transparent gauze portieres" to create a "non-realistic" effect. Carr at times replicates this kind of attention to lighting in *The Mai*. For example, when Robert appears at the end of Act One with the dead Mai in his arms, the lighting is "ghostly" and aspires to create a "ghostly effect" (Carr, *Plays 1*, pp. 147–148).
19. This range of influences, as Carr discusses and Christopher Morash describes, also includes Chekhov and, in the case of *The Mai*, Henrik Ibsen and Flannery O'Connor. See Morash, *A History of Irish Theatre*, p. 265.
20. Paula Murphy, "Staging histories in Marina Carr's Midland Plays," *Irish University Review* 36 (Fall 2006), p. 389. Murphy also employs Derrida to read Carr, but in a very different way than he is employed here. See also James F. Clarity, "A Playwright's Post-Beckett Period," *The New York Times*, November 3, 1994; and Ian Kilroy, "Greek Tragedy, Midlands-Style," *Irish Times*, September 20, 2002. In "Translating Women into Irish Theatre History," in *A Century of Irish Drama: Widening the Stage*, eds. Stephen Watt, Eileen Morgan, and Shakir Mustafa (Bloomington: Indiana University Press, 2000), Mary Trotter defines Beckettian "style" more specifically, noting that Carr "appropriates Beckett's absurdist use of language and space" to express a feminist critique (p. 168).
21. Lyn Gardner, "Woman and Scarecrow," *Guardian*, June 23, 2006.
22. Sam Marlowe, "Woman and Scarecrow," *Times*, June 23, 2006.
23. Scaife, "Mutual Beginnings," p. 13.
24. Bender rhapsodizes about a time when her child becomes Pope and the two of them will sit "side by side" contentedly in the Vatican, "launching crusades, banning divorce, denying evolution, destroying the pill ..." (Carr, *Plays 1*, p. 55).
25. See Tyrus Miller, *Late Modernism*, pp. 190–95.
26. Here I am referring to Cavell's analysis of language in *Endgame* in *Must We Mean What We Say?*, pp. 120–27.
27. Daniel Bensaïd, "Alain Badiou and the Miracle of the Event," in *Think Again: Alain Badiou and the Future of Philosophy*, ed. Peter Hallward (New York: Continuum, 2004), p. 98.
28. Bensaïd, "Alain Badiou," p. 97.
29. Badiou made this remark during the seminar "Politics, Universalism, and the Legacy of the 1960s," Indiana University – Bloomington, November 9, 2007.

30. Bernadette Bourke, "Carr's 'cut-throats and gargilyes,'" p. 139. The Beckettian elements of the play's mise-en-scène were further enhanced by the black, white, and gray set of the 1998 Dublin Theatre Festival production, the only contrast to which was provided by Josie's red pajamas.
31. Anna McMullan, "Unhomely Stages: Women Taking (a) Place in Irish Theatre," in *Druids, Dudes, and Beauty Queens*, ed. Dermot Bolger (Dublin: New Island, 2001), p. 82.
32. McMullan, "Unhomely Stages," p. 82.
33. This list excludes the most infamous employee of slaughterhouses, Francie Brady in Patrick McCabe's *The Butcher Boy* (1992), in whom some reviewers detected traces of Beckett's Moran and Molloy.
34. Marina Carr, *On Raftery's Hill* (Oldcastle: Gallery Press, 2000), p. 24. All further quotations from the play will be followed by page numbers in the text.
35. Millie's monologue at the end of Act One of *The Mai* replicates this motif in which water is associated with the deaths of both women and animals. Millie relates the story of Coillte, young daughter of the mountain god, who bounds across her father's mountain "like a young deer" only to meet her death in Owl Lake (p. 147).
36. Cary Wolfe, "In the Shadow of Wittgenstein's Lion: Language, Ethics, and the Question of the Animal," in *Zoontologies: The Question of the Animal*, ed. Cary Wolfe (Minneapolis: University of Minnesota Press, 2003), pp. 16, 29.
37. Wolfe, "In the Shadow of Wittgenstein's Lion," p. 28.
38. Marina Carr, *Ariel* (Oldcastle: Gallery Books, 2002), p. 55. All further quotations from this play will be followed by page numbers in the text.
39. Derrida, "The Animal That Therefore I Am," quoted in Wolfe, "In the Shadow of Wittgenstein's Lion," p. 30.
40. Marina Carr, *Woman and Scarecrow*, p. 44.
41. Quoted in Catherine Foley, "Kicking up a Storm on Stage," *The Irish Times*, March 17, 2007.
42. Fintan O'Toole, "Metaphors for Modern Times," *The Irish Times*, March 24, 2007.
43. Sam Shepard, *Motel Chronicles* (San Francisco: City Light Books, 1982), p. 102. All further quotations from this anthology will be followed by page numbers in the text.
44. Sam Shepard, *Fool for Love and Other Plays* (New York: Bantam, 1984), p. 30.
45. Sam Shepard, *Seven Plays* (New York: Bantam, 1981), pp. 38, 47. All further quotations from this play will be followed by page numbers in the text.
46. Marc Robinson, *The Other American Drama* (Cambridge and New York: Cambridge University Press, 1994), pp. 62–63.
47. Sam Shepard, *Kicking a Dead Horse* (London: Faber and Faber, 2007), p. 10. All further quotations from the play will be followed by page numbers in the text.

CODA

On retrofitting: Samuel Beckett, tourist attraction

> Do we give up fighting so the tourists come
> or fight the harder so they stay at home?
>
> –Derek Mahon, "An Bonnán Buí" in *The Yellow Book* (1998)

In a recent essay in *The London Review of Books*, Colm Toíbín walked the streets of city centre Dublin, recalling a coffee shop he once frequented, his days reading at the National Library on Kildare Street, and one frightening explosion in 1974 when the Troubles in the North migrated south in the form of a car bomb on South Leinster Street. For Toíbín, these memories and the press of daily responsibilities – paying bills, traipsing along O'Connell Street to the General Post Office (GPO) to mail letters, finding a quiet place to enjoy lunch – usually trump more literary and cultural ruminations. Moreover, he observes, some Dublin streets possess such a "peculiar intensity," a quality that has grown ever "more gnarled and layered" over the years, that the past and the books that record it "hardly matter" any more.[1] He thus admits to seldom thinking of Leopold Bloom's trek along these streets, and yet on this day he does, which through a chain of other associations leads him to the sign "Finn's Hotel" where James Joyce famously met Nora Barnacle. Other flotsam from *Ulysses* drifts into his consciousness, lemon soap and the racehorse Throwaway, for instance, as does one bit of arcana concerning Beckett's novel *Murphy* and the exact distance between the floor of the GPO and the posterior of Cuchulain's statue prominently displayed there. In actuality, Toíbín's essay has nothing to do with Joyce, *Murphy*, or Cuchulain's arse; rather, it offers a snapshot of Jack MacGowran and Patrick Magee, two actors who rose to prominence in the 1950s impersonating Clov and Krapp, respectively, in *Endgame* and *Krapp's Last Tape*. MacGowran in particular, who occupies the limelight in Toíbín's essay, was long associated with Beckett, largely because of his celebrated one-man show comprised of scenes from Beckett's work and his role as the Fool in Peter Brook's famously Beckettian film *King Lear*

(1971), in which Magee played Cornwall. (Here, the term "Beckettian" resonates in an untheorized, almost banal way: lines from Beckett are transposed into Shakespeare's play, Lear's throne room resembles Hamm's shelter in *Endgame*, and of course the presence of MacGowran all motivate the use of this adjective.)

An essay on Beckett's actors that starts with Joyce is perhaps surprising, and it may seem eccentric to pause at the statue of Cuchulain or to recall Joyce and Nora's first date, which began with their rendezvous outside the office of Sir William Wilde's surgery. More intriguing for my purposes are Toíbín's playful allusions to Ireland's largest industry – tourism – and its relation to the nation's literary history and culture. "Tourists must love" the sign at Finn's Hotel, he reflects, just as they flock to see the "funny colourful statue" of Oscar Wilde in Merrion Square opposite the office in which his father practiced, the same statue unveiled in 1997, as Paula Murphy reminds us, that irreverent Dubliners refer to as the "quare on the square."[2] Such thoughts then yield in this network of associations to the attic in which Beckett temporarily resided over his father's quantity-surveying business on nearby Clare Street, which in turn inspires Toíbín's notion of having a plaque inscribed and positioned conspicuously on the building: "'This is where Beckett got away from his God-forsaken mother.'" And then he adds: "Must tell tourist board." In a city littered, if this is not too flippant a term, with statues of well-known figures from Irish mythology, of acclaimed writers and influential politicians, even of fictional characters – the most celebrated being the Anna Livia monument, the so-called "floozy in the jacuzzi" – Toíbín's epiphany seems oddly appropriate, yet prompts an obvious question: Why would tourists, especially those Americans of Irish heritage who pour into Ireland every summer, be interested in Beckett in the first place? True enough, *Waiting for Godot* was once heralded by *Variety* as the "laugh sensation of two continents," but Americans have scarcely crowded into theatres to see Beckett's plays, save perhaps for the 1988 Lincoln Center production of *Waiting for Godot* starring Steve Martin and Robin Williams. And even this was far from an unqualified success.[3]

Toíbín's musings, however, reflect an even more striking phenomenon, one that has transformed the very streets he walks: namely, the robust "Celtic Tiger" economy in which multinational corporations have made enormous investments both in the North and in the Republic. A force driving this economy as, among others, Andrew Kincaid has examined, is cultural tourism and the reimagining of history as "heritage," one example of a larger process in which the Celtic Tiger "appropriates the past to anchor itself more thoroughly and to present itself as the logical outcome of history." In Ireland, the results of this appropriation have contributed to a sharp increase in the number of visitors to the country – during the decade of the 1990s alone, the number soared from 2.2 million per year to some 5.5 million by the decade's end – which in turn has sparked a boom in hotel construction. In Dublin the number of hotels rose from 80 to 115 between 1998 and 2000 with some 20 more in the planning stages, and in 2008 the national tourist board advertised nearly 125 hotels in the Dublin area alone.[4] Those tourists who love garish statues and old signs need to sleep somewhere! But, again, such projects raise more serious questions, ones that like Dublin streets are mottled and nuanced in a number of ways. Paramount among these is perhaps too obvious a query: What damage is done both to Irish culture and history – and to the land itself – in the names of progress and prosperity? More specifically, what sort of operations – or deformations – could turn Beckett into a tourist attraction?

As my epigraph implies, writers like Derek Mahon have expressed palpable unease over such issues; others, like Brian Friel in *The Mundy Scheme* (1969), have lampooned the idiocy of Irish legislators as they pursue American greenbacks and the tourists who dispense them. The "scheme" of Friel's high-flying politicians in *The Mundy Scheme* involves the development of several western counties into cemeteries for foreigners, particularly Americans. After all, as the Minister of External Affairs explains to the Taoiseach in Act One, when cities like New York and London grow, "ground becomes more scarce and therefore more expensive … and as these cities expand, more and more cemeteries are required."[5] The solution? Identify tracts of land unsuitable for farming, preserve their "natural state" except in those locales where "landscaping would be desirable, and the building of all roads, airstrips, and communication links," and create graveyards for wealthy foreigners. In addition, the plan's champions argue, the Mundy scheme could bolster, perhaps even treble, the tourist industry in the West, as families and friends of the deceased will almost certainly make pilgrimages to the gravesites; as a result, the demand for "hotels, souvenir shops, wreaths, headstones," and so on should increase sharply. In short, just as Switzerland is the acknowledged center of world banking, Ireland could become known as the Irish diaspora's "eternal resting place," or so the scheme's proponents argue to wary colleagues.[6]

America, as Friel has revealed in interviews, weighed heavily on his mind while writing this play. While he feared for the futures of Irish writers in an increasingly global market, he was more acutely concerned about a country that was devolving into a "shabby imitation of a third-rate American state." No longer describable as "West Britons," an echo of Molly Ivors' deprecation of Gabriel Conroy in Joyce's "The Dead," Irish men and women were slowly becoming "East Americans."[7] The speakers of several poems in Mahon's volume *The Yellow Book* are equally direct. Recalling his strolls down the sidewalks of New York in "American Deserta," Mahon laments the "post-Cold War, global warming age/of corporate rule, McPeace and Mickey Mao."[8] In this age, the ascent to discursive power of "glib promotional blather" is corroborated daily by the busloads of tourists who descend upon Ireland, "space invaders clicking at the front door/goofy in baseball caps and nylon leisurewear," eager to be thrilled by a "Georgian theme-park" (*The Yellow Book*, pp. 12–13). In "'shiver your tenement,'" he remembers with affection a different sort of visitor in the "demure" 1960s. Then, young would-be writers traveled to Dublin by the busload to crawl down Dawson and Grafton Streets, pursuing at times a night of "roguery," but just as often searching for the rich assembly of writers and intellectuals who frequented pubs there. These neophytes found hospitable gathering places, where they sipped "watery Jamesons" and enjoyed a "life of the mind" among established literati and other artists, who preferred the "unforced pace" of Dublin to the thoughtless speed of London and elsewhere. This was a time before writers were reduced to promotional hucksters:

> Those were the days before tourism and economic growth,
> before deconstruction and the death of the author,
> when pubs had as yet no pictures of Yeats and Joyce
> since people could still recall their faces, their voices. (*Yellow Book*, p. 18)

By contrast, living in the "pastiche paradise of the postmodern," people today feel more at home with the "ersatz, the pop, the phony." This hyperreal Eden, of course, has been supported by tourist dollars, francs, pounds, and euros; and it has necessitated both the leveling of some neighborhoods to make room for the headquarters of multinational corporations and the transformation of others into faux-historical "theme-parks."

If the land itself can be so transformed, what might happen to a figure like Beckett if *Bord Fáilte*, the Irish tourist board, were to act upon Tóibín's puckish suggestion? In what specific ways might Beckett be turned into the "ersatz, the pop, the phony"? In another essay in which Kincaid assesses ways in which the Celtic Tiger induces the Irish diaspora to return home for a visit, a partial answer to these questions emerges, in this instance in the design of landscapes:

> Contemporary artists, architects and landscapers have incorporated the history of emigration into their work, re-writing emigration *on the landscape* ... Cultural geography is a form of history-writing. Contemporary shapers ... do not whitewash its trauma, but they engage in a more subtle glossing-over.[9]

One *not*-so-subtle instance of this process, as Kincaid explains, is Ireland's emergence as a destination for golfers, a project envisioned by Bernard Shaw's Tom Broadbent in *John Bull's Other Island* over a century ago. Shortly after World War II, Irish political leaders were advised that, for the tourism industry to flourish, the country would need not only to expand and improve its hotel accommodations, roads, and airports, but also develop venues for entertainment (golf courses, spas, even casinos were specifically recommended) and a coherent cultural program of attractions, one of which was the checkered *Tóstal* festival.[10] Responding to this call, some 110 new golf courses were built during the 1990s alone, often – as Kincaid wryly observes – "out of the remains of former Anglo-Irish landlords' houses and the remnants of the garden estates that once surrounded them."[11] Even a cursory inspection of the advertising campaigns of some of Ireland's most celebrated newer courses confirms this point. The hotel of the K Club Golf and Spa Resort near Dublin, for example, which opened in 1991 and hosted the prestigious Ryder Cup matches in 2006, was built around Hugh Barton House (1828–31). The K Club's promotional literature sketches the history of the house and foregrounds its "idyllic rural setting," as it also highlights the challenge of the club's thirty-six holes designed by golfing legend Arnold Palmer. The Big House, as Kincaid archly notes in reference to this widespread revision of cultural geography, has now been restored as "the clubhouse."[12]

A lot has happened, in other words, to reverse the admission Seán Lemass made in 1960, the same year in which he assumed the office of Taoiseach, that Ireland was "new to, and somewhat inexperienced in, the organized international tourism business." Indeed, in the early 1950s, when tourism ranked as Ireland's second-leading industry behind agricultural exports, some politicians viewed the nascent project as a kind of anathema.[13] It is no longer. Yet, in the past half century or so since Lemass made this confession to the Congress of International Hotel Associations, the country has scarcely slowed down to draw a deep conceptual breath and consider the entire range of effects of this investment. I intend to speculate about one such case – or, rather, possible effect – of this investment, taking seriously Toíbín's perhaps fanciful suggestion of placing a plaque on William Beckett's surveying office on Clare Street and turning his son Samuel into a tourist attraction. What sorts of refashioning or the cultural equivalent of plastic surgery would this project require? How could Beckett attract tourists to Clare Street after lazy mornings kissing the Blarney stone, playing a round of golf at Lahinch or Ballybunion, or fishing for salmon in the Shannon River?

Acting upon Toíbín's brainstorm would require Ireland's tourist board to engage in a concerted *retrofitting* of Beckett, a process that, as we shall see, is already well underway. I employ the term "retrofitting" purposefully, appropriating it from the architectural jargon in which it initially gained currency. The process connotes the remodeling of an older architectural structure to accommodate a present-day purpose; or, through the installation of more technologically advanced equipment or the redesign of space, retrofitting allows an older structure to comply with safety or other codes enacted since its original construction. One of the more spectacular – and tragic – examples of architectural retrofitting came as the result of the 1980 fire at the "old" MGM Grand Hotel in Las Vegas in which over 80 residents were killed and nearly 700 were injured. After spending between $110 and an estimated $223 million settling claims brought against the Grand after this disaster, owner Kirk Kerkorian – and every other hotel-casino operator in the city – spent millions more installing automatic sprinklers in ceilings, improving emergency exit systems, and implementing a unique array of precautions.[14] If nineteenth-century Big Houses and all they connote about the Great Famine, absentee landlordism, and the class system of nineteenth-century Ireland can be remodeled into clubhouses with all the amenities today's golfers demand, surely a writer, even one as aloof as Beckett was, can be refurbished to satisfy the tastes and pique the curiosities of wealthy visitors. But how?

At least three possibilities present themselves: one adapted from a long-established marketing ploy that induces consumers to visit a place and purchase goods there; another derived from recent staging practices and the repertories of contemporary Irish theatres; and yet a third that finds its provenience in a chameleon-like *presentism* that some commentators believe has already affected our understanding of writers like Beckett and even Shakespeare – for the worse.

The first strategy for retrofitting Beckett has already begun in such projects as the Beckett Centenary Festival of April 2006, one goal of which was to make him more Irish while, at the same time in the words of John O'Donoghue, Minister for Arts, Sport, and Tourism, affirming Ireland as a "cultural destination of quality and note."[15] This stratagem works, to a considerable extent, by positioning Beckett in a tradition within which he is ill-described; and, in so doing, precipitates what can only be regarded as a series of telling ironies. One such irony concerns an analogous "move" in the broader discipline of Irish Studies which James Chandler describes as produced by the "Irishing" of writers through a critical exfoliation of a writer's "Irishable" qualities. This strategy, rather paradoxically, makes Irish writers *more* Irish in a kind of fantasy conflation of writer and nation which, adapting a line from Marianne Moore's poem "Spenser's Ireland," makes Beckett the authorial equivalent of the "greenest place I've never seen."[16] Chandler explains:

> In many of these examples, and Burke's is an especially good case in point, the question of an author's being "Irishable" is intensified by the sense that, internal to his or her *ouevre*, we can find not only another side to the story but beyond this, an anticipation of what it means to be able to see or not to see the story from the other side.[17]

Chandler goes on to ask what the "Irishing" of an author might mean and what effect such a process might exert on our ability to locate this author on a larger "cultural map."[18] That Beckett can very easily be seen as Irishable is beyond question; this has been one of the informing premises of this book. But that he can be located on the precise cultural map created by Irish tourism is another matter altogether.

Nor surprisingly, therefore, when dealing with Beckett, an event like the centenary needed to perform the crucial culture work of repatriation, which it accomplished in several ways. For example, in a session convened at the National Gallery in Dublin, John Banville and several distinguished panelists explored Beckett's association with the visual arts, both European and Irish. To at least some extent, then, "Beckett country" can be constructed as – or is isomorphic with – Irish country. Another prominent means of refashioning this cultural landscape were posters displayed in airports and other public venues of the country's four Nobel Prize winners in literature: William Butler Yeats, Bernard Shaw, Beckett, and Seamus Heaney. One effect of the Nobel poster, based on a stamp collection printed by Sweden Post Stamps in 2004, is to reclaim both Shaw and Beckett, writers who left Ireland at relatively young ages and, in Beckett's case, didn't often look back. To be sure, Shaw took an interest in all things Irish and from afar commented on them, from Home Rule to the stage Irishman, from Irish melodrama to – of all things – Irish tourism (in fact, he wrote an article in 1916 extolling the quality of Irish hotels, of fishing in the Shannon River, and of Irish golf courses).[19] Beckett, conversely, can hardly be accused of a similar fascinations save, perhaps, for his lifelong interest in golf.[20] As Banville observes, Joyce and Beckett, "who took so much from this impoverished little bit of rock on the edge of Europe, had shaken the dust of Ireland from their heels and never looked back."[21] Like Beckett's biographers, Banville emphasizes that Beckett's short stint teaching at Trinity College in 1930–31 only intensified his disdain of Ireland in general and Dublin in particular. "He was not happy in Ireland," Banville notes, finding "Dublin life suffocating …"[22] By December, 1931, Beckett could no

Figure 3. Irish Nobel Laureates in Literature (2004). Reprinted by permission of Sweden Post Stamps

longer tolerate Dublin and escaped to Germany and then Paris, only to "crawl home" again in August of 1932. He remained in Ireland for a little over a year, but again he was unhappy. His father's death in May, 1933 complicated his life even further. Deirdre Bair puts the matter about as strongly as it can be put: "Beckett had no pride in his Irishness; national identity meant nothing to him," and was something to be "avoided at all costs."[23]

But national identity means everything to Irish tourism. Moreover, the iconic gesture of putting four Nobel laureates in a single design – and then positioning the result in crowded venues like the Dublin International Airport, where I first saw it in the summer of 2006 – can be regarded not only as a stratagem of "Irishing," but also as a device of unbridled irony, as anyone who has ever investigated Beckett's reaction to the Nobel Prize must be immediately aware. When his wife Suzanne answered the telephone call in 1969 informing them of the Nobel Committee's decision, for example, she is said to have whispered to him, "*Quelle catastrophe.*"[24] And, while all the major biographies relate slightly different stories about the days and weeks surrounding the announcement – and about the precise ways in which Beckett generously gave away much of the money awarded with the Prize – all agree that he was "distressed," even "perturbed," by the news, for he was acutely aware of "how much his long-term future would be disrupted by the celebrity, in addition to his present peace being shattered."[25] No matter, for, again, the message conveyed by the juxtaposing of this quartet is that these are *all* Irish writers, connected irrevocably to the wild coastline in the background of the stamp celebrating Heaney (See Figure 3). Such a thesis, as I have tried to suggest, is *least* applicable to Beckett, perhaps one reason that the background of his stamp features a duo from *Waiting for Godot* – there, apparently, to support the description of Beckett as a comic dramatist – and not a natural vista or other visual cliché associated with the Irish geography. Nonetheless, the poster intimates unities that do not or did not exist.

One of these, as Pascale Casanova has parsed so effectively, is the Irish writer's relative dependence on the nation, on Ireland itself, in building an international reputation of sufficient dimension to merit consideration for the prize. Discussing the Irish Revival of the fin de siècle, Casanova observes that Yeats, a spearhead of the revival of Irish arts, "came to be regarded in Dublin as in a sense embodying Irish poetry … Later, in 1923, as though his own newly official status in the world of letters had been confirmed through the recognition of Ireland's literary 'difference,' Yeats received the Nobel Prize for literature."[26] But, of course, however separatist Yeats' early political and aesthetic agendas, as Casanova notes, his international celebrity accrued both from Irish National Theatre performances in London and thus from patronage from the very colonialist capitol from which he desired distancing. Conversely, Beckett left Ireland entirely to earn his reputation at considerable remove from his homeland, a distance that none of the other Irish Nobel laureates, even Shaw, achieved.

But there are other glossings over of specific histories as well. Yeats, as is well known, disliked Beckett's early work, disparaging it as "amoral," and he "neither approved of the direction in which Beckett's writing took him, nor did he enjoy reading it."[27] If not quite so censorious as Yeats was of Beckett, Shaw, in his "Preface for Politicians" that preceded the 1906 first edition of *John Bull's Other Island*, recounts Yeats' request of a play to add to the repertory of the nascent Irish Literary Theatre and remarks that in *John Bull*, "Mr Yeats got rather more than he bargained for." From Shaw's perspective, the play is "uncongenial to the whole spirit of the neo-Gaelic movement, which is bent on creating a new Ireland after its own ideal," while he insists instead upon an "uncompromising presentment of the real old Ireland."[28] As a result, *John Bull's Other Island*, which Casanova pointedly describes as a "deliberately anti-Yeatsian play,"[29] opened at the Court Theatre in London to enthusiastic audiences, in part because Shaw's and Yeats' Ireland were very different places (and, more prosaically, because the play's staging demands exceeded the capacity of a young theatre to realize them). Nationalism, as Terry Eagleton observes, "speaks of the entry into full self-realization of a unitary subject known as the people." So, to a great extent, does cultural tourism.[30]

Shaw's "real old Ireland," by contrast, the Ireland of the Great Famine and colonial subjection, of economic hardship and superstition, exerts a limited appeal to tourists. And the fact that Beckett's major influences were either European – Dante, Pirandello, Shakespeare – or other Irish writers, most notably Joyce, would also seem relevant to this assessment of multiplying ironies. In addition to his well-documented admiration of Joyce, as I have mentioned, Beckett enjoyed J. M. Synge's comedies, particularly *The Well of the Saints*, which he had seen at the Abbey Theatre, and the "knockabout comedy" of Sean O'Casey's *Juno and the Paycock* and such one-act "curtain raisers" as *The End of the Beginning*. Indeed, Joyce, O'Casey, and Beckett are permanently linked in Irish cultural history – and, in yet another irony inherent to this topic, in the history of Irish tourism – in a fashion far more substantial than any perception of aesthetic or national unity implied by the stamp series. For in 1958, in connection with *Tóstal*, *Bord Fáilte* announced that the Dublin Theatre Festival, inaugurated a year earlier, would feature O'Casey's new play *The Drums of Father Ned*, a theatrical adaptation of *Ulysses* called *Bloomsday*, and several works of Beckett's because, in the board's own words, "the *Bloomsday* and O'Casey productions would be likely to have the greatest effect toward inducing people to visit Ireland for the festival."[31] What happened then, as Carolyn Swift, cofounder of Dublin's Pike Theatre where *Waiting for Godot* received its first Irish production, describes, was "a hugely complicated comedy of errors typical of the times, with double and triple dealing," the upshot of which was the cancellation of the festival and Beckett's subsequent imposition of a "blanket ban of any of his plays being performed in the Irish Republic."[32]

Christopher Murray underscores the awkwardness and insipidity of the festival's cancellation by recalling that when *Tóstal* was conceived in the early 1950s, its raison d'être was not only to attract tourists to the country, but also to "showcase Ireland in forms which would revive cultural nationalism." Murray quotes Lemass' endorsement of the program as "designed to express the Irish way of life and to revive the spirit which animated the traditional Gaelic festivals for which Ireland was famous when Europe was young."[33] We will never really know how Beckett's plays might have contributed to an expression of the "Irish way of life," because after Archbishop John Charles McQuaid refused to preside over a special mass in protest over the inclusion of Joyce and O'Casey in the festival, the program was rather quickly scuttled. McQuaid felt little need to explain his refusal; according to Murray, he "merely had to sit back" and "let the *Tóstal* committee work itself into a lather over the bad publicity that [his] disapproval would bring."[34] For her part, Carolyn Swift indicted the "utter spinelessness" of a committee that capitulated to the "public and private pressure" exerted upon it by McQuaid's "lay allies, particularly his close associates in the Knights of Saint Columbanus."[35] Beckett was livid at this turn of events.

As the ill-fated 1958 Dublin Theatre festival suggests, cultural tourism in Ireland has not always met with success, as ideological battles – and real ones in the North – have risen to undermine its ambitions. More important for my purposes here, Seán Lemass' understanding of the cultural work such festivals achieve also indicates the extent to which they are calibrated to invoke a nostalgia analogous to that inherent in the practices employed in the marketing of other commodities. In her formulation of the "commodified authentic" cultivated to market consumer goods at such London department stores as Selfridge's earlier in the century, for example, Elizabeth Outka describes how skillfully designed advertising campaigns were combined with the mise-en-scène of the store itself (transforming it into an "urban village") to produce a "nostalgic version of the authentic" for its shoppers. The result was the invocation of an "originary and unified past before mechanical reproduction and fragmentation," a simulation that cast a "misty glow over the production process" of the various commodities available for purchase.[36] A similar process obtains in a promotional campaign that attempts to repatriate Beckett in the way the Nobel Prize poster does, foregrounding the faces of the laureates against an iconically Irish background and thereby connecting all four to the national landscape. Needless to say, the poster remains silent about Beckett's disillusionment with Ireland in the early 1930s, his support of Alan Simpson during his trial for obscenity in producing Tennessee Williams' *The Rose Tattoo*, and his outrage over the power of the Church so strikingly in evidence during the 1958 Irish Theatre Festival fiasco. "Beckett was Beckett," Irish journalist Brian Fallon once quipped, an "odd individualist" who, to become a tourist attraction, has to be made both familiar and "Irishable."[37]

At this point, one might reasonably object that historical distortion inevitably subsists in tourism, especially where celebrities are concerned, and there is doubtless some truth to this. Indeed, that is one of the points I'm laboring to make. More germane to my purposes, Toíbín's fanciful plaque on the Clare Street office – "This is where Beckett got away from his God-forsaken mother" – provides yet another register within which to (mis) read Beckett. For aren't many Irish and Irish American writers, at some point, forced to negotiate an impossible relationship with their mothers? Think here of May Joyce's fatal illness and its effect on her son (and on *Ulysses*); or Ella O'Neill's drug addiction and its centrality to Eugene O'Neill's *Long Day's Journey into Night*; or, to take a more recent example, Brigid Regan's battle with cancer and Paul Muldoon's elegy "Yarrow." Toíbín's imaginary engraving traffics in such romanticized and clichéd portrayals of the pained son-author. Or, to disarticulate stereotypes of nation and gender, take the example of Marianne Moore whose Irishness Laura O'Connor so persuasively explores in *Haunted English* (2006). Some "hindered characters," Moore postulates, may "lack mothers but they all have grandmothers." That is, like the Irish bull O'Connor historicizes, in which an Irishman's attempts at "verbal passing" are rendered laughable by the solecism that invariably exposes the Irish within,[38] both mother and grandmother inhere in, even haunt, Irish writers and in the popular imaginary that romanticizes Irish artists. Toíbín's engraving traffics in such romantic and clichéd portrayals even as it possesses the merit of a partial truth. Beckett in the early 1930s *did* seek refuge above his father's office, though the plaque remains silent about his several reasons for doing so: initially, to flee his mother's intense anger over both his writing and his apparent disinterest in finding gainful employment; and, more important, after his father's fatal heart attack on June 26, 1933, to escape a home that his mother had turned into a "mausoleum" that lasted for "weeks on end." He fled, in his own words, not just his mother but all the "vile worms of melancholy observance."[39] No plaque intended for the perusal of tourists can record all of this.

In this context, finally, it seems important to consider also the suggestions conveyed by the stamp itself, for unlike the majority of books and photographic collections published since Beckett's death in 1989 which underscore an older, contemplative, and even morose figure, the Nobel stamp captures a younger, vital Beckett for the "new Ireland," not an octogenerian or postwar depressive. This Beckett, to be sure, is not a child or adolescent; the wrinkles in the furrowed brow and trail of lines in his face confirm this. But neither is he ancient or brooding, as he has so often been presented in portraits and photographs. John Minahan's photo album *Beckett* (2007), for example, collected from his 2006 exhibitions in Britain, America, and Japan, contains beautiful pictures of Beckett, almost all of which capture him in the early and middle 1980s as he approached his final years. In a few photographs he is actively directing actors or enjoying a Guinness, but the majority of images present a solitary figure drinking coffee, sitting on a bed, or reading a book. To my eye, many of these pictures recall Gisèle Freund's earlier image in *Gisèle Freund – Photographer* (1985) of a solitary Beckett in 1964 seated near a window, which partially illuminates his profile. Lost apparently in meditation, his eyes are downcast as plumes of smoke from a cigarette in his right hand drift lazily toward the light.

Similarly, Anne Atik's *How It Was* contains nine portraits of Beckett by her husband, the painter Avigdor Arikha. In several, Beckett's eyeglasses are perched on his forehead, as he apparently considers what he has just read; in another, he rests his head against his hands, a glass of wine positioned in front of him; and in still another, representing a moment in 1970, he is seated alone with a cigar. To be sure, Atik's memoir also includes photographs of more social moments – at meals, for instance, or one in which her infant daughter sits peacefully on Beckett's lap – yet her husband's portraits represent a thoughtful, withdrawn man. By contrast, the Nobel stamp collection and poster present a very different Beckett: Beckett the author of the "provoking and humorous" play *Waiting for Godot*, as the Swedish postal service explains. His depiction on the stamp supports this construction, in part by softening his wrinkles and virtually eliminating any sense of the pessimistic by directing his gaze forcefully ahead at the viewer.

Were *Bord Fáilte* to act upon Toíbín's suggestion, then, it could once again rely on the Nobel poster to help refashion Beckett as a "commodified authentic" Irish writer. To assist in this kind of marketing strategy – to help conceal the fact that Beckett wrote most of his major works in French, for example – the board might also consider a second kind of retrofitting: namely, the revision of earlier writers' work by way of more contemporary conventions. Such a revisionary process is not entirely new and may prove almost unavoidable, as Jack MacGowran once intimated when describing his impersonation of Fluther Good in a revival of *The Plough and the Stars* after playing in *Waiting for Godot*: "I began to notice Vladimir creeping in. This jovial old Fluther from O'Casey suddenly turned into Vladimir."[40] Beckett, he felt, would have been amused by this; O'Casey might not have been.

A similar, but much more concerted revision of Synge's plays on the twenty-first century stage might help illuminate this point. As Adrian Frazier identified in the Druid Theatre's 2003 production of *The Playboy of the Western World*, director Garry Hynes introduced a kind of "post-modern paddywhackery" into Synge's text by transporting such a sensibility from the plays of Martin McDonagh. Frazier describes the curious result:

> Now in 2004, through a sort of feedback loop in the Syngean tradition of Irish drama, *The Playboy* manifests the traits of these more recent playwrights and productions. Their radical and postmodern aestheticizations of Irish rural life inspire a non-naturalist and almost 19th-century melodramatic extravaganza.[41]

Nicholas Grene responded similarly, connecting *The Playboy* to the Druid's earlier productions not only of McDonagh's plays, but also of John B. Keane's *Sharon's Grave* (2003).[42] Grene employs the term "redesigning" to characterize this redaction of earlier works by way of later ones, but in my view this term is too tame. That is to say, if "Irishing" a writer defines one kind of potential retrofitting of Beckett, this recasting of Synge might better be termed, after Beckett, one of Proustian or "reverse" influence. Recall that in *Proust*, Beckett insists that there is "no escape from yesterday because yesterday has deformed us, or been deformed by us" (p. 2). For much of the previous century, the discipline of literary criticism was obsessed with the former process – the effect of past writers and texts on later ones. A revised cultural criticism needs to privilege the opposite process, defining the ways present aesthetic conventions and thematic preoccupations modify, even deform, the past. Reverse influence, then, may *not* make Synge – or Beckett – more "Irishable," but it may make them more like Martin McDonagh or another figure from the contemporary scene.

Adaptation is perhaps the most familiar form of reverse influence, and here again Synge's plays have proven fertile material for contemporary playwrights: Vincent Woods' *A Cry from Heaven* (2005) adapts *Deirdre of the Sorrows*, and Bisi Adigun and Roddy Doyle have collaborated on a new version of *The Playboy of the Western World* (2007). Among the numerous and significant modernizations of these texts, Woods' play foregrounds both violence and sexual desire in the Deirdre legend that was notably muted in or absent from Synge's unfinished original. Indeed, the play's concluding tableau combines a disturbing reprise of the symbolic oppositions between day and night, sexuality and violence, that underlie the legend and play. And the Adigun/Doyle *Playboy* shifts the scene of the action from Mayo to a Dublin suburb, recasting the play's protagonist as a Nigerian immigrant to Ireland. In addition to both adaptations' repositioning of the canon of Irish drama more centrally in Dublin's postmodern and multinational present, both invariably reread and retrofit the Syngean originals into this cultural moment. Without deprecating either of these more recent plays, this kind of reverse influence suggests the potentially "poisonous ingenuity" of Time that Beckett describes in *Proust*; in so doing, it reveals both a Beckettian form of reverse influence and another model of retrofitting Beckett in the twenty-first century.

The processes of "Irishing" and reverse influence might be subsumed under a third, larger kind of retrofitting: *presentism*, which some critics, especially those in early modern studies, perceive as the warping of a text from the past into a comment on the present moment. One might hope that the mere assertion of Shakespeare or Beckett's contemporaneity does not signal a presentist bias, and certainly the history of Shakespearean adaptations suggests nothing of the sort. Nahum Tate, to cite perhaps the most egregious example in a long chronicle of theatrical and filmic adaptations, actually argued that his *King Lear* rectified an error in Shakespeare's play by rescuing Cordelia from an unwarranted fate. While this perversion might have made the tragedy more appealing to a Restoration audience – rather like casting the witches in *Macbeth* as punk rock druggies in an early 1980s Royal Shakespeare Company production I shall always remember[43] – it does not necessarily conceive of the play as commenting presciently on contemporary realities or dilemmas. Presentism does. In *Hamlet's Heirs* (2006), for example, Linda Charnes offers no Tate-like "improvements" of Shakespeare, but finds persuasive ways of reading George W. Bush's presidency into them. Such a project might thus be regarded as an analogue to Sam Shepard's *Kicking a Dead Horse* which, as I have suggested in the previous chapter, adduces parallels between America's president and Beckett's Krapp.

Is such a presentist reading also an example of retrofitting? Does it necessitate the addition to the original of the interpretive equivalent of sprinkler systems or more effectively illuminated emergency stairwells? Stated differently, such questions assess the extent to which the term "Beckett" or "Beckettian" is socially, hence contingently, constituted, encouraging a meditation of how precisely our historical moment revises the past to suit its own purposes – personal, commercial, ideological – at a time when many are too preoccupied with kicking dead horses to reflect on such matters. To take another example by moving from the desert to the flood, clearly residents of the Lower Ninth Ward in New Orleans responded to *Waiting for Godot* in 2007 in a far different fashion after Hurricane Katrina than they would have before the devastation of their city and the irreparable damage done to many of their lives.

This, the always evolving reception and understanding of Beckett, is the tenor of Lydia Davis' short story "Southward Bound, Reads *Worstward Ho*" from her collection *Varieties of Disturbance: Stories* (2007) in which a woman prepares for a long bus ride by taking two books to read: Beckett's *Worstward Ho* and *West with the Night*. She quite consciously decides to read Beckett during the first half of the trip "when she is fresh" and, however alert and diligent she might be, Davis' narrator describes her several struggles with the text, particularly with one passage:

> Soon after, with confusion she reads: "Said is missaid. Whenever said said said missaid." She misunderstands and reads again: "Whenever said said said missaid." Then a third time, and when she imagines a pause in the middle of it, she understands better.[44]

The myriad ways in which in the twenty-first century Beckett will appear as our contemporary will thus also demand our concerted, critical engagement with such retrofittings as "Irishing," reverse influence, and presentism. That is to say, as the post 9/11 world grows ever more frightening, as a post-Katrina New Orleans struggles to find hope, as it apparently did from *Waiting for Godot*, we shall need to remain, like Davis' reader, "fresh" in contending with the contemporary Becketts with whom we will most assuredly be confronted. Like her and without a Beatrice to guide us though the Dante-like complexities we will always find, we shall need to pause and reflect about how Beckett remains our contemporary.

NOTES

1. Colm Toíbín, "My Darlings: Colm Toíbín on Beckett's Irish Actors," *London Review of Books* 29 (April 5, 2007), p. 3.
2. Paula Murphy, "The Quare on the Square: A Statue of Oscar Wilde for Dublin," in *Wilde the Irishman*, ed. Jerusha McCormack (New Haven: Yale University Press, 1998), p. 127.
3. While audiences seemed entertained, many reviewers were not, blasting in particular Robin Williams' numerous improvisations.
4. Kincaid, *Postcolonial Dublin*, p. 177. Kincaid reports the data on hotel construction on p. 182. In 2008, the website www.tripadvisor.com provided information on over 125 hotels in the Dublin area alone.
5. Brian Friel, *The Mundy Scheme* in *Crystal and Fox and the Mundy Scheme* (New York: Farrar, Straus and Giroux, 1970), pp. 203, 202.
6. Friel, *The Mundy Scheme*, p. 204.
7. Friel, "In Interview with Des Hickey and Gus Smith" (1972), rpt. in Murray (ed.), *Brian Friel: Essays, Diaries, Interviews*, p. 49.
8. Mahon, *The Yellow Book*, p. 46.
9. Kincaid, "What They Left Behind: The Irish Landscape After Emigration," an unpublished manuscript, p. 6. My thanks to Andrew Kincaid for permission to quote from this essay.
10. For a discussion of these plans, see Irene Furlong, "Tourism and the Irish State in the 1950s," in *The Lost Decade: Ireland in the 1950s*, eds. Dermot Keogh, Finbarr O'Shea, and Carmel Quinlan (Cork: Mercier Press, 2004), pp. 164–86.
11. Kincaid, "What They Left Behind," p. 9.
12. Kincaid, "What They Left Behind," p. 10.
13. Furlong "Tourism and the Irish State," notes that in 1950 tourism trailed agricultural exports by some 12 million pounds (p. 173). In the early 1950s, Lemass spearheaded several legislative initiatives to install a tourist board, gradually altering political opinion of this topic.
14. Some insist that as many as 85, or even 87, died in this accident.
15. John O'Donoghue, "Welcome" to the Beckett Centenary Festival, April, 2006. www.beckettcentenaryfestival.ie.
16. I am indebted to Laura O'Connor's reading of Moore as an Irish writer in *Haunted English: The Celtic Fringe, the British Empire, and De-Anglicization* (Baltimore: Johns Hopkins University Press, 2006), pp. 152–87.

17. James Chandler, "A Discipline in Shifting Perspective: Why We Need Irish Studies," *Field Day Review* 2 (2006), p. 27.
18. Chandler, "A Discipline in Shifting Perspective," p. 31.
19. See "Touring in Ireland," *Colliers Magazine*, June 10, 1916, rpt. in *The Matter with Ireland*, eds. David H. Greene and Dan H. Laurence (London: Rupert Hart-Davis, 1962), pp. 92–99.
20. In *Images of Beckett* (Cambridge: Cambridge University Press, 2003), John Haynes and James Knowlson allude to Beckett's interest in sports. He read a French paper dedicated to sports, followed cricket and rugby on television, and discussed golf with a small circle of fellow enthusiasts (pp. 12–13).
21. John Banville, "Memory and Forgetting: The Ireland of de Valera and Ó Faoláin," in Keogh, O'Shea, and Quinlan (eds.), *The Lost Decade*, p. 29.
22. John Banville, "The Painful Comedy of Samuel Beckett," *The New York Review of Books* 43 (November 14, 1996), p. 26.
23. Deirdre Bair, *Samuel Beckett*, p. 120; Fintan O'Toole, "Shadows over Ireland," *American Theatre* (July/August 1998), p. 17.
24. Quoted in Bair, *Samuel Beckett*, p. 604.
25. Knowlson, *Damned to Fame*, p. 505.
26. Casanova, *The World Republic of Letters*, p. 307.
27. Quoted in Bair, *Samuel Beckett*, p. 122.
28. Bernard Shaw, "Preface for Politicians," in *Complete Plays with Their Prefaces*, 6 vols. (New York: Dodd Mead and Company, 1963), vol. II, p. 443.
29. Casanova, *The World Republic of Letters*, p. 313.
30. Terry Eagleton, "Nationalism: Irony and Commitment," in *Nationalism, Colonialism and Literature* (Minneapolis: University of Minnesota Press, 1990), p. 28.
31. Quoted in Gerald Whelan with Carolyn Swift, *Spiked: The Church-State Intrigue and The Rose Tattoo* (Dublin: New Island, 2002), p. 114.
32. Whelan and Swift, *Spiked*, pp. 114–15.
33. Quoted in Christopher Murray, "O'Casey's *The Drums of Father Ned* in Context," in Watt, Morgan, and Mustata (eds.), *A Century of Irish Drama*, p. 124.
34. Murray, "O'Casey's *The Drums of Father Ned*," p. 125.
35. Whelan and Swift, *Spiked*, p. 114.
36. Elizabeth Outka, "Crossing the Great Divides: Selfridges, Modernity, and the Commodified Authentic," *Modernism/Modernity* 12.2 (2005), pp. 314, 316.
37. Brian Fallon, *An Age of Innocence: Irish Culture 1930–1960* (Dublin: Gill and Macmillan, 1999), p. 23.
38. O'Connor, *Haunted English*, p. 166.
39. Knowlson, *Damned to Fame*, p. 167.
40. Quoted in Toíbín, "My Darlings," p. 7.
41. Adrian Frazier, "Postmodern Paddywhackery," in *Playboys of the Western World: Production Histories*, ed. Adrian Frazier (Dublin: Carysfort Press, 2004), p. 124.

42. Nicholas Grene, "Redesigning *The Playboy*," in Frazier (ed.), *Playboys of the Western World*, p. 126.
43. I am referring here to Howard Davies' materialist production of *Macbeth*, which opened at the Royal Shakespeare Company in Stratford in the spring of 1982 and moved later to London to largely hostile reviews.
44. Lydia Davis, "Southward Bound, Reads *Worstward Ho*," in *Varieties of Disturbance: Stories* (New York: Farrar, Straus and Giroux, 2007), p. 70.

Bibliography

Abbott, H. Porter. "Late Modernism: Samuel Beckett and the Art of the Oeuvre." *Around the Absurd*. Eds. Brater and Cohn: pp. 73–96.
Adorno, Theodor W. *Negative Dialectics*. Trans. E. B. Ashton. New York: Continuum Books, 1973.
"Trying to Understand *Endgame*." Trans. Michael T. Jones. *New German Critique* 26 (Spring–Summer 1982): 119–150.
"What Does Coming to Terms with the Past Mean?" *Bitburg in Moral and Political Perspective*. Ed. Hartman: pp. 114–129.
Albright, Daniel. *Beckett and Aesthetics*. Cambridge: Cambridge University Press, 2003.
Allen, Michael. "Rhythm and Revision in Mahon's Development." *The Poetry of Derek Mahon*. Ed. Kennedy-Andrews: pp. 111–129.
Altick, Richard D. *The Art of Literary Research*. Rev. edn. New York: W.W. Norton, 1975.
Alvarez, A. *Samuel Beckett*. New York: Viking Press, 1973.
Appadurai, Arjun. "Introduction: Commodities and the Politics of Value." *The Social Life of Things: Commodities in Cultural Perspective*. Ed. Arjun Appadurai. Cambridge: Cambridge University Press, 1986: pp. 3–63.
Atherton, James S. *The Books at the Wake: A Study of Allusions in James Joyce's Finnegans Wake*. New York: Viking Press, 1960.
Atik, Anne. *How It Was: A Memoir of Samuel Beckett*. 2001. Rpt. New York: Shoemaker & Hoard, 2005.
Augé, Marc. *Non-Places: Introduction to an Anthropology of Super-Modernity*. Trans. John Howe. London: Verso, 1995.
Bachelard, Gaston. *The Poetics of Space*. Trans. Maria Jolas. Boston: Beacon Press, 1964.
Badiou, Alain. *Being and Event*. Trans. Oliver Feltham. New York: Continuum, 2005.
On Beckett. Trans. Nina Power and Alberto Toscano. Manchester: Clinamen Press, 2003.
Polemics. Trans. Steve Corcoran. London: Verso, 2006.
"Roundtable." Indiana University-Bloomington. November 9, 2007.
Theoretical Writings. Ed. and trans. Ray Brassier and Alberto Toscano. New York and London: Continuum, 2004.

Bair, Deirdre. *Samuel Beckett: A Biography*. London: Jonathan Cape, 1978.
Banville, John. *Athena*. New York: Vintage Books, 1996.
"Beckett's Last Words" *Samuel Beckett 100 Years*. Ed. Murray: pp. 122–31.
Eclipse. New York: Vintage Books, 2000.
Ghosts. New York: Vintage Books, 1994.
"Memory and Forgetting: The Ireland of de Valera and Ó Faoláin." *The Lost Decade*. Eds. Keogh, O'Shea, and Quinlan: pp. 21–30.
Nightspawn. 1971. Rpt. Oldcastle: Gallery Press, 1993.
"The Painful Comedy of Samuel Beckett." *The New York Review of Books* 43 (November 14, 1996): 24–29.
Shroud. 2002. Rpt. New York: Vintage Books, 2004.
Barthes, Roland. *Image – Music – Text*. Trans. Stephen Heath. New York: Hill & Wang, 1977.
Bateman, Colin. *Divorcing Jack*. New York: Arcade Publishing, 1995.
Baudrillard, Jean. *For a Critique of the Political Economy of the Sign*. Trans. Charles Levin. St. Louis: Telos Press, 1981.
Beckett, Samuel. *The Collected Shorter Plays of Samuel Beckett*. New York: Grove Press, 1984.
The Complete Short Prose, 1929–1989. New York: Grove Press, 1995.
Disjecta: Miscellaneous Writings and a Dramatic Fragment. Ed. Ruby Cohn. New York: Grove Press, 1984.
Dream of Fair to Middling Women. Eds. Eoin O'Brien and Edith Fournier. New York: Arcade Publishing, 1992.
Endgame. New York: Grove Press, 1958.
Happy Days. New York: Grove Press, 1961.
How It Is. New York: Grove Press, 1964.
Mercier and Camier. New York: Grove Press, 1974.
More Pricks Than Kicks. New York: Grove Press, 1972.
Nohow On: Company, Ill Seen Ill Said, Worstward Ho. New York: Grove Press, 1996.
Poems, 1930–1989. London: Calder Publications, 2002.
Proust. New York: Grove Press, 1957.
Three Novels: Molloy, Malone Dies, The Unnamable. New York: Grove Press, 1955.
Waiting for Godot. New York: Grove Press, 1954.
Watt. New York: Grove Press, 1959.
Bensaïd, Daniel. "Alain Badiou and the Miracle of the Event." *Think Again: Alain Badiou and the Future of Philosophy*. Ed. Peter Hallward. London: Continuum, 2004.
Bew, Paul, Peter Gibbon, and Henry Patterson. *Northern Ireland 1921–1996: Political Forces and Social Classes*. Rev. edn. London: Serif, 1996.
Blechman, Max, Anita Chari, and Rafeeq Hasan. "Human Rights Are the Rights of the Infinite: An Interview with Alain Badiou." Unpublished interview, 2005.
Bloch, Ernst. *The Principle of Hope*. 3 vols. Trans. Neville Plaice, Stephen Plaice, and Paul Knight. Cambridge, MA: MIT Press, 1995: Vol. I.

Bloom, Harold. *The Anxiety of Influence*, 2nd edn. New York: Oxford University Press, 1997.

Boland, Eavan. "Brian Friel: Derry's Playwright." *Hibernia*, February 16, 1973. Rpt. *Brian Friel in Conversation*. Ed. Delaney: pp. 112–116.

Bolger, Dermot, ed. *Druids, Dudes and Beauty Queens: The Changing Face of Irish Theatre*. Dublin: New Island, 2001.

Bourke, Bernadette. "Carr's 'cut-throats and gargiyles': Grotesque and Carnivalesque Elements in *By the Bog of Cats* ..." *The Theatre of Marina Carr*. Eds. Leeny and McMullan: pp. 128–144.

Brater, Enoch, and Ruby Cohn, eds. *Around the Absurd: Essays on Modern and Postmodern Drama*. Ann Arbor: University of Michigan Press, 1990.

Brennan, Rory. "Contemporary Irish Poetry: An Overview." *Poetry in Contemporary Irish Literature*. Ed. Michael Kinneally. Gerrards Cross: Colin Smythe, 1995: pp. 1–25.

Brown, Bill. "Thing Theory." *Critical Inquiry* 28 (Autumn 2001): 1–16.

Burke, Patrick. "'Them Class of People's a Very Poor Judge of Character': Friel and the South." *Irish University Review* 29.1 (Spring/Summer 1999): 42–47.

Carlson, Marvin. *The Haunted Stage*. Ann Arbor: University of Michigan Press, 2001.

Carr, Marina. *Ariel*. Oldcastle: Gallery Books, 2002.

On Raftery's Hill. Oldcastle: Gallery Books, 2000.

Plays 1. London: Faber and Faber, 1999.

Woman and Scarecrow. London: Faber and Faber, 2006.

Carson, Ciaran. *Belfast Confetti*. Winston-Salem, NC: Wake Forest University Press, 1989.

Casanova, Pascale. *Samuel Beckett: Anatomy of a Literary Revolution*. Trans. Gregory Elliott. London: Verso, 2006.

The World Republic of Letters. Trans. M. B. Debevoise. Cambridge, MA: Harvard University Press, 2004.

Cash, John Daniel. *Identity, Ideology and Conflict: The Structuration of Politics in Northern Ireland*. Cambridge: Cambridge University Press, 1996.

Cavell, Stanley. *Must We Mean What We Say?* Cambridge: Cambridge University Press, 1976.

Chambers, Lilian, and Eamonn Jordan, eds. *The Theatre of Martin McDonagh: A World of Savage Stories*. Dublin: Carysfort Press, 2006.

Chambers, Lilian, Ger FitzGerald, and Eamonn Jordan, eds. *Theatre Talk: Voices of Irish Theatre Practitioners*. Dublin: Carysfort Press, 2001.

Chandler, James. "A Discipline in Shifting Perspective: Why We Need Irish Studies." *Field Day Review* 2 (2006): 19–39.

Charnes, Linda. *Hamlet's Heirs: Shakespeare and the Politics of a New Millennium*. New York and London: Routledge, 2006.

Chubb, Kenneth, and the Editors of *Theatre Quarterly*, "Metaphors, Mad Dogs, and Old Time Cowboys: Interview with Sam Shepard." 1974. Rpt. Bonnie Marranca, ed. *American Dreams: The Imagination of Sam Shepard*. New York: PAJ Publications, 1981: pp. 187–209.

Clarity, James F. "A Playwright's Post-Beckett Period." *The New York Times*, November 3, 1994. Late Edition.

Cleary, Joe. *Outrageous Fortune: Capital and Culture in Modern Ireland*. Dublin: Field Day Publications, 2007.

"The World Literary System: Atlas and Epitaph." *Field Day Review* 2 (2006): 197–219.

Coleridge, Samuel Taylor. *The Complete Works*. 3 vols. Ed. W. T. G. Shedd. New York: Harper, 1860.

Conlon, Gerry. *In the Name of the Father*. 1990. Rpt. New York: Plume, 1993

Connor, Steven. "Over Samuel Beckett's Dead Body." *Beckett in Dublin*. Ed. S. E. Wilmer: pp. 100–8.

Samuel Beckett: Repetition, Theory and Text. Oxford: Basil Blackwell, 1988.

Cotter, Holland. "A Broken City. A Tree. Evening." *The New York Times*, December 2, 2007, p. 21.

Cronin, Anthony. *Collected Poems*. Dublin: New Island, 2004.

Samuel Beckett: The Last Modernist. London: HarperCollins, 1996.

Davis, Lydia. *Varieties of Disturbance: Stories*. New York: Farrar, Straus and Giroux, 2007.

Dawe, Gerald. "Heirs and Graces: The Influence and Example of Derek Mahon." *The Poetry of Derek Mahon*. Ed. Kennedy-Andrews: pp. 49–56.

Deane, Seamus. *Celtic Revivals: Essays in Modern Irish Literature, 1880–1980*. London: Faber and Faber, 1985.

"Introduction." *Brian Friel: Selected Plays*. London: Faber and Faber, 1984: pp. 12–22.

Debord, Guy. *The Society of the Spectacle*. Detroit: Black and Red, 1983.

Delaney, Paul, ed. *Brian Friel in Conversation*. Ann Arbor: University of Michigan Press, 2000.

Deleuze, Gilles. "The Exhausted." *Essays Critical and Clinical*. trans. Daniel W. Smith and Michael A. Greco. Minneapolis: University of Minnesota Press, 1997.

Deleuze, Gilles, and Félix Guattari. *Kafka: Toward a Minor Literature*. Trans. Dana Polan. Minneapolis: University of Minnesota Press, 1986.

Dentith, Simon. *Bakhtinian Thought: An Introductory Reader*. London: Routledge, 1995.

Derrida, Jacques. "The Law of Genre." *Glyph 7: Textual Studies*. Ed. Samuel Weber. Baltimore: Johns Hopkins University Press, 1980: pp. 176–232.

Specters of Marx: The State of the Debt, the Work of Mourning, and the New International. Trans. Peggy Kamuf. New York and London: Routledge, 1994.

Devlin, Anne. *Ourselves Alone*. London: Faber and Faber, 1986.

Dolar, Mladen. *A Voice and Nothing More*. Cambridge, MA: MIT Press, 2006.

Duffy, Brian. "Banville's Other Ghost: Samuel Beckett's Presence in John Banville's Eclipse." *Études Irlandaises* 28.1 (2003): 85–106.

Eagleton, Terry. *After Theory*. New York: Basic Books, 2003.

The Illusions of Postmodernism. Oxford: Basil Blackwell, 1996.

"Introduction." Pascale Casanova. *Samuel Beckett: Anatomy of a Literary Revolution*. London: Verso, 2006: pp. 1–9.

"Nationalism: Irony and Commitment." *Nationalism, Colonialism and Literature*. (Minneapolis: University of Minnesota Press, 1990): pp. 23–39.

Esslin, Martin. "Introduction." Jan Kott. *Shakespeare Our Contemporary*. Trans. Boleslaw Taborski. New York: W.W. Norton, 1964: pp. xi–xxi.

Evans, G. Blakemore, ed. *The Riverside Shakespeare*. Boston: Houghton Mifflin, 1997.

Fairleigh, John, ed. *Far from the Land: Contemporary Irish Plays*. London: Methuen, 1998.

Fallon, Brian. *An Age of Innocence: Irish Culture 1930–1960*. Dublin: Gill and Macmillan, 1999.

Foley, Catherine. "Kicking Up a Storm on Stage." *The Irish Times*, March 17, 2007.

Foster, R. F. *Modern Ireland 1600–1972*. London: Penguin Books, 1988.

Frazier, Adrian, ed. *Playboys of the Western World: Production Histories*. Dublin: Carysfort Press, 2004.

"Postmodern Paddywhackery." *Playboys of the Western World*. Ed. Adrian Frazier: pp. 115–124.

Friel, Brian. *Crystal and Fox* and *The Mundy Scheme*. New York: Farrar, Straus and Giroux, 1970.

Performances. Oldcastle: Gallery Press, 2003.

Selected Plays. London: Faber and Faber, 1984.

Volunteers. London: Faber and Faber, 1979.

Furlong, Irene. "Tourism and the Irish State in the 1950s." *The Lost Decade*. Eds. Keogh, O'Shea, and Quinlan: pp. 164–86.

Gardner, Lyn. "Woman and Scarecrow." *Guardian*, June 23, 2006.

Garner, Jr., Stanton B. *Bodied Spaces: Phenomenology and Performance in Contemporary Drama*. Ithaca: Cornell University Press, 1994.

Gibson, Andrew. *Beckett and Badiou: The Pathos of Intermittency*. Oxford: Oxford University Press, 2006.

Glassie, Henry. *All Silver and No Brass: An Irish Christmas Mumming*. 1975. Rpt. Philadelphia: University of Pennsylvania Press, 1983.

Passing the Time in Ballymenone: Culture and History of An Ulster Community. 1982. Rpt. Bloomington: Indiana University Press, 1995.

Glendinning, Robin. *Three Plays: Mumbo Jumbo, Donny Boy, Summerhouse*. Belfast: Lagan Press, 2004.

Gordon, Lois. *The World of Samuel Beckett, 1906–1946*. New Haven: Yale University Press, 1996.

Grene, Nicholas. "Redesigning *The Playboy*." *Playboys of the Western World*. Ed. Frazier: pp. 125–28.

Hartman, Geoffrey, ed. *Bitburg in Moral and Political Perspective*. Bloomington: Indiana University Press, 1986.

Haughton, Hugh. "'The Importance of Elsewhere': Mahon and Translation." *The Poetry of Derek Mahon*. Ed. Kennedy-Andrews: pp. 145–83.

Hay, Malcolm, and Philip Roberts. *Bond: A Study of His Plays*. London: Eyre Methuen, 1980.

Haynes, John, and James Knowlson. *Images of Beckett*. Cambridge: Cambridge University Press, 2003.

Heaney, Seamus. "Digging Deeper." *Times Literary Supplement* (January–March 1975): 306. Rpt. *Preoccupations: Selected Prose 1968–1978*. London: Faber and Faber, 1980: 214–20.

Finder's Keepers: Selected Prose, 1971–2001. London: Faber and Faber, 2002.

North. London: Faber and Faber, 1975.

Horne, Jed. "Is New Orleans Waiting for Godot?" *The Huffington Post*, November 14, 2007: www.huffingtonpost.com.

Jaffe, Aaron. *Modernism and the Culture of Celebrity*. Cambridge: Cambridge University Press, 2005.

Jameson, Fredric. *The Political Unconscious: Narrative as a Socially Symbolic Act*. Ithaca: Cornell University Press, 1981.

Johnston, Jennifer. *The Railway Station Man*. London: Penguin Books, 1984.

Jones, Marie. *A Night in November*. Dublin: New Island Books, 1995.

Joyce, James. *Dubliners*. 1914. Rpt. London: Penguin Books, 1976.

Finnegans Wake. New York: Viking Press, 1939.

Kearney, Richard. *Transitions: Narratives in Modern Irish Culture*. Dublin: Wolfhound Press, 1988.

The Wake of Imagination: Towards a Postmodern Culture. Minneapolis: University of Minnesota Press, 1988.

Keller, John Robert. *Samuel Beckett and the Primacy of Love*. Manchester: Manchester University Press, 2002.

Kendall, Tim. *Paul Muldoon*. Brigend, Wales: Seren, 1996.

Kendall, Tim, and Peter McDonald, eds. *Paul Muldoon: Critical Essays*. Liverpool: Liverpool University Press, 2004.

Kennedy-Andrews, Elmer. *Fiction and the Northern Irish Troubles Since 1969: (De)-Constructing the North*. Dublin: Four Courts Press, 2003.

ed. *The Poetry of Derek Mahon*. Gerrards Cross: Colin Smythe, 2002.

Keogh, Dermot, Finbarr O'Shea, and Carmel Quinlan, eds. *The Lost Decade: Ireland in the 1950s*. Cork: Mercier Press, 2004.

Kerrigan, John. "Paul Muldoon's Transits: Muddling Through after *Madoc*." *Paul Muldoon: Critical Essays*. Eds. Kendall and McDonald: pp. 125–49.

Kiberd, Declan. *Irish Classics*. Cambridge, MA: Harvard University Press, 2001.

Kilroy, Thomas. "The Early Plays." *The Cambridge Companion to Brian Friel*. Ed. Roche: pp. 6–17.

The Shape of Metal. Oldcastle: Gallery Press, 2003.

Kincaid, Andrew. *Postcolonial Dublin: Imperial Legacies and the Built Environment*. Minneapolis: University of Minnesota Press, 2006.

"What They Left Behind: The Irish Landscape after Emigration." Unpublished manuscript.

Knowlson, James. *Damned to Fame: The Life of Samuel Beckett*. 1997. New York: Grove Press, 2004.

Knowlson, James, and Elizabeth Knowlson. *Beckett Remembering Remembering Beckett: A Centenary Celebration*. New York: Arcade Publishing, 2006.

Kott, Jan. *Shakespeare Our Contemporary*. Trans. B. Taborski. New York: W.W. Norton, 1964.

Kristeva, Julia. *Black Sun: Depression and Melancholia*. Trans. Leon S. Roudiez. New York: Columbia University Press, 1989.

Desire in Language: A Semiotic Approach to Literature and Art. Trans. Leon S. Roudiez. New York: Columbia University Press, 1980.

Leeney, Cathy, and Anna McMullan, eds. *The Theatre of Marina Carr: "before rules was made."* Dublin: Carysfort Press, 2003.

Levene, Nancy. "Roundtable with Alain Badiou." Indiana University-Bloomington, November 9, 2007.

Lloyd, David. "Republics of Difference: Yeats, McGreevy, Beckett." *Field Day Review* 1 (2005): 43–69.

Longley, Michael. *Collected Poems*. London: Jonathan Cape, 2006.

Lowry, David R. "Internment: Detention without Trial in Northern Ireland." *Human Rights* 5 (1975–76): 261–331.

Luckhurst, Mary. "Martin McDonagh's *The Lieutenant of Inishmore*: Selling (-Out) to the English." *The Theatre of Martin McDonagh*. Eds. Chambers and Jordan: pp. 116–29.

Lynch, Brian. *Pity for the Wicked*. Dublin: Duras Press, 2005.

Lynch, Martin, Conor Grimes, and Alan McKee. *The History of the Troubles (accordin' to my Da)*. Belfast: Lagan Press, 2005.

Lyons, Charles R. "Beckett, Shakespeare, and the Making of Theory." *Around the Absurd*. Eds. Brater and Cohn: pp. 97–127.

Machacek, Gregory. "Allusion." *PMLA* 122 (March 2007): 522–536.

MacLaverty, Bernard. *The Anatomy School*. New York: W.W. Norton, 2002.

Cal. London: Jonathan Cape, 1983.

Grace Notes. New York: W.W. Norton, 1997.

The Great Profundo and Other Stories. New York: Grove Press, 1987.

Lamb. New York: George Braziller, 1980.

Matters of Life & Death and Other Stories. London: Jonathan Cape, 2006.

Secrets and Other Stories. 1977. Rpt. New York: Viking, 1984.

A Time to Dance and Other Stories. New York: George Braziller, 1982.

Walking the Dog and Other Stories. London: Penguin Books, 1994.

Mahon, Derek. *Collected Poems*. Oldcastle: Gallery Press, 1999.

The Hudson Letter. Oldcastle: Gallery Press, 1995.

Journalism: Selected Prose, 1970–1995. Ed. Terence Brown. Oldcastle: Gallery Press, 1996.

The Yellow Book. Winston-Salem, NC: Wake Forest University Press, 1998.

McCarthy, Dermot. "Belfast Babel: Postmodern Lingo in Eoin McNamee's *Resurrection Man*." *Irish University Review* 30 (Spring/Summer 2000): 132–48.

McDonagh, Martin. *The Pillowman*. London: Faber and Faber, 2003.

McDonald, Ronán. "Between Hope and History: The Drama of the Troubles." *Druids, Dudes and Beauty Queens*. Ed. Bolger: pp. 231–49.

McNamee, Eoin. *Resurrection Man*. London: Picador, 1994.

Mercier, Vivian. *The Irish Comic Tradition*. New York and London: Oxford University Press, 1962.

Miller, Tyrus. *Late Modernism: Politics, Fiction, and the Arts Between the World Wars*. Berkeley: University of California Press, 1999.

Morash, Christopher. *A History of Irish Theatre: 1601–2000*. Cambridge: Cambridge University Press, 2002.

Morrison, Conall. *Hard to Believe. Far From the Land*. Ed. Fairleigh: pp. 309–40.

Muldoon, Paul. *The Annals of Chile*. New York: The Noonday Press, 1994.

The End of the Poem. New York: Farrar, Straus and Giroux, 2006.

"Getting Round: Notes Toward an *Ars Poetica*." *Essays in Criticism* 48 (April 1998): 107–28.

Hay. New York: Farrar, Straus and Giroux, 1998.

Horse Latitudes. New York: Farrar, Straus and Giroux, 2006.

Moy Sand and Gravel. New York: Farrar, Straus and Giroux, 2002.

Poems 1968–1998. New York: Farrar, Straus and Giroux, 2001.

To Ireland, I. Oxford: Oxford University Press, 2000.

Six Honest Serving Men. Oldcastle: Gallery Press, 1995.

Murphy, Paula. "The Quare on the Square: A Statue of Oscar Wide for Dublin." *Wilde the Irishman*. Ed. Jerusha McCormack. New Haven: Yale University Press, 1998: pp. 127–39.

"Staging Histories in Marina Carr's Midland Plays." *Irish University Review* 36 (2006): 389–403.

Murphy, Tom. *Plays: 2*. London: Faber and Faber, 1997.

Murray, Christopher. "The Cripple of Inishmaan Meets Lady Gregory." *The Theatre of Martin McDonagh*. Eds. Chambers and Jordan: pp. 79–95.

"O'Casey's *The Drums of Father Ned* in Context." *A Century of Irish Drama*. Eds. Watt, Morgan, and Mustafa: pp. 117–29.

ed. *Brian Friel: Essays, Diaries, Interviews: 1964–1999*. London: Faber and Faber, 1999.

ed. *Samuel Beckett 100 Years: Centenary Essays*. Dublin: New Island, 2006.

Ni Anluain, Cliodhna, ed. *Reading the Future: Irish Writers in Conversation with Mike Murphy*. Dublin: Lilliput Press, 2000.

Nixon, Mark. "'Guess Where': From Reading to Writing in Beckett." *Genetic Joyce Studies* 6 (Spring 2006): www.antwerpjamesjoycecenter.com.

Norfolk, Lawrence. "The Abundant Braes of Yarrow." *TLS*, October 7, 1994: 32–33.

O'Brien, Edna. *House of Splendid Isolation*. New York: Farrar, Straus and Giroux, 1994.

O'Connor, Laura. *Haunted English: The Celtic Fringe, the British Empire, and De-Anglicization*. Baltimore: Johns Hopkins University Press, 2006.

O'Donoghue, John, T. D. "Welcome." Beckett Centenary Festival, April 2006: www.beckettcentenaryfestival.ie

O'Kelly, Fachtna, "Can the Critics Kill a Play?" *Brian Friel in Conversation*. Ed. Delaney: pp. 117–19.

O'Leary, Joseph S. "Beckett's Intertextual Power." *Journal of Irish Studies* 18 (2003): 87–101.

O'Toole, Fintan. *Critical Moments: Fintan O'Toole on Modern Irish Theatre*. Eds. Julia Furay and Redmond O'Hanlon. Dublin: Carysfort Press, 2003.

"Metaphors for Modern Times: Review of Sam Shepard's *Kicking a Dead Horse*." *The Irish Times*, March 24, 2007.

"Shadows over Ireland." *American Theatre* (July/August 1998): 16–19.

Outka, Elizabeth. "Crossing the Great Divides: Selfridges, Modernity, and the Commodified Authentic." *Modernism/Modernity* 12.2 (2005): 311–328.

Parrott, Jeremy. *Change All the Names: A Samuel Beckett Onomasticon*. Szeged, Hungary: The Kakapo Press, 2004.

Pearson, Nels C. "'Outside of Here It's Death': Co-dependency and the Ghosts of Decolonization in Beckett's *Endgame*." *ELH* 68.1 (2001): 215–239.

Pelaschiar, Laura. "Transforming Belfast: The Evolving Role of the City in Northern Irish Fiction." *Irish University Review* 30 (Spring/Summer 2000): 117–31.

Pilkington, Lionel. *Theatre and State in Twentieth-Century Ireland: Cultivating the People*. London and New York: Routledge, 2001.

Pine, Richard. *Brian Friel and Ireland's Drama*. London and New York: Routledge, 1990.

"Friel's Irish Russia." *The Cambridge Companion to Brian Friel*. Ed. Roche: pp. 104–16.

Poster, Mark, ed. *Jean Baudrillard: Selected Writings*. Stanford: Stanford University Press, 1988.

Pratt, William. "World Literature in Review: English – Review of *The Annals of Chile*." *World Literature Today* 69 (Spring 1995): 365.

Quinn, Eamon, and Alan Cowelle. "Ulster Factions Agree to a Plan for Joint Rule." *New York Times*, March 27, 2007: Foreign Desk 1.

Rabaté, Jean-Michel. "Unbreakable B's: From Beckett and Badiou to the Bitter End of Affirmative Ethics." *Alain Badiou: Philosophy and Its Conditions*. Ed. Gabriel Riera. Albany: State University of New York Press, 2005: pp. 87–108.

Redmond, John. "Indicting the Exquisite: Paul Muldoon: *The Annals of Chile*." *Thumbscrew* 1 (Winter 1994–95): 72–81.

"Muldoon and Pragmatism." *Paul Muldoon: Critical Essays*. Eds. Kendall and McDonald: pp. 96–109.

Rees, Catherine. "The Politics of Morality: *The Lieutenant of Inishmore*." *The Theatre of Martin McDonagh*. Eds. Chambers and Jordan: pp. 130–40.

Richards, Shaun. "'The Outpouring of a Morbid, Unhealthy Mind': The Critical Condition of Synge and McDonagh." *The Theatre of Martin McDonagh*. Eds. Chambers and Jordan: pp. 246–63.

Ricoeur, Paul. *Memory, History, Forgetting*. Trans. Kathleen Blamey and David Pellauer. Chicago: University of Chicago Press, 2004.

Robinson, Marc. *The Other American Drama*. Cambridge and New York: Cambridge University Press, 1994.

Roche, Anthony. *Contemporary Irish Drama: From Beckett to McGuinness*. Dublin: Gill & Macmillan, 1994.

"Samuel Beckett: The Great Plays after *Godot*." *Samuel Beckett 100 Years*. Ed. Murray: pp. 59–69.

ed. *The Cambridge Companion to Brian Friel*. Cambridge: Cambridge University Press, 2006.
Said, Edward W. *The World, The Text, and the Critic*. Cambridge, MA: Harvard University Press, 1983.
Sands, Bobby. *Writings from Prison*. Dublin: Mercier Press, 1998.
Scaife, Sarahjane. "Mutual Beginnings: Marina Carr's *Low in the Dark*." *The Theatre of Marina Carr*. Eds. Leeney and McMullan: pp. 1–16.
Scholes, Robert. *Protocols of Reading*. New Haven: Yale University Press, 1989.
Semiotics and Interpretation. New Haven: Yale University Press, 1982.
Shaffer, Peter. *Lettice and Lovage*. London: Andre Deutsch, 1988.
Shaw, Bernard. *Complete Plays with Their Prefaces*. 6 vols. New York: Dodd, Mead and Company, 1963.
"Touring in Ireland." 1916. Rpt. *The Matter with Ireland*. Eds. David H. Greene and Dan H. Laurence. London: Rupert Hart-Davis, 1962: pp. 92–99.
Shepard, Sam. *Fool for Love and Other Plays*. New York: Bantam, 1984.
Kicking a Dead Horse. London: Faber and Faber, 2007.
Motel Chronicles. San Francisco: City Lights Books, 1982.
True West. Shepard. Seven Plays. New York: Bantam, 1981: pp. 1–59.
Sheridan, Peter. *44 Dublin Made Me: A Memoir*. New York: Viking, 1999.
Smith, Stan. "The Twilight of the Cities: Derek Mahon's Dark Cinema." *The Poetry of Derek Mahon*. Ed. Kennedy-Andrews: pp. 249–71.
Smyth, Gerry. "'The Same Sound but with a Different Meaning': Music, Repetition, and Identity in Bernard Mac Laverty's *Grace Notes*." *Éire-Ireland* 37.3–4 (Fall/Winter 2002): 5–24.
Stewart, Bruce. "'Solving Ambiguity': The Secular Mysticism of Derek Mahon." *The Poetry of Derek Mahon*. Ed. Kennedy-Andrews: pp. 57–81.
Sword, Helen. *Ghostwriting Modernism*. Ithaca: Cornell University Press, 2002.
Taggart, Ashley. "An Economy of Pity: McDonagh's Monstrous Regiment." *The Theatre of Martin McDonagh*. Eds. Chambers and Jordan: pp. 162–73.
Taylor, Paul. "Theatre: Master of the Empty Space." *The Independent*, November 4, 1998: 7.
Tillinghast, Richard. "Poets Are Born, Then Made." *New York Times Book Review* 144 (December 11, 1994): 25–26.
Toíbín, Colm. *The Master*. New York: Scribner, 2004.
"My Darlings: Colm Toíbín on Beckett's Irish Actors." *London Review of Books* 29 (April 5, 2007): 3–8.
The South. London: Penguin Books, 1990.
Trotter, Mary. "Translating Women into Irish Theatre History." *A Century of Irish Drama*. Eds. Watt, Morgan, and Mustafa: pp. 163–78.
Vendler, Helen. "Anglo-Celtic Attitudes." *The New York Review of Books*, November 6, 1997: 57–60.
"Fanciness and Fatality." *The New Republic*, November 9, 2006: 26–33.
Wall, Eamonn. *From the Sin-é Café to the Black Hills: Notes on the New Irish*. Madison: University of Wisconsin Press, 1999.

Watt, Stephen. "007 and 9/11: Specters and Structures of Feeling." *Ian Fleming and James Bond: The Cultural Politics of 007*. Eds. Edward P. Comentale, Stephen Watt, and Skip Willman. Bloomington: Indiana University Press, 2005: pp. 238–59.

"The Politics of Bernard MacLaverty's *Cal*. *Éire-Ireland* 28 (Fall 1993): 130–146.

Watt, Stephen, Eileen Morgan, and Shakir Mustafa, eds. *A Century of Irish Drama. Widening the Stage*. Bloomington: Indiana University Press, 2000.

Whelan, Gerald, with Carolyn Swift. *Spiked: Church-State Intrigue and The Rose Tattoo*. Dublin: New Island Books, 2002.

White, Hayden. *Meta-History: The Historical Imagination in Nineteenth-Century Europe*. Baltimore: Johns Hopkins University Press, 1983.

"The Politics of Historical Interpretation: Discipline and De-Sublimation." *The Politics of Interpretation*. Ed. W. J. T. Mitchell. Chicago: University of Chicago Press, 1983: pp. 119–43.

Whittaker, Stephen. "Joyce and Skeat." *James Joyce Quarterly* 24 (Winter 1987): 177–92.

Widgery, Lord. *Bloody Sunday, 1972: Lord Widgery's Report of Events in Londonderry, Northern Ireland, on 30 January 1972*. London: The Stationery Office, 2001.

Wills, Clair. *Reading Paul Muldoon*. Newcastle: Bloodaxe Books, 1998.

Wilmer, S. E., ed. *Beckett in Dublin*. Dublin: The Lilliput Press, 1992.

Wilson, Robert McLiam. *Eureka Street*. New York: Ballantine Books, 1996.

Ripley Bogle. 1989. Rpt. New York: Ballantine Books, 2000.

Wimsatt, Jr., W. K., and Monroe C. Beardsley. *The Verbal Icon*. 1954. Rpt. New York: Noonday Press, 1958.

Woods, Vincent. *At the Black Pig's Dyke. Far From the Land*. Ed. Fairleigh: pp. 1–61.

Worth, Katharine. "Beckett's Ghosts." *Beckett in Dublin*. Ed. Wilmer: pp. 62–74.

Young, James E. "Memory and Monument." *Bitburg in Moral and Political Perspective*. Ed. Hartman: pp. 103–13.

Zuidervaart, Lambert. *Adorno's Aesthetic Theory: The Redemption of Illusion*. Cambridge MA: MIT Press, 1991.

Zurbrugg, Nicholas. "*Ill Seen Ill Said* and the Sense of an Ending." *Beckett's Later Fiction and Drama*. Eds. James Acheson and Kateryna Arthur. London: Macmillan, 1987: pp. 145–59.

Index

CPSIA information can be obtained at www.ICGtesting.com
Printed in the USA
BVOW011221270412

288848BV00005B/30/P